Sabre, MiG-15 & Hunter

Stewart Wilson

Original Illustrations
by
Juanita Franzi & John Allen

INTRODUCTION

I am proud to introduce the first in our new series of books, *Legends of the Air*, and presenting a broad history of three of the classic fighter aircraft of the 1950s and beyond, the North American F-86 Sabre, MiG-15 and Hawker Hunter. Each played a significant role in the history and development of the jet fighter, between them these most important fighters of their era serving with some 100 nations around the world.

The key to greatness in any aircraft design seems to lie in its ability to be 'the right aircraft at the right time', and the North American F-86 Sabre jet fighter certainly was, blooded in the Korean War and serving with distinction with the air forces of no fewer than 38 nations.

Regarded by many as the greatest fighter of the 1950s, the Sabre was far in advance of the jet fighters which immediately preceded it and was an outstanding commercial success with nearly 9,000 built in five countries in nine major variants to fill day fighter, all weather fighter and fighter-bomber roles. Add to that the more than 1,100 Fury naval fighter variants which were produced and the result is a classic of its time.

The West was shaken out of its complacent attitude towards Soviet fighter capabilities in the skies over Korea in November 1950 with the unexpected appearance of the MiG-15. Suddenly, the equation had changed and the allied air forces operating in Korea had a fight on their hands.

The MiG-15 had its flaws, but in the hands of a skilled pilot could be a match for anything else during the early 1950s, including the F-86 Sabre. Simple in concept, design and engineering, the MiG-15 proved ideal for service with just about every country whose sympathies lay with the Soviet Union. For many of these countries it was the ideal first fighter and nearly 40 of them operated the type, built on production lines in Russia, China, Poland and Czechoslovakia.

One of the best loved of all British aircraft, the Hunter represented several areas of importance: it was Britain's first transonic fighter and it was one of the first genuinely multi role jet combat aircraft, at least in its mature form.

The Hunter had its problems early in its career but with development and the exploitation of its true potential, a classic fighting aeroplane emerged and served with 28 nations. Fewer than 2,000 were built thanks mainly to the short sightedness of British politicians during the 1950s. The result was that the manufacturer established a lucrative refurbishing and reselling business around the Hunter in the 1960s and '70s as it tried to fill the demand for an aircraft which should have been built in larger numbers and developed further.

I hope that what follows provides some insight into these three important aircraft. Some invaluable help was given in the preparation of this book and I gratefully acknowledge the following: Philip J Birtles, Brian Pickering of Military Aircraft Photographs, Peter R March, Commodore Norman Lee RAN (ret), Air Vice Marshal Bill Collings RAAF (ret), Jim Thorn, Gerard Frawley, Maria Davey, Juanita Franzi and John Allen.

Stewart Wilson
Buckingham 1995

Published by Aerospace Publications Pty Ltd (ACN: 001 570 458), PO Box 3105, Weston Creek, ACT 2611, publishers of monthly Australian Aviation magazine.
Production Manager: Maria Davey

ISBN 1 875671 12 9

CONTENTS

LEGENDS OF THE AIR

North American F-86 Sabre

Three F-86As (top) and a single F-86E Sabre (bottom) from Nellis AFB, Las Vegas, over Nevada in the early 1950s. The F-86E is from the Block 15 production batch which combined the F-86F airframe with the F-86E's less powerful engine. (NAA)

NORTH AMERICAN F-86 SABRE

The key to greatness in any aircraft design seems to lie in its ability to be 'the right aircraft at the right time'. The North American F-86 Sabre jet fighter certainly was, blooded in the Korean war and serving with distinction with the air forces of no fewer than 37 nations (including second hand purchasers) in the 1950s, 1960s and in some cases beyond.

The Sabre was produced in many day and all weather fighter variants by North American Aviation and its licencees. A total of 8,681 F-86s were built: 6,233 by the parent company, 1,815 by Canadair, 112 by the Commonwealth Aircraft Corporation in Australia, 221 assembled by Fiat in Italy and 300 assembled by Mitsubishi in Japan. To this must be added 1,115 examples of the carrier based version developed for the US Navy, the Fury.

Overall, an impressive tally for an aircraft which is generally regarded as the best fighter of its era because of its excellent combat record in Korea, its technical achievements – it was far in advance of the jet fighters which immediately preceded it – and its outstanding commercial success. For North American Aviation the success of the Sabre was doubly significant in that it enabled the company to follow the classic piston engined P-51 Mustang with another classic aircraft,

something which very few of the fighter manufacturers of World War II could achieve. By the end of the 1940s once pre-eminent companies such as Curtiss and Supermarine were virtually spent forces in the fighter business, a situation which would have seemed laughably improbable a handful of years earlier.

The Growth of NAA

North American Aviation's dominance of the military aircraft field in the 1940s and 1950s was due to a series of successful designs which kept the company at the forefront for many years. Formed in 1928, NAA initially operated as a holding company for other aviation concerns such as Curtiss, Sperry and the airline TWA and had no aircraft designs of its own, instead funding these other companies and their designs.

NAA was reorganised in 1933 when it came under the control of James H ('Dutch') Kindelberger, one of the leading lights in military aircraft design in the years ahead and formerly chief engineer at Douglas Aircraft. Joining Kindelberger was John Leland 'Lee' Attwood, the two men together establishing the manufacturing division of North American Aviation at the old Curtiss-Caproni plant at Dandalk, Maryland.

The revamped NAA's first design

was the model GA-15 two seat observation monoplane of 1935 powered by a 975hp (725kW) Wright R-1820 Cyclone radial engine. Ordered for the US Army Air Corps as the O-47, 239 were built. Most were based in the USA where they were used for training and general duties, although some saw limited service in the early weeks of the Pacific war.

NAA followed the O-47 with the aircraft which really made the company, the NA-16 family of basic trainers which evolved into the hugely successful T-6 Texan/Harvard series of advanced and combat trainers. USAAC contracts for the early models allowed NAA to build the factory with which it is most readily associated – at Inglewood, California, located on the perimeter of Mines Field, or Los Angeles International Airport.

The NA-16/T-6 family was built in huge numbers as it became the standard trainer of its type with many allied nations during World War II, armed versions even seeing combat with some. North American alone built more than 17,000 (which necessitated the building of a second factory at Dallas Texas), to which must be added 755 built in Australia as the CAC Wirraway and 2,910 Harvards by Noorduyn Aviation in Canada for the Royal Air Force, Royal Canadian Air Force and USAAF.

F-86D-60s on the ramp at NAA's Inglewood facility in company with F-100 Super Sabres. (NAA)

North American Aviation's wartime heritage (top to bottom): T-6 Texan/Harvard, B-25 Mitchell and P-51 Mustang. These aircraft established the company as a major supplier of military aircraft. (David Foote/NAA)

'Rockwells'. NAA and the Rockwell Corporation had merged in 1967 creating the 'North American-Rockwell' brand name, with the former disappearing a few years later.

In the meantime, the company had continued producing successful, technologically advanced designs for both civil and military markets: the B-45 Tornado of 1947, the first US heavy multi engined jet; the T-28 Trojan trainer (successor to the Texan); the T-2 Buckeye jet trainer for the US Navy; the AJ Savage composite powered large naval bomber and reconnaissance aircraft; the T-39 Sabreliner military and civil light jet transport (one of the first bizjets); the A-5 Vigilante advanced supersonic naval bomber; the XB-70 Valkyrie Mach 3 experimental strategic bomber; and the extraordinary X-15 rocket powered research aircraft which achieved a speed of Mach 6.72 and an altitude of 354,200 feet (107,960m).

From Jet Mustang to Sabre

By the end of 1943, North American Aviation – along with several other manufacturers – was beginning to look at the possibilities of jet powered aircraft. Indeed, by that time the first two British jets to achieve production, the Gloster Meteor and de Havilland Vampire, had already made their first flights. In the United States, the Bell XP-59 Airacomet had been in the air for a year and the Lockheed XP-80 Shooting Star would be airborne when 1944 was just eight days old. Republic, too, would soon be working on its F-84 Thunderjet series although it wouldn't fly until after the war had ended.

Early NAA design studies revolved around various 'Jet Mustangs', one of them a mixed powerplant piston/jet design incorporating a modified Mustang fuselage combined with forward swept wings and tricycle undercarriage.

A 1944 design study resulted in NAA's first jet aircraft, the original straight winged FJ-1 Fury for the US Navy, which took to the air for the first time in November 1946. The swept wing and substantially redesigned XP-86 (later F-86) Sabre would not fly for nearly another year.

This delayed first flight was another example of the imaginative leadership of 'Dutch' Kindelberger, the man who in 1940 had rejected a British proposal that his company licence build Curtiss P-40s for the Royal Air Force. Kindelberger promised a new and much better fighter aircraft to be designed and built in record time instead. It was, and the world was given the classic P-51 Mustang.

The company developed from there, producing two of the classic combat aircraft of World War II, the B-25 Mitchell medium bomber and the P-51 Mustang fighter. As noted earlier, the end of the war saw several manufacturers which had previously been leading lights in the designing and building of military aircraft – notably fighters – fall by the wayside in that area. NAA was not one of them

thanks to the subject of this account, the Sabre, but carried on even after that with the F-100 Super Sabre.

At its peak during World War II, NAA employed some 91,000 workers and during the war years built more than 42,000 military aircraft, or 14 per cent of all US production.

The name North American remained at the fore until the early 1970s when its aircraft became known as

In the case of the Sabre, Kindelberger made another deliberate and on the face of it risky decision when he delayed what would become the F-86 programme for a year while his designers, J Lee Atwood, Ray Rice and Ed Schmued, investigated the benefits of swept wings from captured German data and redesigned their original efforts to incorporate such wings. In doing so, North American surrendered the short term jet fighter market to other manufacturers but benefited substantially in the longer term.

The aircraft which would become the original FJ-1 Fury for the US Navy had been given the company designation NA-134. This single seat fighter featured a straight wing which was essentially the laminar flow unit of the P-51 Mustang, a tricycle undercarriage, unswept tail surfaces and a tubby fuselage with a nose intake and rear jet pipe for the single 4,000lb (17.9kN) thrust Allison J35 axial flow turbojet engine. A fully blown canopy completed the Fury's appearance.

The performance the FJ-1 offered was reasonable for its era if not spectacular: a top speed of 494 knots (914km/h) at low level, an initial climb rate of 3,300 feet (1,005m) per minute and a modest service ceiling of 32,000 feet (9,750m). Only 30 FJ-1 Furys were built; later aircraft with the same FJ designation and Fury name would be totally different naval aircraft based on the F-86 Sabre.

In order to meet a United States Army Air Force requirement for an advanced fighter which could fly day intercept, escort and dive bomber missions, North American decided in 1944 to propose a land based development of the NA-134 designated NA-140. This was basically an NA-134 without the equipment necessary for carrier operations but with some other modifications including a longer fuselage, a development of the Mustang wing with a slightly reduced thickness/chord ratio (which significantly increased critical Mach number from 0.8 to 0.9) and increased fuel capacity.

North American in the jet age (top to bottom): F-100 Super Sabre, A-5 Vigilante and F-107, the latter marking the end of the road for the company as a builder of fighters.

Powered by the same Allison powerplant as the NA-134, the new aircraft offered a top speed of 506 knots (936km/h) at 10,000 feet, a ceiling of 46,000 feet (14,020m), a climb rate of 5,850 feet (1,783m) per minute and a combat radius of 258 nautical miles (478km) on the standard internal fuel capacity of 410 US gallons (1,552 litres). Maximum take off weight was 11,500lb (5,216kg).

Considering the NA-140's estimated top speed did not meet the USAAF's requirement of 522 knots (965km/h) and its overall performance was inferior to that projected for the well advanced Republic XP-84 Thunderjet, it's perhaps surprising that the USAAF accepted the design and signed a contract for three prototypes in May 1945. The aircraft was given the designation XP-86 but subsequent events would ensure that none would be built in this straight winged form.

The USAF's review of the XP-86 mock up was completed in June 1945, by which time the war in Europe had ended and vast amounts of German data dealing with jet engines, high speed aerodynamics and swept wings was beginning to come into the hands of American, British and Soviet aeronautical engineers. Teams from these countries were flown to Germany to inspect this information, the Americans photocopying and microfilming anything that looked interesting and sending it all back to the USA. Documents passed on to NAA were translated by the company's Head of Design Aerodynamics, Larry Green, and the application of this information to a new fighter aircraft studied by engineer Harrison Storms.

Sweeping Changes

It soon became obvious that the Germans were way ahead of the Allies in the field of high speed aero-

The extraordinary XB-70 Valkyrie experimental strategic bomber capable of Mach 3.

dynamics. Reports dealing with swept back wing surfaces to delay the effects of compressibility near the speed of sound went back as far as 1940 as a result of using models in wind tunnels. Other aspects of this complicated subject abounded, and all pointed to the need for swept back wings on jet fighters to gain the maximum benefit from the new jet powerplants.

Other reports had a direct bearing on the development of what would become the North American F-86 Sabre. One of them confirmed that swept wings delayed and reduced the drag rise at near supersonic speeds but also emphasised some undesirable effects on stability, particularly at low speed. This was a factor which resulted in the highly successful Messerschmitt Me 262 twin jet fighter featuring an only moderately swept wing in an attempt to find a compromise between high speed and acceptable handling at the other end of the scale.

The Germans had attempted to solve this problem by incorporating automatic leading edge slats into their swept wing designs. These slats popped out when the airspeed/angle of attack equation reached a certain level, providing in effect an increase in wing area (which reduced the stalling speed) and also smoothing out the airflow over the wing. Unfortunately, they had not fully succeeded in developing such a system as there had been no suitable airframe on which to experiment.

Faced with all this information and the possibility of a breakthrough in fighter design, North American Aviation took the bold step in August 1945 of deciding to incorporate a swept wing into the XP-86, the effect of which would be a marked increase

in top speed. The project was given the company designation RD-1369.

These radical changes necessarily delayed the programme by a full year, but the results were more than worthwhile, changing the original design from a mediocre performer into the world beater the Sabre became. The wing finally used for the XP-86 was in fact a development of a Messerschmitt design intended for the Me 262 but abandoned because of its designers' inability to properly cure the instability problem. As a result of extensive testing, North American's engineers were able to develop a satisfactory fully automatic leading edge slat which matched the characteristics of the wing's 35 degree sweep, 4.79 aspect ratio and thickness/chord

ratio varying from eleven per cent at the root to ten per cent at the tip.

Covering almost the entire leading edges of the wings, the slats opened and closed in response to aerodynamic forces. The critical point was at 290 knots in unaccelerated flight at low level. Above that, they remained firmly shut and flush with the wing.

In September 1945 North American Aviation submitted the swept wing XP-86 design to the USAAF which on the first day of the following November authorised the new aircraft to go ahead. Final designs revealed an elegant fighter aircraft with all flying surfaces swept, inwards retracting main undercarriage legs, provision for an ejection seat and cockpit pressurisation, the standard USAAF

The FJ-1 Fury naval fighter, North American's first jet aircraft. The prototype was flown in November 1946 and 30 were built.

An FJ-1 Fury under tow. The photograph clearly shows the top fuselage engine access hatch removed. Despite the FJ-1 being of tubby design with straight wings, some characteristics which would shortly emerge in the Sabre are evident.

armament of six 0.5 inch Browning machine guns (mounted in the nose) and hydraulically boosted elevators.

Speedbrakes were fitted on each side of the rear fuselage. These were operated by a hydraulic jack and could be opened at any speed. The original intention had been to install these in the wings, but the structural innovations incorporated in the wing design (as described below) made this impossible.

The bottom line of all this was simply that here was an aircraft which was not just a collection of piston engine airframe design principles modified to accept jet engines, it was in fact in many ways as advanced as technology and knowledge would allow it to be in the immediate post war era, a second generation jet fighter, in fact.

In the meantime, work continued on the very much first generation FJ-1 Fury naval fighter, the prototype recorded its first flight (as the XFJ-1) on 27 November 1946. The jet era at North American Aviation had begun, but much better was just around the corner.

Considering its development history it is perhaps not surprising that the detail design of the wing involved some innovations. Some of these were described by a North American Aviation technical bulletin: "A double skin structure with hat sections between layers extends from the centre section to the outboard edges of the outer panel fuel tanks, replacing the conventional rib and stringer construction in that region. Tapered skins have been used to save weight.

"The inboard upper skin, for example, is 0.250 inches thick at the wing root and 0.064 inches at the joint where it joins the outboard skin; the latter tapers from 0.064 inches at the joint to 0.032 inches at the wing tip. Specially equipped milling machines, using carbide tipped fly cutters up to 12 inches in diameter were set up in North American's main plant to solve new fabrication problems presented by these skins. The most complicated skin, on which three operations are required to obtain compound tapers, is completely matched in only 45 minutes.

"Use of 75S aluminium alloy throughout to provide a maximum strength/weight ratio has also complicated the production process; as have the extremely close tolerances required by both structural and aerodynamic considerations. As an example, a tolerance of only 0.002 inches [five hundredths of a millimetre!] is allowable on external rivet heads; this makes it necessary to shave about 15 per cent of them after assembly.

"The need for maximum fuel space in the new thin structure has further complicated design. This requirement, heightened by the rapid increase in fuel consumption accompanying higher speeds, has been the factor chiefly responsible for the growth in size of fighter aircraft that has marked the post war period. The XF-86, for example, is some 40 per cent heavier than the F-51H Mustang."

This report, which was compiled in 1948, refers to the Sabre prototype as the 'XF-86' rather than 'XP-86' in the last line quoted above. USAAF fighter aircraft were given the role prefix 'P' (for 'Pursuit') until June 1948 when this was changed to 'F' for 'Fighter'. This also explains the use of the term 'F-51H' Mustang.

Towards First Flight

By the end of 1946 construction of the first of three prototype XP-86s had begun and the USAAF had placed orders for 33 production P-86As (company designation NA-151)

The prototype XP-86 at the time of its rollout in August 1947. It would fly less than three months later.

A fine portrait of the first of three XP-86 Sabre prototypes, 45-59597. This aircraft was first flown by George Welch on 1 October 1947. (NAA)

but this was soon increased to 221 aircraft. The name 'Sabre' was not endowed on the aircraft until production models were undergoing service tests early in 1949. The 1st Fighter Group, the initial unit to receive the aircraft, sponsored a competition to find an appropriate name and out of 78 entries 'Sabre' was selected and officially adopted in March of that year.

The major design features of the Sabre as it would shortly be revealed to the world included wings which swept back at 35 degrees at 25 per cent chord with maximum thickness at 50 per cent of chord. They comprised an all metal two spar structure with upper and lower skins between which was sandwiched two sheets milled to tapering thickness (as described above) separated by 'hat' section extrusions. Split flaps were fitted inboard of the ailerons.

The tail unit was of the all metal cantilever monoplane type with all surfaces swept back 35 degrees like the wings. The tailplane was of conventional fixed stabiliser/elevator design on the prototypes and early production models, but the later F-86E introduced an 'all flying design' in which the elevators and tailplane were geared together and moved differentially with movements of the control column to provide in-flight trim.

The fuselage was of an oval section all metal structure with flush riveted stressed skin. Air for the engine entered by a single nose intake. Airbrakes were incorporated on either side of the rear fuselage, and these were innovative in that they could be opened at any speed or attitude. These opened frontwards (ie, were hinged from the rear) on the prototypes but operated in the reverse sense on production Sabres. The prototypes also featured an under-fuselage airbrake which was deleted on production models.

Access to the engine was achieved by a 'break' in the rear fuselage midway between the aft end of the canopy and the leading edge of the fin fillet. By simply disconnecting the fuselage at that point, the engine was exposed.

The tricycle undercarriage features single wheels on each unit and was hydraulically actuated. The main-wheels retracted inwards while the steerable nosewheel retracted rearwards into a bay under the forward fuselage. This area also housed the Sabre's gun armament, initially the standard USAAF fit of six 0.50in Browning M-3 machine guns. Armament variations and the development of the Sabre generally are described in the following chapter.

The single pilot sat in a pressurised cockpit on an ejection seat under a powered sliding 'bubble'

The second XP-86 Sabre (45-59598) was withdrawn from service in 1953 after logging just 202 flying hours. Note the P-82 Twin Mustangs behind. (NAA)

This shot of an Ellis based F-86A's forward fuselage shows the installation of three 0.50in machine guns on the starboard side. The installation was repeated on the port side. (NAA)

canopy which gave a view unsurpassed for the era.

Main dimensions were: wing span 37ft 1.4in (11.31m), length 37ft 6.5in (11.44m) and height 14ft 8.9in (4.49m). The XP-86 weighed 9,730lb (4,413kg) empty and 13,395lb (6,076kg) maximum takeoff.

The first prototype (45-59597) was completed at North American Aviation's Ingelwood, California, plant in August 1947 and from there transported to the USAAF's Lake Muroc (now Edwards Air Force Base) a few weeks later for preparations leading up to first flight. The pilot chosen to take the XP-86 up for the first time was George Welch, an NAA test pilot for three years and a man who achieved some fame on 7 December 1941, when as a P-40 pilot at Pearl Harbour had been the first to take off in an attempt to intercept the Japanese raiders who brought the USA into World War II. Welch had retired from the military as a Major with 16 kills to his credit before joining North American. Intimately involved in NAA's jet fighter test programmes, 'Wheaties' Welch was killed in 1954 while testing an F-100 Super Sabre.

Powered by a 3,750lb (16.8kN) thrust Allison J35-C-3 engine (similar to that which powered the FJ-1 Fury but built under licence by Chevrolet), George Welch took the unarmed XP-86 into the air for the first time on 1 October 1947, just under three months before its future rival in Korea, the Soviet MiG-15. That maiden flight resulted in a rather longer effort than the planned ten minute hop when the nosewheel leg jammed in the half extended position on the landing approach. For the next 40 minutes Welch attempted to rock the leg free but failed to do so. Fortunately, the jolt of landing on the mainwheels did the trick, and the errant nosewheel leg was correctly positioned and locked before it came down onto the runway following a skilled piece of flying by the test pilot.

Otherwise, the Sabre's first flight had been a success, the aircraft exhibiting fine handling characteristics which were to be confirmed as time went on. As proof of the success of the leading edge slats, pilots who flew the aircraft during its testing period commented on its docility at low speeds, providing sufficient power was available to keep the aircraft in the air. Stall the wings and/or fall off the back of the 'drag/power'

The cockpit of an F-86A, with the gunsight missing from its mounting position on the top of the coaming. It is generally considered that the cockpits of American military aircraft were better organised than their British counterparts then and for some time afterwards.

curve and the aircraft would perform what was referred to as the 'Sabre Dance', in which it would flail about in the air regardless of how much power was applied.

One solution was to have more engine power available and it was intended that production aircraft would be fitted with the General Electric J47 axial flow turbojet producing over 5,000lb (22.4kN) thrust.

Performance figures were revealed as the tests continued and with the slightly more powerful (3,920lb/ 17.6kN thrust) J35-A-5 version of the Allison engine installed, the prototype Sabre was significantly faster than the similarly powered but straight winged FJ-1 Fury despite the modest amount of available thrust. Top speed at a weight of 13,790lb (6,255kg) was 521 knots (964km/h) at sea level, 537 knots (995km/h) at 14,000 feet and 500 knots (925km/h) at 35,000 feet, the latter representing a Mach number of 0.875. Maximum rate of climb was logged at 4,000ft (1,219m) per minute and the service ceiling was 41,300 feet (12,588m).

In a shallow dive, the Sabre was supersonic. This milestone was first achieved in April 1948 when George Welch put the first prototype (now fit-

ted with a production standard 5,200lb/23.3kN thrust J47-GE-3 engine) through the so-called 'sound barrier' and caused sonic booms to bounce around the city of Los Angeles. Going supersonic was a significant event for the Sabre as it was the world's first combat aircraft capable of doing so and only the second US aircraft to achieve that feat. The first was the air launched Bell X-1 experimental aircraft flown by Charles Yeager the previous year.

Prototype testing was conducted in three phases: Phase I was initial testing conducted by the manufacturer and comprised 30 flying hours; Phase II was 11 service evaluation flights (totalling just over 10 hours in the air) conducted by Major Ken Chiltern in December 1947; and Phase III was an extensive period of testing lasting several months using all three prototypes. It was during this period that George Welch went supersonic in the first prototype.

45-59597 was destroyed in a crash during September 1952 after recording 280 flight hours. The second and third XP-86s (45-59598 and 45-59599) were withdrawn from service in 1953 after logging 202 and 75 hours, respectively.

Preserved by the RAAF and still flying in the 1990s, CAC Sabre A94-983 (top) once served with Malaysia. A JASDF RF-86F Sabre (bottom) of the 501st Tactical Reconnaissance Squadron. (Ray Berghouse/MAP)

Operators of second hand Sabres: a Yugoslav F-86D (top) and Colombian F-86F. (MAP)

Two South African Canadair Sabre Mk.6s in very different colour schemes. The lower aircraft was operated by 85 AFS when photographed in 1977. (MAP/Philip J Birtles)

European operated Sabres included this West German Canadair Mk.6 (top) and Portuguese F-86F. (MAP)

Most of Japan's 435 F-86F Sabres were built by Mitsubishi like this one from the Blue Impulse aerobatic team (top); while French F-86Ks (bottom) were built in Italy by Fiat. (MAP/Philip J Birtles).

A well worn Italian F-86K (top) and Turkish Canadair Sabre (bottom) display contrasting colour schemes. It's interesting that neither of these Sabres were built in the USA. (MAP)

Sharpening The Blade – Sabre Variants

F-86A SABRE

The initial US Air Force contract for 33 P-86A Sabre day fighters had been placed in December 1946 and was subsequently extended to include 190 examples of the ultimately stillborn P-86B variant. The P-86B was cancelled in December 1947, and 188 P-86As plus two F-86Cs (see below) substituted for them instead. Total 'A' model Sabre production eventually reached 554 aircraft before it was replaced on North American's production lines by the next day fighter variant, the F-86E.

The first production P-86A (47-605) flew on 20 May 1948, less than two weeks before the newly autonomous (since September 1947) US Air Force changed the role prefix in the Sabre's designation from 'P' for 'pursuit' to 'F' for 'fighter'. From now on all US Sabres would be known as F-86s.

The first 33 F-86As were Block 1 aircraft (F-86A-1), and in effect were pre production models used for service trials and evaluation. They differed from the prototypes mainly in having gun armament installed and General Electric J47-GE-1 axial flow turbojets of 4,850lb (21.7kN) thrust in place of the original J35. The remaining 521 F-86A-5 Sabres were fitted with 5,200lb (23.3kN) thrust J47-GE-3, -7, -9 and 13 engines, resulting in greatly enhanced performance when compared with the prototypes and contemporary jet fighters. With a maximum speed of 590 knots (1,093km/h) at sea level, the F-86A was nearly 80 knots (148km/h) faster than the straight winged Lockheed F-80 Shooting Star and Gloster Meteor F.8.

Standard armament was the usual six 0.50in Browning M-3 machine guns with 267 rounds each, mounted in easily installed and removed boxes in the lower forward fuselage. These boxes were capable of holding 300 rounds per gun, but the lower number was normally carried. Most F-86As had a Mark 18 lead computing gyroscopic gunsight installed, although the final 24 had an A-ICM sight coupled with AN/APG-30 radar mounted in the upper lip of the nose intake.

This radar had a sweep range of between 150 and 3,000 yards (137–2,740m) and automatically locked on to and tracked a target, projecting the sight image onto the Sabre's windshield in the form of an early 'head up display' (HUD). The system could be used for gun, rocket and bomb aiming and although theoretically a much improved aiming system, suffered from unreliability in a harsh operating environment such as in Korea. Many F-86A-5s were retrofitted with this sighting system and redesignated F-86A-7s.

Other detail differences between the F-86A and the prototypes included the fitting of rearwards opening speed brakes and the deletion of the underfuselage brake and the relocation of the pitot tube from the fin to the starboard wing tip.

The initial batch of F-86A-1s also featured an interesting door system over the six gun ports. In the interests of streamlining, the ports remained shut until the guns were fired, at which point the doors opened inwards. This feature was eliminated on the F-86A-5 aircraft, which was in effect the first combat capable version. The A-5 also received an armoured glass windscreen, heated gun compartments and the ability to carry a variety of stores on two underwing pylons. These could include 120US gal (455 litre) drop tanks, 500 or 1,000lb (227 or 454kg) bombs or unguided 5 inch (12.7cm) HVAR rockets.

An additional F-86A sub variant was the RF-86A reconnaissance aircraft, about 11 of which were converted from fighters serving with the USAF's 4th Fighter Interceptor Wing in Korea. Under the name Project Ashtray, the conversion involved removing all but two of the Sabre's guns, ammunition bays and associated equipment and installing a pair of K-24 cameras in their place. As the cameras were mounted horizontally, a system of mirrors had to be devised to gain vertical coverage. Some RF-86As were also fitted with a K-22 'dicing camera' in the lip of the nose.

Into Service and Records

As the majority of the 33 F-86A-1s were used for service tests and evaluation (particularly those involving armament trails), the F-86A-5 was the first Sabre variant to see enter regular operational service with the USAF. First equipped with the new fighter was the 1st Fighter Group (FG) at March AFB, California, the

Two F-86A-5s of the USAF's 81st Fighter Interceptor Group taxying out at Hatfield in early 1952 during a visit to the United Kingdom. Sabres from this group were the first to cross the Atlantic the previous year. (via Philip J Birtles)

F-86A-5s of Cadillac Flight, Las Vegas. These aircraft are from the first major Sabre production batch.

94th Fighter Interceptor Squadron (FIS) receiving initial deliveries for the Group in March 1949. Interestingly, the 1st FG was responsible for the air defence of the Los Angeles area, which included North American Aviation's Inglewood factory.

Four other USAF Fighter Groups were rapidly equipped with F-86A Sabres: the 4th (Langley AFB) defending Washington DC, the 81st (Kirtland AFB) which included the atomic bomb plant at Alamogordo, New Mexico, among its responsibilities; the 33rd and 56th. F-86A service with the Air National Guard began as early as December 1950 when aircraft were accepted by the 116th FIS of the Washington ANG, while a further five ANG squadrons were subsequently equipped with the type. For

the record, the average F-86A Sabre cost the US taxpayer $US178,400 per aircraft.

Probably the best known of the five USAF Fighter Groups which operated the F-86A Sabre is the 4th due to its exploits in the Korean War. Although this conflict is covered in greater detail later, it's worth recounting here that the unexpected appearance of the Soviet MiG-15 fighter in Korean skies in November 1950 changed the aerial situation completely. Up to that point the US and its allies had almost uncontested air superiority and the 4th FG's Sabres were rushed to the area to counter the new threat.

Sabre operations in Korea began on 13 December and the first MiG 'kill' was recorded four days later

when the 336th FIS's Lt Col Bruce Hinton shot one down during a patrol near Sinuiji. It was the first of 792 claimed MiG-15 kills Sabre pilots would make over the remainder of the war.

When it entered service, the Sabre was the fastest production jet fighter extant, so attempts on the world's air speed record were perhaps inevitable. By the time the Sabre entered service the record was 650.796mph (1,047.3km/h), set in August 1947 by a Douglas Skystreak research aircraft.

The Sabre's first attempt to break the record in September 1948 during the National Air Races at Cleveland, Ohio (in front of 80,000 people!) was officially unsuccessful, although there is little doubt the necessary speed was achieved. The rules required the

An F-86A ripple fires its 5 inch HVAR rockets. Sixteen could be carried underwing.

Major Robert Johnson (second from right) talks to NAA personnel just before setting a new world's air speed record of 670.98mph (1,079.8km/h) in September 1948 flying F-86A-1 47-611.

aircraft to make two passes in each direction over a three kilometre course at a height not exceeding 328 feet (100 metres). Flying the fourth production F-86A-1 (47-608), Major Richard Johnson made six passes over the course but three were not timed due to problems with the recording equipment, bumpy weather restricted the aircraft's speed on two and other problems like stray aircraft wandering onto the course meant that the rules' requirements were not fully met.

Despite all this, three measured runs did reveal an average speed of 669.480mph (1,077.4km/h), well above the previous mark but not eligible to enter the record books.

Another attempt was made ten days later, on 15 September over the dry lake at Muroc. This time there were no mistakes, Major Johnson achieving an average speed of 670.981mph (1,079.8km/h) over the four runs and having that ratified by the *Federation Aeronautique International* as the new world record. Later on, F-86D Sabres would raise the record even further.

> **F-86A-5 SABRE**
> **Powerplant:** *One 5,200lb (23.3kN) thrust General Electric J47-GE-7 axial flow turbojet; internal fuel capacity 432 USgal (1,636 l), provision for two 120 USgal (454 l) underwing drop tanks.*
> **Dimensions:** *Wing span 37ft 1.4in (11.31m); length 37ft 6.5in (11.44m); height 14ft 8.9in (4.49m); wing area 288sq ft (26.75m²).*
> **Weights:** *Empty 10,093lb (4,578kg); takeoff (clean) 14,108lb (6,399kg), with external tanks 15,876lb (7,201kg), maximum 16,223lb (7,362kg).*
> **Armament:** *Six 0.50in Browning M-3 machine guns in nose with 267 rounds per gun; underwing 500 or 1,000lb (227 or 454kg) bombs or 16 5in HVAR rockets.*
> **Performance:** *Max speed 589kt (1,089km/h) at sea level, 523kt (967km/h) at 35,000ft; cruising speed 463kt (857km/h); maximum rate of climb 7,470ft (2,277m)/min, time to 40,000ft 10.4min; service ceiling 48,000ft (14,630m); combat radius (internal fuel) 287nm (530km); max range (with drop tanks) 915nm (1,694km).*

F-86B SABRE

This stillborn variant was designed to meet a USAF requirement for a Sabre with larger wheels and tyres and heavier brakes. Based on the F-86A, it would have featured a seven inches (18cm) wider fuselage to accommodate these but the requirement was dropped when it was realised that improvements in wheel and tyre design made it unnecessary. As a result, the F-86B was never built.

The USAF ordered 190 F-86Bs in October 1947 but when the project was cancelled 188 of these were allocated to extra F-86As and the remaining two became orders for the F-86C, as described below.

F-86C/YF-93A SABRE

Intended as a long range escort fighter version of the basic Sabre, the extent of the F-86C's modifications over the standard aircraft were such that the two examples built were redesignated YF-93As. The two aircraft were serialled 48-317 and -318 and the first of them was flown in January 1950 in the hands of George Welch. An order for 118 production aircraft was placed in June 1948 but cancelled the following year, although the two prototypes were built. The advent of high speed jet strategic bombers such as the Boeing B-47 Stratojet made the YF-93C unnecessary.

The F-86C/YF-93A embodied several radical changes over the standard Sabre, resulting in a much different looking aircraft. The J47 engine was replaced by an 8,000lb (35.8kN) thrust (with afterburning) Pratt & Whitney J48 centrifugal flow

F-86A-5 Sabre 48-205 of the USAF's 56th Fighter Group at Chicago O'Hare.

The YF-93A (right) at Lake Muroc with the prototype YF-86D. The differences between the two aircraft are marked, while the F-86D was itself very different to the day fighter Sabres.

turbo jet (Rolls-Royce Tay licence), the larger engine necessitating a longer and fatter fuselage which in turn housed a vastly increased fuel capacity of 1,581 US gallons (5,985 l).

Engine air was provided by NACA intakes mounted flush on the forward fuselage sides (replaced by protruding intakes later on), the previous nose intake giving way to a radome housing SCR-720 search radar. A taller undercarriage was fitted with dual wheels on the main legs, the proposed armament was six 20mm cannon in the nose, the side fuselage speed brakes were replaced by a single 'slab' brake under the forward fuselage and at 26,516lb (12,027kg), the maximum weight was nearly twice that of the F-86A.

Despite the cancellation of the F-86C/YF-93A programme, the two prototypes flew on well into the 1950s as chase and test aircraft for the National Advisory Committee for Aeronautics (NACA).

F-86C/YF-93A SABRE

Powerplant: One Pratt & Whitney J48-P-1 (Rolls-Royce Tay) centrifugal flow turbojet rated at 8,000lb (35.8kN) thrust with afterburner; internal fuel capacity 1,581 USgal (5,985 l).
Dimensions: Wing span 38ft 11in (11.86m); length 44ft 1in (13.43m); height 15ft 8in (4.77m).
Weights: Maximum loaded 26,516lb (12,027kg).
Armament: Six 20mm cannon.
Performance: Max speed 616kt (1,139km/h) at sea level, 541kt (1,001km/h) at 35,000ft; initial climb 11,960ft (3,645m)/min; service ceiling 46,800ft (14,264m); max range 1,711nm (3,165km).

F-86D SABRE

The most numerically important version of the Sabre, with 2,506 built including two prototypes, the F-86D – or 'Sabre Dog' as it was popularly known – all weather fighter was also

the first major redesign of the basic Sabre to attain production. The changes were such that only 25 per cent of the original remained untouched (mainly the wings and undercarriage) and at the time of the prototype's first flight on 22 December 1949, the 'D' was regarded as a new aircraft by the USAF and was designated the F-95A. Political expediency then took a hand – it was easier to get funding for developed versions of existing aircraft than for new ones – and the F-95A became the F-86D Sabre in July 1950.

Conceived in the era of the early days of the Cold War and intended to intercept Soviet bombers which would undoubtedly be carrying nuclear weapons in a time of war, the F-86D introduced several 'firsts' to the art of fighter design and service, notably in that it was the first single seat all weather (or 'night') fighter (the traditional second crew member was replaced by electronic fire control and target location wizardry) and it was the first fighter in regular service to entirely dispense with guns and carry rocket armament instead.

Compared with the day fighter Sabres which proceeded it, the F-86D had an afterburning version of the J47 engine, a nose radome for the radar under which was placed a widened engine air intake, a rear hinged 'clamshell' canopy in place of the previous aft sliding type, an 'all flying' tailplane with no separate elevators and no dihedral, hydraulically powered flight controls, a longer, wider and deeper fuselage and an electronic fuel management system which significantly reduced the pilot's workload.

The major area of commonality with the day fighter Sabres was in the use of the F-86A's slatted wing and undercarriage design, the latter coping with increased maximum weights which were eventually some 20 per cent greater than the F-86A's.

Flush intakes identify the YF-93A/F-86C in its early configuration.

An F-86D Sabre unleashes its underbelly pack of up to 24 Mighty Mouse Rockets. The firing sequence took about half a second to complete. (NAA)

As the F-86D was designed to shoot down bombers, it was decided to dispense with the gun armament and replace it with 24 2.75in (70mm) Mighty Mouse FFAR (Folding Fin Aircraft Rocket) rockets which would almost guarantee a 'kill' if fired accurately. The rockets were accommodated in the lower forward fuselage area below the cockpit, and when fired, the retractable tray on which they were mounted would pop out and the selected number of rockets dispatched towards the target. The firing sequence took only half a second to complete while the rocket carried a 7.55lb (3.42kg) warhead and had a range of up to 2.5 miles (4.1km).

Fire Control

The F-86D's fire control system was the heart of the aeroplane. It was highly complicated and because of this – and the general state of 'black box' technology at the time – proved to be notoriously unreliable at first with its miles of cable looms and countless vacuum tubes. The equipment was also extremely heavy as the era of solid state electronics and computer chips was still a long way off in 1950. In 1952-53 many F-86Ds were sitting idle at the North American factory awaiting the installation of the black boxes associated with the radar, fire control and engine control systems while the components' manufacturers tried to sort out problems at their end. Incorrect wiring and fitting of components – a lack of quality control, in other words – meant that many of the electronics had to be returned to the manufacturer for rectification work even before they had seen service.

At one stage it was reported that no fewer than 320 F-86Ds were awaiting these vital components – just as well, then, that the Soviet bombers the aircraft was intended to fight off hadn't been dispatched on a mission at that particular time!

The weapons control system comprised two basic components, the Hughes AN/APG-36 search radar mounted in the nose and the Hughes E-3 (early aircraft) or E-4 Fire Control System, all controlled by an AN/APA-84 computer. These allowed the F-86D's pilot to engage a target on a 'collision course' basis (from a side angle) rather than from the traditional rear attack position. This gave better op-

portunities for an effective engagement and enhanced self protection at the cost of enormous complexity in the Sabre's electronics systems.

The system proved to be very effective once the 'bugs' had been ironed out, the nose radar capable of detecting a target up to 30 miles (48km) away. Once acquired, the target showed as a blip on the pilot's radar screen with range and direction

The first prototype YF-86D/F-95A (50-0577) with a very different rear end configuration compared with production aircraft. Note the tall fin, low set tailplane and the shape of the tailpipe area.

The second prototype YF-86D (serial 50-0578) over Lake Muroc in 1950 during early tests.

A trio of F-86D-1 Sabres from the first production batch formate for the camera. These aircraft are the sixth, eighth and ninth production F-86Ds, built in 1951. (NAA)

Air Force F-86D Sabre
NORTH AMERICAN AVIATION, INC.

A look inside the F-86D, revealing the radar, underfuselage rocket tray and the vast array of heavy and complicated 'black boxes' which made the fire control system work – sometimes! (NAA)

F-86D-40 52-3840 of the 520th FIS, the 'Geiger Tigers'.

indicated. Once the radar had locked onto the target, the system's computer calculated a lead collision course, the pilot following its directions from a dot on the radar screen.

With the target calculated to be less than 20 seconds away, the pilot selected the number of rockets he wanted to fire (six, 12 or all 24) and squeezed the trigger to arm the weapons. At this point the firing control systems took over, calculating the moment when it would automatically fire the rockets, usually when the Sabre was about 500 yards away from the target.

When it worked, this pioneering fire control system was very success-ful, although the numerous F-86D sub variants which were eventually produced resulted in a large fleet of aircraft with major variations in component details, meaning a spares provisioning nightmare. A better degree of commonality was subsequently achieved with the USAF's Project Pull-Out, under which aircraft were withdrawn from service and sent to the NAA factory for refurbishment, modernisation and installation of equipment which resulted in much better commonality.

Afterburning Engines and Records

As mentioned above, the F-86D was the first Sabre variant to feature an afterburning version of the General Electric J47 engine. The proto-type YF-95A/YF-86Ds (Nos 50-0577 and 50-0578) were fitted with non afterburning J47-GE-7 engines rated at 5,200lb (23.3kN) thrust while the first production block of 37 F-86D-1s had 5,400lb (24.2kN) (dry) and 7,350lb (32.9kN) (afterburner) -17 engines. Early production F-86Ds had -17Bs rated at 7,500lb (33.6kN) thrust with afterburner, and later aircraft had 7,650lb (34.3kN) thrust (with afterburning) -33 engines installed.

The extra power provided by the afterburning engines in the F-86D more than compensated for the aircraft's increased operating weights and this was twice illustrated by the setting of new World's Air Speed Records.

The first of them was set in November 1952 when the previous mark of 670.981mph (1,079.8km/h) established by an F-86A in 1948 was beaten by Captain J Slade Nash in an F-86D-20 (51-2945) at Salton Sea, California. Nash recorded an average 698.505mph (1,124.1km/h) over the three kilometre course and carried a fully load of Mighty Mouse rockets while doing it.

This record didn't last long and was topped in July 1953 when another F-86D (51-6145, a Block 35 aircraft) flown by Lt Col William Barnes reached an average 715.745mph

The second of two F-86Ds which set world's air speed records in 1952-53. This is F-86D-35 51-6145 which set a new mark of 715.74mph (1,151.8km/h) in July 1953 in the hands of Lt Col William Barnes. (NAA)

(1,151.8km/h) at the same location. Barnes' aircraft also carried a load of rockets during the record attempt.

Barnes was able to achieve a 17mph (27km/h) advantage over the previous mark for two main reasons: a modified afterburner and the fact that at 105°F (40°C) it was a very hot day. In the days when speed records had to be set at very low altitude, seeking a hot day to attempt them became the sensible thing to do because the speed of sound increases with temperature. On a standard 59°F/15°C day it is 760mph (1,223km/h) at sea level while on the day Barnes made his attempt it was 797mph (1,283km/h). This materially allows the aircraft to go faster as although its limiting Mach number stays the same, that number represents a greater speed at the higher temperature.

The Sabre's record was short lived as the modified prototype Hawker Hunter took it to 727.63mph (1,170.9km/h) just two months later flying in the temperate conditions of England. The next mark of 735.70mph (1,183.9km/h) was established almost immediately afterwards by a Supermarine Swift which took advantage of the heat of the Libyan desert to do so.

F-86D Variations

The 2,405 production F-86Ds were divided between 15 production blocks, all of them manufactured at NAA's Los Angles facility. Deliveries to the USAF began in December 1951, two years after the first prototype had flown. The first production F-86D-1 was serialled 50-0455. The final F-86D-60 (53-1071) was handed over to the USAF in September 1955, meaning the average production rate of this most produced Sabre version was more than 650 per annum.

The various F-86D production blocks incorporated numerous detail changes to the basic aircraft's specification, particularly in regard to its electronics. The more obvious changes were the introduction of the E-4 fire control system on the F-86D-5, the F-86D-15 had single point refuelling, the F-86D-20 had the more powerful J47-GE-33 engine (this sub variant was initially called the F-86G but the designation was changed before deliveries began), provision was made for the installation of 120 USgal (454 litre) underwing drop tanks in the F-86D-25, the F-86D-35 had omni directional ranging radar, the F-86D-45 was the first fitted with a tail mounted braking parachute and it and the F-86D-60 were also fitted with the -33 engine.

The importance of the 'Sabre Dog' to the US Air Force can be gauged by the fact that in early 1956, no fewer than 20 of Air Defence Command's 30 Interceptor Wings were equipped with the pioneering single seat all weather fighter.

A major conversion programme involving more than 800 'Sabre Dogs' was carried out from 1956 and the aircraft involved were redesignated F-86Ls. This model is described later.

As the 1950s drew to a close, many of the USAF's F-86Ds which had not been converted to 'L' standards and were now regarded as obsolete were exported to several nations, Turkey, Greece, Taiwan, South Korea, Japan, Yugoslavia, Denmark and the Philippines among them.

F-86D-45 SABRE

Powerplant: One General Electric J47-GE-33 axial flow turbojet rated at 5,550lb (24.9kN) dry thrust and 7,650lb (34.3kN) thrust with afterburner; fuel capacity 608 USgal (2,301 l), provision for two 120 USgal (454 l) drop tanks.
Dimensions: Wing span 37ft 1.4in (11.31m); length 40ft 3.1in (12.27m); height 15ft 0in (4.57m); wing area 288sq ft (26.75m²).
Weights: Empty 13,518lb (6,132kg); normal loaded 18,160lb (8,237kg); maximum loaded 19,975lb (9,060kg).
Armament: 24 2.75in (70mm) Mighty Mouse FFAR missiles in retractable ventral tray.
Performance: Max speed 603kt (1,115km/h) at sea level, 536kt (991km/h) at 40,000ft; typical cruising speed 478kt (885km/h); initial climb 12,150ft (3,703m)/min; time to 40,000ft 6.9min; service ceiling 49,750ft (15,164m); combat radius (clean) 287nm (531km), combat radius (drop tanks) 435nm (804km); ferry range 889nm (1,645km).

F-86E SABRE

Very much an interim model and a relatively simple evolution of the F-86A, the F-86E Sabre differed from its day fighter predecessor with the incorporation of various aerodynamic and systems improvements. Powered by a 5,200lb (23.3kN) thrust J47-GE-13 engine, 336 were built for the USAF by North American and a further 60 were supplied from Canadair's production line. Each F-86E cost an average $US219,457.

The first F-86E (50-0579) during early testing in 1950. This interim model introduced the all flying tailplane to the Sabre line and formed the basis of the Canadair versions. (NAA)

Nice portrait of the 21st F-86E-1 (50-0599) on the ground showing plenty of detail. Like most American military aircraft, this Sabre seems to have a large part of its maintenance manual stencilled on the airframe! (NAA)

The major change incorporated in the F-86E was the introduction of an 'all flying' tailplane where the elevators and tailplane were linked for coordinated movement. The tailplane was hydraulically actuated (all flying controls were powered for the first time) with the elevator linked to it mechanically, the whole assembly pivoting around its rear spar through eight degrees up or down movement. This new system eliminated many of the effects of compressibility and pro-

vided better control responses generally. The F-86E's powered controls were irreversible and had an artificial feel system incorporated.

The first F-86E-1 (50-0579) was flown on 23 September 1950 and production ended in April 1952 with the introduction of the definitive US built day fighter Sabre, the F-86F. Front line USAF service was relatively brief with aircraft being transferred to Air National Guard Units as early as 1956. In the meantime, the F-86E

served the USAF both at home and with the 4th and 51st Fighter Interceptor Groups in Korea.

Four production blocks were manufactured: the initial F-86E-1 and similar F-86E-5; the F-86E-10 with an optically ground, armoured flat windscreen instead of the previous 'V' shaped unit; and the F-86E-15, an F-86F airframe fitted with the E's J47-GE-13 powerplant due to shortages of the F's more powerful engine.

The sixty Canadair built Sabre

Some of Japan's F-86F-40s (with long span, increased chord and slatted wing) were converted to RF-86F configuration with three cameras in the lower forward fuselage. Note the equipment bulge below the cockpit.

Several F-86Fs (and Es) were fitted with a quartet of 20mm cannon in place of the usual six machine guns in an attempt to increase the Sabre's hitting power. The aircraft were modified under Project Gun-Val. One of the cannon armed F-86Fs is shown above, while the cutaway illustrates the installation of the weapons. (NAA)

Mk.2s supplied to the USAF were designated F-86E-6. These were supplied in 1952 for use in Korea, the aircraft being delivered to the USA for the fitting of equipment and then sent to the front.

Four F-86E-10s were used in the 'Gun-Val' project (as described later), intended to improve the Sabre's firepower by replacing the standard six 0.50in machine guns with a quartet of 20mm cannon.

F-86E-5 SABRE
Powerplant: One 5,200lb (23.3kN) thrust General Electric J47-GE-13 axial flow turbojet; internal fuel capacity 432 USgal (1,636 l), provision for two 120 USgal (454 l) underwing drop tanks.
Dimensions: Wing span 37ft 1.4in (11.31m); length 37ft 6.5in (11.44m); height 14ft 9.5in (4.51m); wing area 288sq ft (26.75m²).
Weights: Empty 10,845lb (4,919kg); normal loaded 16,512lb (7,490kg); maximum 17,806lb (8,077kg).
Armament: Six 0.50in Browning M-3 machine guns in nose with 267 rounds per gun; underwing 500 or 1,000lb (227 or 454kg) bombs or 16 5in HVAR rockets.
Performance: Max speed 579kt (1,072km/h) at sea level, 522kt (966km/h) at 35,000ft; initial climb rate 7,250ft (2,210m)/min; service ceiling 47,200ft (14,386m); combat radius 380nm (704kmm); max range (with drop tanks) 1,060nm (1,965km).

F-86F SABRE

The final development of the basic Sabre day fighter airframe, the F-86F embodied a number of refinements resulting from experience in Korea, where the MiG-15 was proving to be a better dogfighter than expected, only the superior quality of the American pilots providing the edge.

The need for more power in the Sabre prompted the fundamental change in the F-86F over the previous models, particularly in the area of rate of climb where the MiG-15 had a marked advantage. Combat experience also revealed a need for enhanced manoeuvrability, resulting in the development of the so called '6-3' wing with leading edge slats removed. This significant modification was introduced to the F-86F about one-third of the way through its production run and was subsequently retrofitted to many earlier aircraft. With this modification installed, the Sabre was able to out-turn a MiG-15 and its high altitude/high Mach number manoeuvrability was considerably enhanced.

The F-86F Sabre was powered by the J47-GE-27 engine rated at 5,910lb (26.5kN) thrust, a 13 per cent improvement on the A and E models. This resulted in greater speeds but

The F-86F was the final development of the basic Sabre day fighter theme, introducing a more powerful engine and aerodynamic refinements as production went on. (NAA)

also a significantly improved rate of climb – in the order of 25 per cent at sea level – although this was still slightly inferior to the MiG-15.

The first F-86F-1 (51-2850) was flown on 19 March 1952 and production began immediately with an eventual total of 2,239 Fs built by NAA between then and December 1956, of which 280 were for export. A further 300 were assembled in Japan by Mitsubishi from North American kits.

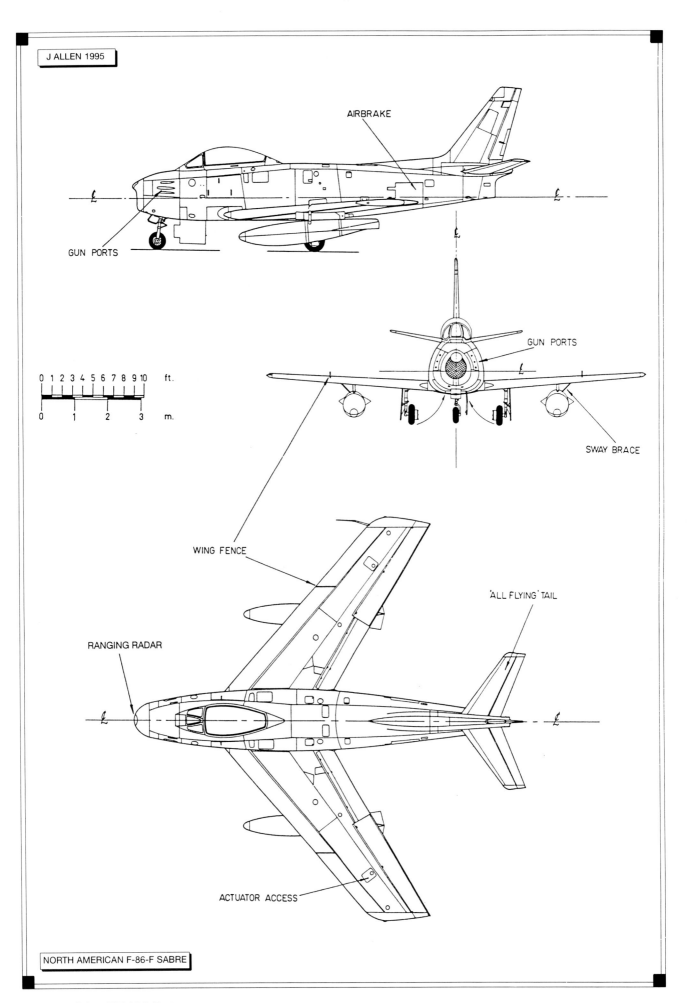

AIRBRAKE

GUN PORTS

GUN PORTS

SWAY BRACE

0 1 2 3 4 5 6 7 8 9 10   ft.

0   1   2   3   m.

WING FENCE

'ALL FLYING' TAIL

RANGING RADAR

ACTUATOR ACCESS

NORTH AMERICAN F-86-F SABRE

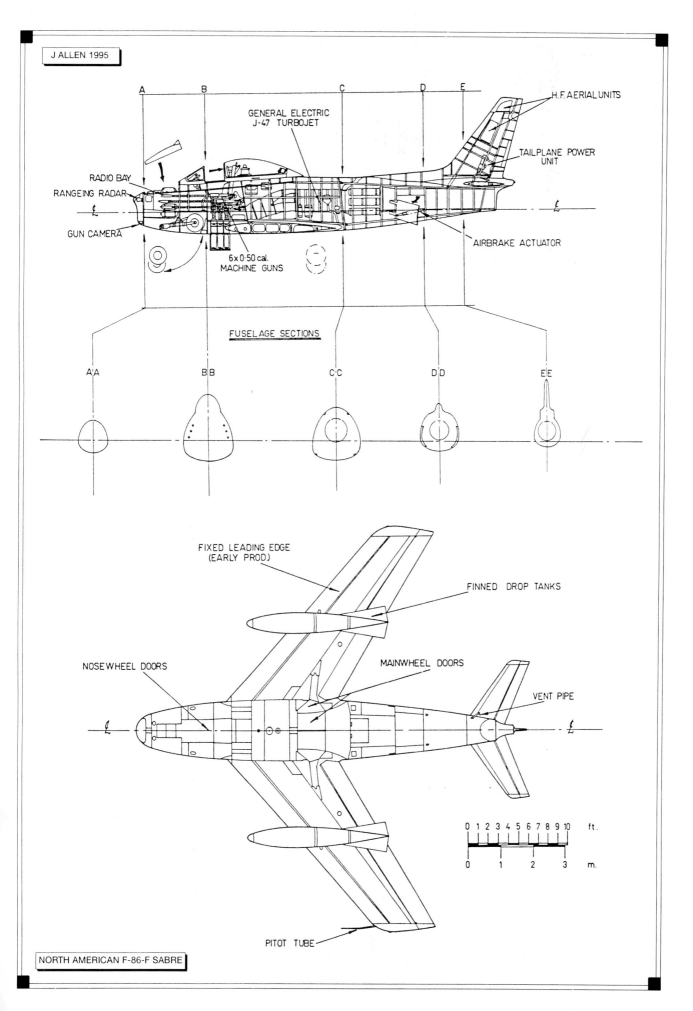

A   B   C   D   E

GENERAL ELECTRIC
J-47 TURBOJET

H.F. AERIAL UNITS

TAILPLANE POWER
UNIT

RADIO BAY

RANGEING RADAR

GUN CAMERA

AIRBRAKE ACTUATOR

6 x 0·50 cal.
MACHINE GUNS

FUSELAGE SECTIONS

A·A   B·B   C·C   D·D   E·E

FIXED LEADING EDGE
(EARLY PROD.)

FINNED DROP TANKS

NOSEWHEEL DOORS

MAINWHEEL DOORS

VENT PIPE

PITOT TUBE

NORTH AMERICAN F-86-F SABRE

0 1 2 3 4 5 6 7 8 9 10   ft.

0   1   2   3   m.

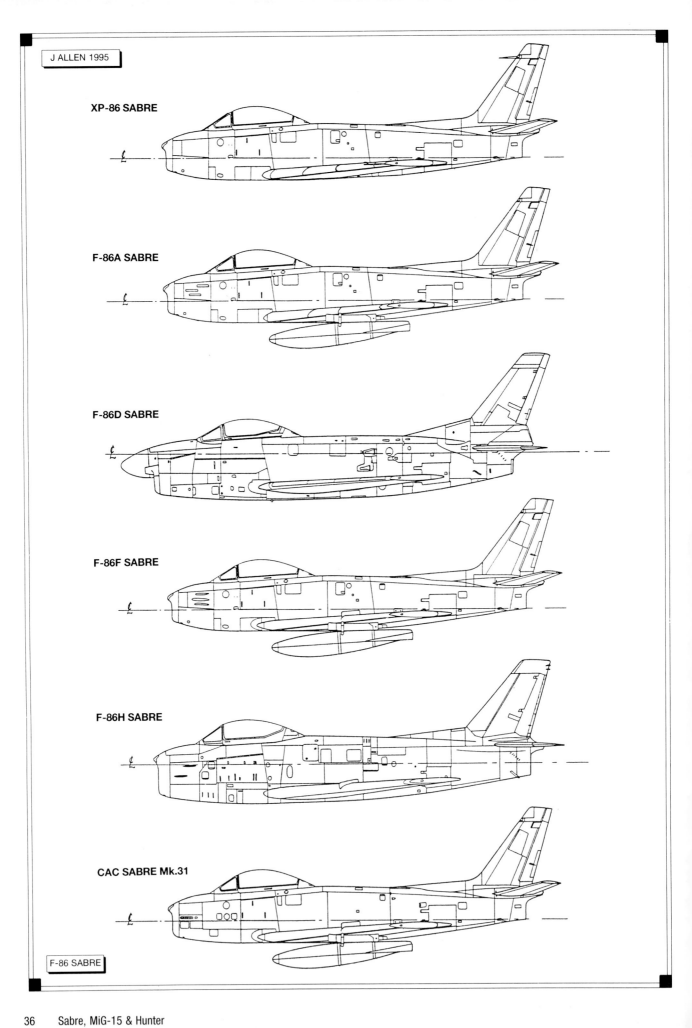

J ALLEN 1995

XP-86 SABRE

F-86A SABRE

F-86D SABRE

F-86F SABRE

F-86H SABRE

CAC SABRE Mk.31

F-86 SABRE

F-86Fs were built at NAA's Los Angeles plant and at the former Curtiss factory at Columbus, Ohio. This plant was reopened by NAA in 1950 to help cope with the ever increasing production rates prompted by the demands of the Korean war and it contributed 700 of the overall F-86F production tally.

Each F-86F cost the American taxpayer an average $US211,111, about four per cent less than the F-86E.

F-86F Variants

The initial 78 F-86F-1s were similar to the F-86E apart from the installation of the more powerful J47-GE-27 engine. The F-86F-5 was capable of carrying two 200 USgal (757 l) underwing drop tanks rather than the previous 120 USgal (454 l) units (bringing with it a useful 20 minutes increase in loiter time), the F-86F-10 introduced the simpler A-4 radar ranging gunsight and the F-86F-20 had an upgraded cockpit and armour protection for the tailplane operating mechanism.

Only seven F-86F-15s were built due to delays in the production of the J47-GE-27 engine with the result that 93 were fitted with the lower powered -13 engine and redesignated F-86E-15s.

The most important innovations came with the F-86F-25 and -30, built at the Columbus and Los Angeles plants, respectively. Between them these production blocks accounted for 1,459 of the F-86F total. All Sabres in these blocks were equipped with the 'dual store' wing with attachment points for two drop tanks or other stores below each wing rather than the previous one. With two 200 and two 120 US gallon (two 757 l and two 454 l) drop tanks under the wings these Sabres had a ferry range of nearly 1,400 nautical miles (2,570km). Alternatively, a 1,000lb (454kg) bomb could be carried on the inner hardpoints.

NAA began investigations into what become the '6-3' wing in the second half of 1952 and three F-86Fs were test flown with it installed from August of that year. The new wing dispensed with the leading edge slats and substituted a fixed leading edge instead. This extended the wing's chord by six inches (15cm) at the root and three inches (8cm) at the tip (thus '6-3'), increased the wing area from 288 to 303 square feet (26.7 to 28.1m²), provided reduced drag (and a small speed gain) and improved manoeuvrability. The addition of a small wing fence at about 70 per cent span completed the package, this reducing transonic buffet and helping the Sabre execute tighter turns at higher speeds.

The '6-3' wing was incorporated into F86F-25 and F86F-30 Sabres on the production line from early 1953 and was retrofitted to earlier aircraft. As is always the case with things aeronautical, you don't get "nuthin' for nuthin'" and in the case of the Sabre the enhanced manoeuvrability created by the new wing was at the cost of the low speed docility so carefully designed into the original wing with leading edge slats. With the '6-3' wing, stalling speed was increased by about 15 knots (28km/h) to 125 knots (231km/h).

The final F-86F variants were the -35 and -40. The F-86F-35 was capable of carrying a 100 kiloton 'special store' (atomic bomb). Weighing 1,200lb (544kg), this was carried under the port wing while drop tanks were mounted under the starboard wing. The F-86F-35 featured a Low Altitude Bombing System (LABS) enabling the 'loft bombing' technique to be used.

The F-86F-40 was the final Sabre day fighter subvariant. Developed for use by Japan, it had a curious mix of wing features. In order to restore the previous low speed docility and reduce the stalling speed, the leading edge slats were reinstated and each wing tip extended by 12 inches (30.5cm), resulting in an overall wingspan of 39ft 1.4in (11.92m) and wing area increased to 313.4sq ft (29.1m²). The result was a stalling speed some 17 knots (32km/h) below that of the F-86F with '6-3' wing.

NAA built 280 F86F-40s and a further 300 were assembled in Japan by Mitsubishi between 1956 and 1961. Some were capable of carrying Sidewinder air-to-air missiles and the USAF later modified many of its F-86Fs to have the extended and slatted wing.

Reconnaissance and Gun-Val

Earlier attempts to modify F-86A Sabres for photo-reconnaissance duties in Korea under Project Ashtray were only partially successful, so another attempt was made with the F-86F. This time the modification programme was made under the name Project Haymaker, using the F-86F-30 as the base and redesignating converted aircraft as the RF-86F.

The programme encompassed only a handful of aircraft which were fitted with one K-17 and two K-22 cameras mounted side by side in the Sabre's lower fuselage immediately forward of the wings. Bulged camera fairings in this area and a larger equipment bulge on the port side of the fuselage below the canopy provided external clues to the conversion. Most RF-86Fs had the guns removed and their ports faired over, although a couple retained two 'fifties' as defensive armament. Some of Japan's F-86Fs were also converted to 'RF' specifications and the type also flew in South Korean colours.

The development of the F-86F with more power and the '6-3' wing solved most of the shortcomings exhibited by the Sabre against the MiG-15. One area which caused ongoing problems was the lack of 'hitting power' provided by the Sabre's six 0.50in machine guns. The MiG-15, by comparison, carried a much heavier punch with its one 37mm and two 23mm cannon. Combat analyses in Korea had revealed that of every three MiGs hit by the Sabre's guns, two were getting away. It was estimated that it took an average 1,024 rounds of fifty calibre ammunition to destroy a MiG-15, or nearly two-thirds of the Sabre's capacity.

This problem was investigated by Project Gun-Val, under which six F-86F-1s and four F-86E-10s were fitted with a quartet of the new T-160 20mm cannon. These aircraft were redesignated as F-86F-2s and two other F-86F-1s were fitted with Oerlikon type 20mm cannon and called F-86F-3s. The main thrust of the trials revolved around the T-160 which later went into production as the M39. This weapon had a revolving drum feed which was capable of delivering the very high rate of fire of 1,600 rounds per minute.

Operational testing was carried out by the 4th Fighter Interceptor Wing in Korea from March 1953, eight F-86F-2s taking part. There were early problems, the main one being the discovery that it was usually only possible to fire two of the four guns at once due to the blast from the full complement causing airflow problems within the Sabre's intake and resulting in compressor stall of the engine. This problem also arose with the Australian built CAC Sabre (which had two 30mm Aden cannon) and with the Hawker Hunter.

The Gun-Val Sabres remained in Korea for four months, and despite the limitations imposed by using only two of the available four guns, fired at 41 MiG-15s and scored six definite kills, three probables and 13 damaged.

The T-160 gun never found its way onto production day fighter Sabres, but as the M39 it was installed in the F-86H fighter-bomber. It also equipped the F-100 Super Sabre, McDonnell F-101 Voodoo and Northrop F-5.

F-86F-25 SABRE

Powerplant: One 5,910lb (26.5kN) thrust General Electric J47-GE-27 axial flow turbojet; internal fuel capacity 437 USgal (1,654 l), provision for two 200 US gal (757 l) and/or two 120 USgal (454 l) underwing drop tanks.
Dimensions: Wing span 37ft 1.4in (11.31m); length 37ft 6.5in (11.44m); wing area 303sq ft (28.1m²).
Weights: Empty 10,950lb (4,967kg); normal loaded 16,860lb (7,648kg); maximum 20,357lb (9,234kg).
Armament: Six 0.50in Browning M-3 machine guns in nose with 267 rounds per gun; four underwing hardpoints for drop tanks or two 1,000lb (454kg) on inboard points; alternatively 16 5in HVAR rockets.
Performance: Max speed 604kt (1,118km/h) at sea level, 530kt (981km/h) at 35,000ft; cruising speed 423-452kt (782-838km/h); initial climb 9,300ft (2,835m)/min; service ceiling 48,000ft (14,630m); combat radius (two 1,000lb bombs) 275nm (508km); combat radius (max external fuel) 400nm (740km); range with internal fuel 683nm (1,263nm); ferry range (max external fuel) 1,327nm (2,454km).

TF-86F SABRE

The development of a two seat conversion trainer Sabre variant began in February 1953 and resulted in two prototypes being built. The project got no further than that due to the planned production of a two seat version of the Sabre's successor, the F-100 Super Sabre.

Both TF-86s were based on F-86F airframes, the modifications involving stretching the fuselage by nearly 63 inches (1.6m) to accommodate the tandem cockpits, which were under a very large single piece, aft hinging 'clamshell' canopy. The rear (instructor's) cockpit was in the normal place and the fuselage stretch forward of that provided space for the student's cockpit. The F-86F's J47-GE-27 engine was retained and both aircraft were fitted with the standard slatted wing which was moved eight inches (20cm) forward.

The first TF-86 (modified from F-86F-30 52-5016 and retaining that serial number) was first flown on 14 December 1953. This aircraft survived only until the following March when it was destroyed in an accident which killed test pilot Joseph Lynch.

A second TF-86 was then authorised (53-1228) and it was based on an F-86F-35. Its main physical characteristics were similar to the original aircraft but it differed in underwing hard points and a pair of 0.50in machine guns in the nose for gunnery practice. '1228 was first flown in August 1954 and despite the need for a Sabre Trainer failing to materialise, this aircraft flew well into the 1960s as a chase aircraft at the Edwards Air Force base Flight Test Centre.

TF-86F SABRE

Powerplant: One 5,910lb (26.5kN) thrust General Electric J47-GE-27 axial flow turbojet.
Dimensions: Wing span 37ft 1.4in (11.31m); length 42ft 9in (13.03m); height 14ft 9.5in (4.51m); wing area 288sq ft (26.75m²).
Weights: Normal loaded 14,836lb (6,730kg), maximum loaded 18,040lb (8,183kg).
Armament: (Second aircraft only) two 0.50in Browning M-3 machine guns in nose; underwing hardpoints for drop tanks or bombs.
Performance: Max speed 602kt (1,113km/h) at sea level; initial climb 10,300ft (3,139m)/min; service ceiling 50,500ft (15,392m); ferry range 1,125nm (2,081km).

F-86H SABRE

The F-86H was the last major development of the Sabre line and also the first version designed from the start as a fighter-bomber. The aircraft was substantially different from the day fighter models which preceded it, featuring a much more powerful engine, a largely redesigned fuselage to accommodate the powerplant and in all but the first production batch, cannon armament instead of the previous machine guns.

The powerplant selected for the F-86H was the General Electric J73 turbojet rated at 8,920lb (40.0kN)

The second of only two TF-86 Sabre trainers, based on the F-86F. The large canopy was in one piece, opening upwards from the rear. (NAA)

The F-86H was the last major development of the Sabre line and the first version designed from the outset as a fighter-bomber. A more powerful engine, redesigned fuselage and four cannon armament in all but the earliest aircraft were features. This aircraft is an early F-86H-1 with six machine guns. (NAA)

thrust, a 50 per cent increase in the power provided by the F-86F's J47. The F-86H was the only production application for this engine.

The new engine was naturally larger and heavier than its predecessor and demanded considerably greater airflow to feed it and therefore a larger inlet. This resulted in a major redesign of the Sabre's fuselage, which was deepened by six inches (15cm). Other physical changes included the fitting of a rear hinged clamshell canopy, a larger tailplane with no dihedral, strengthened undercarriage with a longer nosewheel leg,

upgraded ejection seat and a 28 per cent increase in internal fuel capacity to 562 US gallons (2,127 litres).

The '6-3' wing was initially installed on production F-86Hs but later aircraft were fitted with the extended and slatted wing fitted to late production F-86Fs. This was subsequently retrofitted to the earlier aircraft. The F-86H's armament also changed during the course of production, the 113 aircraft from the first production block (F-86H-1) having the hitherto standard fixed armament of six 0.50in machine guns while the remaining F-86H-5s and -10s were

equipped with four 20mm M39 cannon, the production version of the T-160 rotary magazine weapon previously tested on E and F model Sabres under Project Gun-Val.

The F-86H featured four underwing hardpoints capable of carrying drop tanks or a variety of offensive stores including 1,000lb (454kg) bombs, 750lb (340kg) napalm bombs, eight 5in HVAR rockets or a 100-kiloton atomic bomb weighing 1,200lb (544kg). Operational equipment included the LABS low altitude bombing system, AN/APG-30 radar and A-4 gunsight.

An F-86H-10 with definitive four cannon armament. (NAA)

LABS ensured accurate delivery of the atomic 'special store' by allowing the pilot to 'lob' the bomb at the appropriate moment and then make an escape before the blast got him.

The first YF-86H (52-1975) flew on 30 April 1953 and was followed by another test aircraft (52-1976) and 473 production models. The prototypes were built at NAA's Los Angeles plant and all production aircraft came out of the Columbus, Ohio, facility. The F-86H was rather more expensive than the day fighter versions had been, each one costing an average $US582,839.

Initial deliveries were to the USAF's 312th Fighter Bomber Wing at Clovis AFB, New Mexico, and after a relatively short production run, the last F-86H was handed over in October 1955. The type equipped five USAF fighter-bomber wings but by mid 1958 all had been passed onto the Air National Guard.

One sad note is part of the F-86H story, the death of the USAF's top Korean ace, Captain Joe McConnell in August 1954 while performing a test flight. 1954 was not a good year for accidents in North American jet aircraft. Apart from McConnell, fatalities included test pilot Joe Lynch in the first TF-86 trainer and the legendary George 'Wheaties' Welch (who took the first Sabre on its maiden flight) in an F-100 Super Sabre.

F-86H-5 SABRE
Powerplant: One 8,920lb (40.0kN) thrust General Electric J73-GE-3D axial flow turbojet; internal fuel capacity 562 US gal (2,127 l), provision for 120 and 200 USgal (454/757 l) underwing drop tanks.
Dimensions: Wing span 39ft 1.4in (11.92m); length 38ft 10in (11.83m); height 15ft 0in (4.57m); wing area 313.4sq ft (29.1m²).
Weights: Empty 13,836lb (6,276kg); combat weight 18,683lb (8,475kg); maximum loaded 24,296lb (11,020kg).
Armament: Four 20mm Pontiac M39 cannon in nose; underwing hardpoints for two 1,000lb (454kg) bombs, two 750lb (340kg) napalm bombs, eight 5in HVAR rockets or one 1,200lb (544kg) 100-kiloton atomic bomb.
Performance: Max speed 602kt (1,113km/h) at sea level, 537kt (993km/h) at 35,000ft; typical cruise speed 480kt (888km/h); max rate of climb 12,900ft (3,932m)/min; service ceiling 50,800ft (15,484m); combat radius (clean) 451nm (835km); combat radius (two 1,000lb bombs) 350nm (648km); max ferry range (external fuel) 1,575nm (2,913km).

F-86K SABRE

This simplified development of the F-86D 'Sabre Dog' was developed for use by several NATO nations which had need of an all weather fighter. Under the Mutual Defence Assistance Programme (MDAP), it was subject to a co-production deal with Fiat in Italy and of the 341 F-86Ks eventually built (plus two prototypes), 221 were assembled by the Italian company.

The fundamental differences between the F-86K and the D were the replacement of the latter's all rocket armament with four 20mm Colt M24A-1 cannon and the sophisticated Hughes E-4 fire control system replaced with the new and simpler MG-4 system with optical gunsight. The E-4 was still high on the USAF's secret list at the time and was not prepared to let it be fitted to aircraft for export.

The result was a still sophisticated all weather fighter with those changes and the simpler (and export cleared) AN/APG-37 radar installed. F-86K pilots still had a semi automatic fire control system at their disposal but this led them to an astern rather than collision course firing position.

F-86Ks were powered by either the 7,500lb (33.6kN) thrust (with afterburning) J47-GE-17B or 7,650lb (34.3kN) thrust -33 engines and were originally fitted with the standard Sabre slatted wing. The last 45 Fiat assembled aircraft had the extended span wing from the F-86F-40 and most were subsequently upgraded to this standard. Another modification applied to many F-86Ks was the ability to carry a pair of AIM-9B Sidewinder air-to-air missiles.

Two prototype YF-86Ks were built (52-3630 and 52-3804) both of them converted from F-86Ds. The first aircraft recorded its maiden flight in July 1954 and after service tests, both were delivered to Fiat.

The first YF-86K (52-3630) was converted from an F-86D. This version was developed for use by NATO nations and had the D's rocket armament and complicated fire control system replaced with four 20mm cannon and simpler firing systems. (NAA)

US BUILT SABRES and FURYS – PRODUCTION SUMMARY

F-86 SABRE

Note: Most F-86 Sabres were built at North American's Inglewood (Los Angeles) plant but some were manufactured at the company's Columbus, Ohio, facility. These are the F-86F-20 and -25 production blocks plus all F-86Hs except for the first two aircraft.

Variant	NAA No	USAF Serials	Qty	Remarks
XP-86	NA-140	45-59597/59599	3	prototypes
F-86A-1	NA-151	47-605/637	33	initial production batch
F-86A-5	NA-151	48-129/316	188	
F-86A-5	NA-161	49-1007/1339	333	49-1069 to Canada, CL-13 prototype
YF-86C		48-317/318	2	also known as YF-93A
YF-86D	NA-164	50-0577/0578	2	initially YF-95A
F-86D-1	NA-165	50-0455/0491	37	
F-86D-5	NA-165	50-0492/0517	26	E-4 fire control system
F-86D-10	NA-165	50-0518/0553	36	
F-86D-15	NA-165	50-0554/0576	23	
F-86D-15	NA-165	50-0704/0734	31	single point refuelling
F-86D-20	NA-177	51-2944/3131	188	J47-GE-33 engine
F-86D-25	NA-173	51-5857/5944	88	provision for drop tanks
F-86D-30	NA-173	51-5945/6144	200	
F-86D-35	NA-173	51-6145/6262	118	omni directional radar ranging
F-86D-35	NA-173	51-8267/8499	232	
F-86D-40	NA-190	52-3598/3897	300	
F-86D-45	NA-190	52-3898/4197	300	braking parachute
F-86D-50	NA-190	52-4198/4304	107	
F-86D-50	NA-190	52-9983/10176	194	
F-86D-55	NA-201	53-0557/0781	225	
F-86D-60	NA-201	53-0782/1071	399	
F-86E-1	NA-170	50-0579/0638	60	
F-86E-5	NA-170	50-0639/0689	51	
F-86E-10	NA-172	51-2718/2849	132	flat armoured windscreen
F-86E-15	NA-172	51-12977/13069	93	F-86F-15 with J47-GE-13 engine
F-86F-1	NA-172	51-2850/2927	78	
F-86F-5	NA-172	51-2928/2943	16	larger drop tanks
F-86F-10	NA-172	51-12936/12969	34	A-4 radar ranging gunsight
F-86F-15	NA-172	51-12970/12976	7	see F-86E-15
F-86F-20	NA-176	51-13070/13169	100	upgraded cockpit, tailplane armour
F-86F-25	NA-193	51-13170/13510	341	dual store wing, '6-3' wing
F-86F-25	NA-193	51-5272/5530	259	
F-86F-30	NA-191	52-4305/5163	859	
F-86F-35	NA-191	52-5164/5271	108	nuclear store capability, LABS
F-86F-35	NA-202	53-1072/1228	157	
F-86F-40	NA-227	55-3816/4095	280	for export, long span slatted wing
F-86F-40		55-5048/5117	70	assembled in Japan by Mitsubishi
F-86F-40		56-2773/2882	110	assembled in Japan by Mitsubishi
F-86F-40		57-6338/6457	120	assembled in Japan by Mitsubishi
YF-86H-1	NA-187	52-1975	1	
F-86H-1	NA-187	52-1976	1	
F-86H-1	NA-187	52-1977/2089	113	machine gun armament
F-86H-5	NA-187	52-2090/2125	35	cannon armament
F-86H-5	NA-187	52-5729/5753	25	
F-86H-10	NA-203	53-1229/1528	300	
YF-86K	NA-205	52-3630	1	converted F-86D-40
YF-86K	NA-205	52-3804	1	converted F-86D-40
F-86K	NA-207	53-8273/8322	50	assembled in Italy by Fiat
F-86K	NA-213	54-1231/1350	120	for export
F-86K	NA-221	55-4811/4880	70	assembled in Italy by Fiat
F-86K	NA-232	55-4881/4936	56	assembled in Italy by Fiat
F-86K	NA-242	56-4116/4160	45	assembled in Italy by Fiat

FJ FURY

Note: All production Furys were built at the Columbus, Ohio, plant. The three prototype XFJ-2s were built at Inglewood.

Model	NAA No	USN Serials	Qty	Remarks
XFJ-2	NA-179	133754	1	J47 engine, machine guns
XFJ-2	NA-179	133755	1	
XFJ-2B	NA-185	133756	1	first to fly, cannon armament
FJ-2	NA-181	131927/132126	200	folding wings, all flying tailplane
FJ-3	NA-194	135774/136162	389	J65 Sapphire engine
FJ-3/M	NA-215	139210/139278	69	six plyon wing
FJ-3/M	NA-215	141364/141443	80	
FJ-4	NA-208	139279/139280	2	prototypes
FJ-4	NA-209	139281/139323	43	four hardpoints
FJ-4	NA-209	139424/139530	107	
FJ-4B	NA-209	139531/139555	25	strengthened wing, six hardpoints, LABS
FJ-4B	NA-229	141444/141489	46	
FJ-4B	NA-244	143493/143643	151	

A US built F-86K deploys its braking parachute on landing. Most Ks were assembled in Italy by Fiat. (NAA)

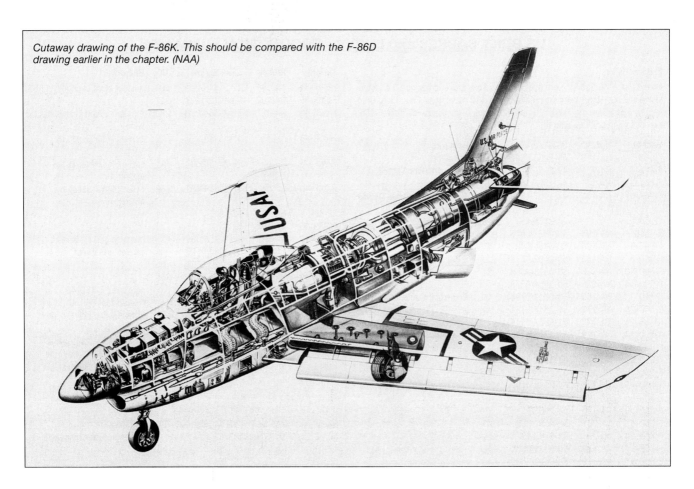

Cutaway drawing of the F-86K. This should be compared with the F-86D drawing earlier in the chapter. (NAA)

Plan view of an F-86K. 54-1231 was the first of 120 production models built in the USA. Fiat assembled 221 more in Italy. (NAA)

NAA built 120 complete F-86Ks at Inglewood for Norway and the Netherlands, while the 221 Fiat assembled aircraft were delivered to the air forces of Italy, France and West Germany. The first Italian assembled F-86K was flown in May 1955 and local content increased as the production run progressed.

F-86K SABRE

Powerplant: One General Electric J47-GE-17B axial flow turbojet rated at 5,425lb (24.3kN) thrust (dry) and 7,500lb (33.6kN) thrust with afterburner; internal fuel capacity 608 USgal (2,301 l), provision for two 120 USgal (454 l) underwing drop tanks.
Dimensions: Wing span 39ft 1.3in (11.92m); length 40ft 11in (12.47m); height 15ft 0in (4.57m); wing area 313.3sq ft (29.1m²).
Weights: Empty 13,367lb (6,063kg); normal loaded 18,379lb (8,337kg); maximum 20,171lb (9,150kg).
Armament: Four 20mm M24A-1 cannon in nose with 132 rounds per gun; two AIM-9B Sidewinder air-to-air missiles on some aircraft.
Performance: Max speed 602kt (1,113km/h) at sea level, 532kt (985km/h) at 40,000ft; cruising speed 478kt (885km/h); initial climb rate 12,000ft (3,658m)/min; time to 40,000ft 7.3min; service ceiling 49,600ft (15,119m); range (internal fuel) 474nm (877km); ferry range 647nm (1,197km).

F-86L SABRE

This final US Sabre variant was not a new aircraft but a substantially modified F-86D, the large conversion programme associated with it involving the upgrading of no fewer than 827 'Sabre Dogs' from the F-86D-10

to -60 production blocks to F-86L standards between 1956 and 1960. The programme was conducted under the auspices of Project Follow On and was intended to enable the Sabre to operate effectively in the all weather interception role until the supersonic Convair F-102 and F-106 were available in numbers.

The basis of the conversion was the installation of the latest state-of-the-art avionics in several of the aircraft's systems, including a new electronic data link between ground controller and pilot. Known as the SAGE (Semi Automatic Ground Environment) system, the new equipment comprised an onboard digital computer which was capable of receiving, processing and displaying air surveillance data from ground radar. The AN/ARR-39 data link provided the pilot with the necessary target heading, speed, altitude, bearing and range information and the equipment automatically positioned the aircraft for a collision course attack. Other parts of the SAGE package were AN/ARC-34 command radio, AN/APX-25 identification radar and a new glide slope receiver.

The F-86L retained the original E-4 fire control system, radar and FFAR rocket armament but the conversion was a complex one involving stripping the aircraft and completely replacing its wiring. As for the airframe, the F-86L received the long span slatted wing as installed on the F-86F-40 day fighter.

The first F-86L conversion was flown in October 1956, the upgrading job being shared between NAA's Inglewood and Fresno plants.

FJ FURY

Although outside the broad scope of this account, the FJ Fury shipborne naval fighter-bomber requires a brief description here as it began life as a navalised version of the F-86 Sabre. What must be remembered is that the swept wing FJ-2, FJ-3 and FJ-4 Furys had little or no relationship to the original straight winged FJ-1 Fury of 1946-48, production of which was limited to 33 aircraft including three prototypes.

The fact that the second generation Fury carried the same name and US Navy designation (FJ) as its predecessor was simply a case of political expediency. The motivation was funding – it was considerably easier to convince the US Congress that allocating funds for the Fury's development and production was a good idea if the perception was created that the aircraft was merely a development of an existing aircraft rather than a new one. The name 'Sea Sabre' was seriously considered for a time, but dropped for the reasons stated above.

Much the same thing had happened with what was originally called the F-95A Sabre when it was redesignated the F-86D by the USAF in order to minimise the chances of funding being restricted.

The first swept wing Fury – the FJ-2 – was in simple terms a navalised version of the slatted wing F-86E and F with the necessary airframe changes to make carrier operation possible.

The first of three Los Angeles built XFJ-2 Fury prototypes (USN serials 133754-756) flew on 27 December 1951 with Bob Hoover at the controls.

The F-86L was a conversion of the F-86D for the USAF involving a major upgrade of the aircraft's avionics and systems and installing long span slatted wings. The first F-86L was flown in October 1956 and 827 conversions were performed.

Powered by the F-86E's J47-GE-13 engine, these aircraft differed from their land based brethren by having vee frame arrester hooks, catapult points and lengthened nosewheel legs to set the aircraft at the correct angle of attack for a catapult launch. The third prototype (which was actually the first to fly) had the F-86E/F's six 0.50in machine guns replaced with four 20mm Colt Mk.12 cannon, this becoming the standard fixed armament of the production version.

Following testing (including carrier qualification trials aboard the USS *Coral Sea* in December 1952), deliveries of 200 production FJ-2s began, these aircraft differing from the prototypes in having hydraulically actuated folding wings, 'all flying' horizontal tail surfaces (with the dihedral removed), a 6,000lb (26.9kN) thrust J47-GE-2 engine (essentially the naval version of the F-86F's J47-GE-27), a reprofiled and deeper cockpit canopy, and the four cannon arma-

ment. With its naval equipment installed the FJ-2 was about 1,000lb (454kg) heavier than the F-86F but still recorded a maximum speed of 588 knots (1,088km/h) at sea level and 524 knots (969km/h) at high altitude. Initial climb rate was 7,230 feet (2,203m) per minute and service ceiling 41,700 feet (12,710m).

All FJ-2 and subsequent Furys were built at NAA's Columbus, Ohio, plant and this first production version served exclusively with US Marine Corps operational squadrons, starting with VMF-122 at Cherry Point, North Carolina from January 1954. Six USMC fighter squadrons were ultimately equipped with the FJ-2.

British Power

Attempts to rectify some of the problems experienced with the FJ-2 Fury – notably a need to improve performance – resulted in the next production version, the FJ-3 powered by a 7,700lb (34.5kN) thrust Wright J65-W-2 turbojet, a licence built version of the British Armstrong-Siddeley Sapphire. At virtually no cost in extra weight, the Sapphire delivered some 28 per cent greater thrust, allowing slightly higher speeds (maximum 592kt at sea level) but much improved rate of climb (8,450ft/min) and ceiling (49,000 feet).

The first FJ-3 (135774) was flown in December 1953 and the 538th and last example was handed over in August 1956. Several running changes were introduced during the FJ-3's production life: the wings' leading edge slats were replaced with extended fixed leading edges (allowing an increase in fuel capacity); four additional underwing stores pylons were incorporated (bringing the total to six and allowing the carriage of bombs, rocket pods and fuel tanks); and the capability to carry a pair of Sidewinder air-to-air missiles. Existing Furys modified to carry Sidewinders were redesignated FJ-3Ms and aircraft from number 345 on were built to this standard. Late production aircraft were fitted with an in flight refuelling probe under the port wing.

The FJ-3/M Fury served with 18 US Navy and six Marine Corps squadrons, the latter in the main replacing FJ-2s.

The Ultimate Fury

The final Fury variant – the FJ-4 – represented a substantial redesign resulting in a highly capable attack fighter. Although the FJ-4's powerplant remained the Wright J65 Sapphire, the fuselage was virtually new, being deeper and shorter than before and featuring a prominent dorsal spine running from the rear of the redesigned canopy to the base of the taller fin which incorporated a smaller

The first prototype XFJ-2 Fury naval fighter (133754). Based on the F-86E Sabre, the aircraft featured an arrester hook, catapult launching points and lengthened nosewheel leg. Folding wings appeared on the production FJ-2. (NAA)

XFJ-2 Fury 133754 departs the USS Coral Sea *during carrier trials in December 1952. (USN)*

An FJ-3M Fury powered by a licence built version of the British Armstrong Siddeley Sapphire engine and capable of carrying Sidewinder air-to-air missiles. This one belongs to US Navy Squadron VF-142 from the USS Hornet*. It was photographed in 1957.*

rudder. Internal fuel capacity was 50 per cent greater than the FJ-3, giving a range on this capacity alone of 1,290 nautical miles (2,388km).

The wing was entirely new, featuring a substantially thinner section (the thickness chord ratio was reduced from ten to six per cent), greater span and chord, mid span ailerons, redesigned flaps and drooped leading edges. The wing fold point was now at about two-thirds (rather than half) span and the undercarriage featured a revised lever suspension design with increased track. The FJ-4 retained the four 20mm cannon fixed armament and the four underwing pylons were capable of carrying the usual mix of fuel tanks, bombs and rocket pods as well as Sidewinder missiles on all of them if necessary.

The first FJ-4 (139279) was flown on 28 October 1954 and the first production aircraft came off the Columbus production line in February 1955. Production of the basic FJ-4 Fury amounted to 152 aircraft and these were followed by 222 FJ-4Bs between December 1956 and May 1958.

This variant was optimised for attack duties and featured six stores points under the strengthened wing, an additional speed brake under each side of the rear fuselage and provision for a 'Buddy' aerial refuelling pack. If used as an interceptor, the FJ-4B could carry a Sidewinder on each of its six hardpoints and at the other end of the scale it had Low Altitude Bombing System (LABS) equipment so as to ensure accurate and safe delivery of a nuclear 'special store'. A later service modification incorporated in the FJ-4B allowed the carriage of up to five Martin Bullpup air-to-surface radar guided missiles along with their guidance pod.

The basic FJ-4 Fury served with three USMC fighter squadrons and the FJ-4B was used by 10 US Navy and three Marines attack squadrons. Front line service began to diminish from 1959 when newer types started to come on line, and by late 1962 surviving aircraft were in the hands of Reserves units. By then the FJ-4 and FJ-4B had been redesignated F-1E and AF-1E, respectively, in line with a general reorganisation of US military aircraft designations.

Underside view of an FJ-3M Fury showing the Sidewinder missile installation. (USN)

A prototype FJ-4 Fury taking off from dry land at NAA's Columbus, Ohio, factory. The FJ-4 was a virtually new design and intended from the start as an attack fighter. (NAA)

One of two experimental FJ-4Fs converted from production FJ-4s. The -4F was built for mixed powerplant research and had a 6,000lb (26.9kN) thrust rocket engine at the base of fin, above the standard turbojet. The nose radome housed various instruments. (USN)

FJ-4B FURY
Powerplant: One 7,700lb (34.5kN) thrust Wright J65-W-16A (Armstrong-Siddeley Sapphire) axial flow turbojet.
Dimensions: Wing span 39ft 1in (11.91m); length 36ft 4in 11.07m); height 13ft 11in (4.24m); wing area 338.6sq ft (31.45m²).
Weights: Empty 13,780lb (6,251kg); normal loaded 20,130lb (9,131kg); maximum overload 26,000lb (11,794kg).
Armament: Four 20mm Colt Mk.12 cannon in nose with 576 rounds per gun; six underwing stores pylons capable of carrying combinations of drop tanks, 500 or 1,000lb (227 or 454kg) bombs, rocket pods, AIM-9 Sidewinder AAMs, AGM-12A Bullpup ASMs or atomic weapon.
Performance: Max speed 591kt (1,094km/h) at sea level, 549kt (1,015km/h) at 35,000ft; typical cruise 464kt (859km/h); initial climb 7,660ft (2,335m)/min; service ceiling 46,800ft (14,265m); range (internal fuel) 1,292nm (2,390km); range with two 200USgal (757 l) drop tanks 1,757nm (3,250km); range with max external fuel 2,350nm (4,345km).

A Canadair Sabre Mk.5 powered by the locally developed Avro Orenda turbojet. Otherwise, it was similar to the F-86F-30 with '6-3' wing. (via Philip J Birtles)

CANADAIR SABRE

With the end of World War II's hostilities came the need for most countries to consider their post war defence policies and order the necessary equipment to fill their needs. Among them was Canada, which with the establishment of the North Atlantic Treaty Organisation (NATO) in 1949 needed to think about not only its domestic requirements but also its substantial overseas NATO commitments, particularly in Germany.

High on the list of priorities was the purchase of a new jet fighter and the Sabre was selected in 1949 to fill this role. Early discussions centred around purchasing aircraft from North American's production lines but this way of thinking was quickly changed to licence production. Canadian Sabres would be based on the F-86E and F day fighters and would be built by Canadair at its Cartierville Airport facility near Montreal. Canadair was established in December 1944 from the former aircraft division of Canadian Vickers Ltd.

An initial quantity of just 100 Canadair Sabres was planned, but by the time production ended in 1958,

the Canadian company had contributed no fewer than 1,815 aircraft to the Sabre total, more than half of them for export. Early Canadair Sabres contained about 10 per cent local content, but this increased to 90 per cent later in the production run. A large part of this proportion came from the use of the Canadian designed and built Avro Canada Orenda axial flow turbojet in the later marks, earlier aircraft being virtually identical to their American contemporaries (including use of the J47 engine) apart from specific items of equipment. All retained the American aircraft's six 0.50in machine gun fixed armament.

Canadair built six Sabre versions under the company designation CL-13. The first aircraft (RCAF serial

19101) was the sole Mk.1, flown for the first time on 9 August 1950 with Canadair's chief test pilot, A J 'Al' Lilly at the controls. This aircraft was in reality a North American built F-86A-5 merely assembled by Canadair. A few days after its maiden flight, this Sabre became the first Canadian aircraft to exceed the speed of sound, again with Lilly at the controls.

Series production of the Canadair Sabre began in 1951 with the Mk.2, equivalent to the F-86E. A total of 350 Sabres Mk.2 was built, 290 of them going to the RCAF and the remaining 60 to the USAF for use in Korea. These aircraft were delivered between April and June 1952 and after fitting out at NAA's Fresno, California, facility, were sent to Korea. In USAF service these Sabres were given the designation F-86E-6.

The one and only Sabre Mk.3 was the 100th aircraft to come from Canadair's line and was the prototype Orenda powered aircraft. Powered by the 6,000lb (26.9kN) thrust Orenda 3, this aircraft was used by famed aviatrix Jacqueline Cochrane to establish two world wom-

CANADAIR SABRE PRODUCTION SUMMARY			
Variant	RCAF Nos	Qty	Remarks
CL-13 Mk.1	19101	1	prototype assembled from F-86A-5
CL-13 Mk.2	19102-19199	98	
CL-13 Mk.2	19201-19452	252	60 to USAF, 3 to RAF
CL-13 Mk.3	19200	1	Orenda powered prototype
CL-13 Mk.4	19453-19890	438	428 to RAF
CL-13A Mk.5	23001-23370	370	all to RCAF
CL-13B Mk.6	23371-23760	390	all to RCAF
CL-13B Mk.6	–	6	for Colombia
CL-13B Mk.6	–	34	for SAAF
CL-13B Mk.6	–	225	for Luftwaffe

en's speed records in June 1953 at Edwards Air Force Base. The first record of 652.552mph (1,050.15km/h) was over a 100 kilometre course and the second of 692.471mph (1,114.39km/h) was over a 100 kilometre closed circuit.

Production continued with the Sabre Mk.4 (similar to the F-86E-10), of which all but 10 of the 438 built were delivered to the Royal Air Force in 1952-53 as the Sabre F.1. The RAF's aircraft were supplied with help from the United States Mutual Defence Assistance Programme and became necessary due to delays in the development of Britain's own swept wing fighters, the Hawker Hunter and Supermarine Swift. Most RAF Sabres were deployed to West Germany, where it had been realised that the existing Vampires and Meteors would be no match for the MiG-15s which lurked in East Germany and other nearby Soviet *Bloc* countries. The RAF also received three Mk.2s from the RCAF, but these were returned to Canada when deliveries of the Mk.4 were underway.

Powered By Avro

The last two Canadair Sabre variants were the CL-13A Mk.5 and CL-13B Mk.6, both based on the F-86F airframe but powered by the local Avro Orenda powerplant. Offering considerably more power than the standard J47, the Orenda-Sabre (along with the Australian CAC Avon-Sabre, described below) represented the pinnacle of Sabre day fighter development with much better performance than the American equivalents. With a maximum speed of 710mph

A Royal Canadian Air Force Sabre Mk.6, the definitive version of the Canadian built Sabre. Total Canadair production reached 1,815 aircraft, of which many were exported.

(618kt/1,142km/h) at sea level, the Mk.6 was the fastest of all the Sabres.

Compared with the J47 engine it replaced, the Orenda was shorter, of greater diameter but of similar weight. Its extra diameter (some 5.25in/13.3cm) necessitated some minor redesign of the fuselage to accommodate it (including larger frame apertures) but nothing of the scale which confronted CAC's engineers when they decided to install the Rolls-Royce Avon in Australian Sabres.

The first CL-13A Sabre Mk.5 was flown in July 1953 and production

amounted to 370 aircraft, of which 75 were transferred from the RCAF to the Federal German *Bundesluftwaffe*. In Canadian service, the Mk.5 was used mainly to replace earlier marks.

The Sabre Mk.5 was powered by the 6,355lb (28.5kN) thrust Orenda 10 and was otherwise similar to the F-86F-30 with slatless '6-3' wing. Compared with the Mk.2, the Mk.5 offered a leap forward in performance capability, especially in the area of rate of climb where the time to reach 40,000 feet was almost halved to nine minutes.

Britain's Royal Air Force was a major customer for the Canadair Sabre, taking more than 400 Mk.4s as a stopgap while problems with the Hawker Hunter were being sorted out. Like its predecessors, the Mk.4 was very similar to the American F-86E. (via Philip J Birtles)

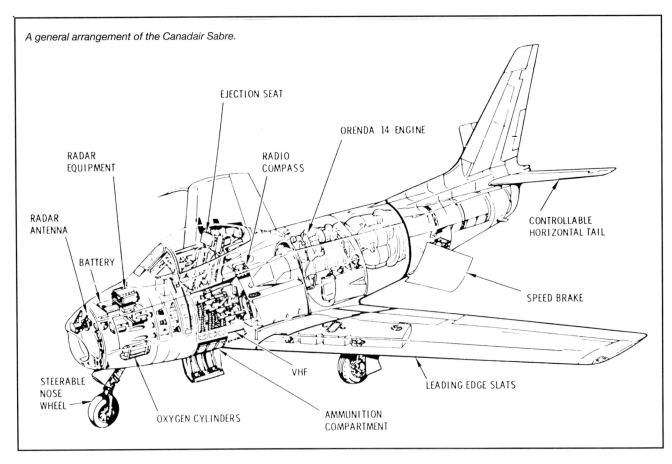

A general arrangement of the Canadair Sabre.

EJECTION SEAT

RADIO COMPASS

ORENDA 14 ENGINE

RADAR EQUIPMENT

RADAR ANTENNA

BATTERY

CONTROLLABLE HORIZONTAL TAIL

SPEED BRAKE

STEERABLE NOSE WHEEL

VHF

LEADING EDGE SLATS

OXYGEN CYLINDERS

AMMUNITION COMPARTMENT

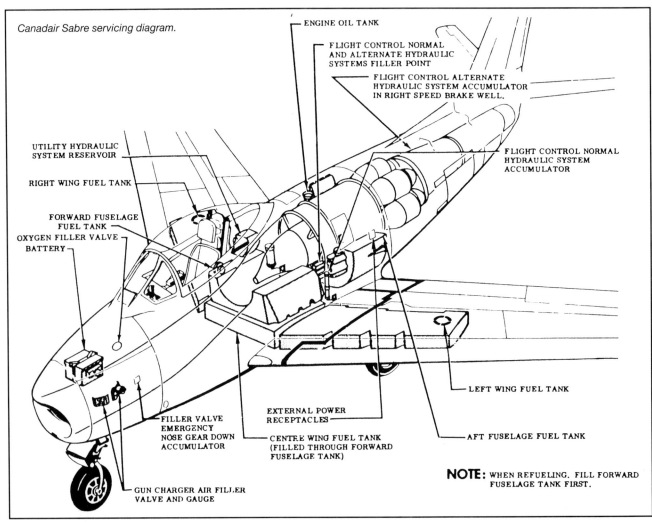

Canadair Sabre servicing diagram.

ENGINE OIL TANK

FLIGHT CONTROL NORMAL AND ALTERNATE HYDRAULIC SYSTEMS FILLER POINT

FLIGHT CONTROL ALTERNATE HYDRAULIC SYSTEM ACCUMULATOR IN RIGHT SPEED BRAKE WELL.

UTILITY HYDRAULIC SYSTEM RESERVOIR

FLIGHT CONTROL NORMAL HYDRAULIC SYSTEM ACCUMULATOR

RIGHT WING FUEL TANK

FORWARD FUSELAGE FUEL TANK

OXYGEN FILLER VALVE

BATTERY

FILLER VALVE EMERGENCY NOSE GEAR DOWN ACCUMULATOR

EXTERNAL POWER RECEPTACLES

CENTRE WING FUEL TANK (FILLED THROUGH FORWARD FUSELAGE TANK)

LEFT WING FUEL TANK

AFT FUSELAGE FUEL TANK

GUN CHARGER AIR FILLER VALVE AND GAUGE

NOTE: WHEN REFUELING, FILL FORWARD FUSELAGE TANK FIRST.

One RAF Sabre (XB982) was used by Bristol Siddeley as an engine testbed and fitted with Orpheus turbojets of between 4,850lb (21.7kN) and 6,105lb (27.4kN) thrust.

Even better performance was offered by the definitive Canadair Sabre, the CL-13B Mk.6. Powered by a 7,275lb (35.6kN) thrust Orenda 14, this variant also featured the '6-3' wing on early aircraft but this was soon replaced with a wider chord wing with leading edge slats, the idea being to restore some of the more friendly low speed handling characteristics which had been lost with the fitting of the '6-3' wing.

The first Mk.6 was flown in November 1954 and production ended in October 1958 when the 655th and last example was rolled out. Of these, 390 were delivered to the RCAF, six to Colombia, 34 to the South African Air Force and 225 (the final batch) to the Luftwaffe. The West German aircraft were subsequently modified to carry a pair of Sidewinder air-to-air missiles. Second hand Canadair Sabres were later sold to several nations – including Italy, Yugoslavia, Greece and Turkey – and sales of new aircraft to Argentina and Israel were frustrated by a lack of funds and the 1956 Arab-Israeli war, respectively. One RAF Mk.4 (XB982) was used by Bristol Siddeley as a testbed for the Orpheus engine.

Several other Sabre variants were projected by Canadair, two of which reached the prototype stage. The CL-13C was powered by an afterburning version of the Orenda and this configuration was test flown in a converted Mk.6 (serial 23544). A converted Mk.5 (23021) resulted in the CL-13E with area ruled fuselage but no obvious improvement in performance.

Unbuilt projects were the CL-13D with Armstrong-Siddeley Snarler booster rocket, the CL-13G two seat operational trainer, the radar equipped CL-13H all weather fighter and the afterburner equipped CL-13J.

CL-13B SABRE Mk.6
Powerplant: One 7,275lb (35.6kN) thrust Avro Canada Orenda 14 axial flow turbojet; internal fuel capacity 357imp gal (1,623 l), provision for two 100imp gal (454 l) or 167imp gal (759 l) underwing drop tanks.
Dimensions: Wing span 37ft 1in (11.30in); length 37ft 6in (11.43m); height 14ft 7in (4.44m); wing area 304sq ft (28.24m²).
Weights: Empty 11,143lb (5,054kg); normal loaded 16,426lb (7,450kg), maximum 17,611lb (7,988kg).
Armament: Six 0.50in Browning M-3 machine guns in nose with 267 rounds per gun; provision for underwing bombs, rockets and drop tanks.
Performance: Max speed 618kt (1,143km/h) at sea level, 591kt (1,094km/h) at 10,000ft, 539kt (998km/h) at 36,000ft; initial climb 11,800ft (3,597m)/min; time to 40,000ft 6.0min; service ceiling 54,000ft (16,459m); tactical radius (clean) 316nm (584km); max range (with drop tanks) 1,300nm (2,406km).

CAC SABRE

The Australian built Commonwealth Aircraft Corporation (CAC) Sabre was the most radically changed of the Sabre day fighter variants, considerable redesign of the fuselage becoming necessary with the decision to replace the standard General Electric J47 engine with a 7,500lb (33.6kN) thrust Rolls-Royce Avon. The usual six machine gun armament was also changed to a pair of 30mm Aden Cannon.

CAC built 112 Sabres between 1953 and 1961, all of them delivered to the Royal Australian Air Force,

Even as the RAAF's first operational jet fighter – the de Havilland Vampire – was entering service in 1949, investigations were underway to find a more modern replacement, with local licence production consid-

ered a necessary part of the project.

Early possibilities which were considered included the Grumman Panther naval fighter and various of the evolutionary designs produced by Hawker in the late 1940s and early 1950s which eventually resulted in the Hunter. One of these was the swept wing Hawker P.1081, 72 of which were actually ordered for the RAAF in 1950 but cancelled the following year when it was realised the proposed delivery schedule was highly optimistic and even the British were showing no interest in the aircraft.

The choice for the RAAF's new fighter was then narrowed down to either the Sabre (favoured by CAC's influential general manager, Lawrence Wackett) and the Hunter. CAC's long association with North American (its first product, the Wirraway, was a licence built version of the NA-16-2K and P-51 Mustangs were built by the company between 1945 and 1951) and well founded doubts about the Hunter's early availability resulted in the Sabre being selected in February 1951, an initial order for 70 aircraft being placed.

But this was to be no ordinary Sabre thanks to the change of engine, the result of Wackett and Rolls-Royce's Lord Hives having unofficial talks about CAC producing the Avon under licence, all this going on well before the Sabre was ordered. CAC eventually built 218 Avons in several versions for both the Sabre and the Canberra bomber, which was also manufactured under licence in Australia.

Major Changes

The major changes necessitated by the installation of the Avon in the Sabre resulted in a fuselage design which retained only 40 percent of the original. The Avon was a shorter and lighter engine of greater diameter than the J47 it replaced but required considerably more airflow to sustain it. The result of all this was an engine mounted further aft in order to maintain centre of gravity, a relocated fuselage 'break' line and an enlarged intake with rerouted ducting.

In order to achieve the necessary increase in inlet size, the fuselage was in effect split horizontally and a new section inserted whilst retaining the original cross section profiles of the fuselage frames. In association with this came a multitude of detail changes and some of a more major nature including providing adequate structural cooling around the engine. This resulted in the fuel lines, engine control units, fuel pumps and hydraulic pumps being moved to a position forward of the firewall.

The prototype CAC CA-26 Sabre (A94-101) recorded its first flight in August 1953 after a substantial redesign of the basic aircraft in order to accommodate the Rolls-Royce Avon engine. (via Stewart Wilson)

The CAC production line at Fisherman's Bend, Melbourne. (via Stewart Wilson).

The definitive Australian Sabre, the Mk.32, equipped with Sidewinder air-to-air missiles. CAC built 112 Sabres between 1953 and 1961 in three sub variants. (RAAF)

The new gun armament also required some substantial changes including redesigning the side fuselage frames, blast panels and skins in the nose area, reinforcing the gun access panels, modifying the ammunition box frames and providing new access doors to the guns. Interestingly, the Avon-Sabre suffered engine surge when the guns were fired, similar to the problem which also occupied engineers involved with the Avon powered and Aden armed Hawker Hunter for some time. In the case of the Sabre, redesigned gun blast panels and an improved engine which incorporated a 'dipper' mechanism which reduced engine revs as the guns were fired solved the problem after extensive testing had been carried out.

CAC ordered 100 sets of F-86F major components to help expedite production, and the prototype CAC CA-26 Avon-Sabre (RAAF serial A94-101) was flown by Flt Lt Bill Scott, RAAF, from the Department of Supply's Avalon airfield on 3 August 1953. Power was provided by an imported RA.7 Avon 20 (identical to those which would be installed in the first production batch) and flew on a pair of standard F-86F slatted wings.

This and subsequent Sabres were built at CAC's Fisherman's Bend (Melbourne) factory and then trucked the 60 kilometres to Avalon for flight testing after reassembly. The prototype's first flight was originally scheduled for April 1952, this highly optimistic target slipping by 16 months as the complexity of the redesign came into play.

Production Avon-Sabres

The initial production model was designated the CA-27 Sabre Mk.30, the first of 22 examples (RAAF serials A94-901 to 922) making its first flight from Avalon on 13 July 1954 and was handed over to the RAAF on 18 August. A lengthy series of service trials followed – much of them concerned with solving the engine surge problem – and the Sabre finally entered RAAF service in April 1955, by which

time 18 aircraft had been flown.

All Sabre Mk.30s were fitted with the slatted wing and all but the last six were powered by imported Avon 20s, the latter aircraft having CAC built examples of the same engine.

The next 20 Sabres (A94-923 to 942) were designated Mk.31 and delivered between July 1955 and September 1956. The Mk.31 differed from the initial model mainly by having the '6-3' wing installed. This wing was fitted to all subsequent CAC Sabres and was retrofitted to the earlier aircraft as they underwent major servicing. Thus modified, these Sabres were redesignated as Mk.31s. Eleven of the 20 new build Mk.31s had locally built Avons, the remainder had imported engines.

Two Sabre 31s featured a major modification installed on the production line which would become standard equipment on future aircraft: substantially increased internal fuel capacity thanks to a local modification which allowed fuel to be carried in the leading edges of the wings. Previously, the internal fuel had been carried in the normal Sabre fuselage and wing tanks, giving a total capacity of 352 Imperial gal-

CAC SABRE PRODUCTION SUMMARY				
Variant	RAAF Nos	Qty	Delivery	Remarks
CA-26	A94-101	1	ff 08/53	prototype
CA-27 Mk.30	A94-901/922	22	08/54-07/55	slatted wing
CA-27 Mk.31	A94-923/942	20	07/55-09/56	6-3 wing, CAC Avons
CA-27 Mk.32	A94-943/970	28	09/56-07/57	Avon 26, dual store wing, Sidewinder AAMs, extra fuel
CA-27 Mk.32	A94-971/990	20	07/57-12/58	
CA-27 Mk.32	A94-351/371	21	10/59-12/61	

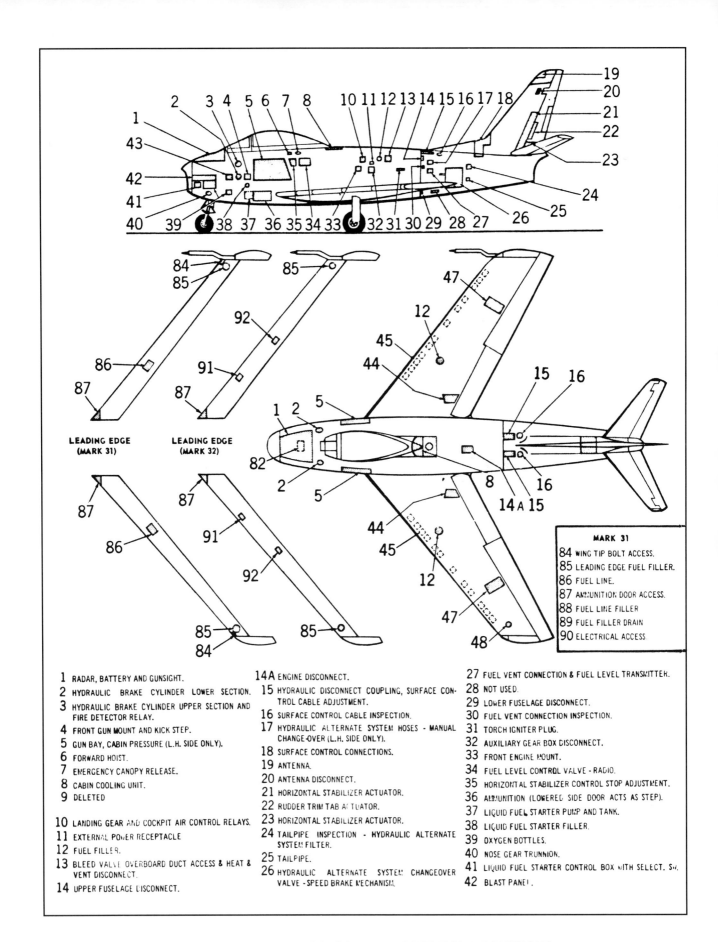

MARK 31

84 WING TIP BOLT ACCESS.
85 LEADING EDGE FUEL FILLER.
86 FUEL LINE.
87 AMMUNITION DOOR ACCESS.
88 FUEL LINE FILLER
89 FUEL FILLER DRAIN
90 ELECTRICAL ACCESS.

LEADING EDGE (MARK 31)

LEADING EDGE (MARK 32)

1 RADAR, BATTERY AND GUNSIGHT.
2 HYDRAULIC BRAKE CYLINDER LOWER SECTION.
3 HYDRAULIC BRAKE CYLINDER UPPER SECTION AND FIRE DETECTOR RELAY.
4 FRONT GUN MOUNT AND KICK STEP.
5 GUN BAY, CABIN PRESSURE (L.H. SIDE ONLY).
6 FORWARD HOIST.
7 EMERGENCY CANOPY RELEASE.
8 CABIN COOLING UNIT.
9 DELETED

10 LANDING GEAR AND COCKPIT AIR CONTROL RELAYS.
11 EXTERNAL POWER RECEPTACLE
12 FUEL FILLER.
13 BLEED VALVE OVERBOARD DUCT ACCESS & HEAT & VENT DISCONNECT.
14 UPPER FUSELAGE DISCONNECT.

14A ENGINE DISCONNECT.
15 HYDRAULIC DISCONNECT COUPLING, SURFACE CONTROL CABLE ADJUSTMENT.
16 SURFACE CONTROL CABLE INSPECTION.
17 HYDRAULIC ALTERNATE SYSTEM HOSES - MANUAL CHANGE-OVER (L.H. SIDE ONLY).
18 SURFACE CONTROL CONNECTIONS.
19 ANTENNA.
20 ANTENNA DISCONNECT.
21 HORIZONTAL STABILIZER ACTUATOR.
22 RUDDER TRIM TAB ACTUATOR.
23 HORIZONTAL STABILIZER ACTUATOR.
24 TAILPIPE INSPECTION - HYDRAULIC ALTERNATE SYSTEM FILTER.
25 TAILPIPE.
26 HYDRAULIC ALTERNATE SYSTEM CHANGEOVER VALVE - SPEED BRAKE MECHANISM.

27 FUEL VENT CONNECTION & FUEL LEVEL TRANSMITTER.
28 NOT USED.
29 LOWER FUSELAGE DISCONNECT.
30 FUEL VENT CONNECTION INSPECTION.
31 TORCH IGNITER PLUG.
32 AUXILIARY GEAR BOX DISCONNECT.
33 FRONT ENGINE MOUNT.
34 FUEL LEVEL CONTROL VALVE - RADIO.
35 HORIZONTAL STABILIZER CONTROL STOP ADJUSTMENT.
36 AMMUNITION (LOWERED SIDE DOOR ACTS AS STEP).
37 LIQUID FUEL STARTER PUMP AND TANK.
38 LIQUID FUEL STARTER FILLER.
39 OXYGEN BOTTLES.
40 NOSE GEAR TRUNNION.
41 LIQUID FUEL STARTER CONTROL BOX WITH SELECT. SW.
42 BLAST PANEL.

CAC CA-27 SABRE ACCESS AND INSPECTION PROVISIONS

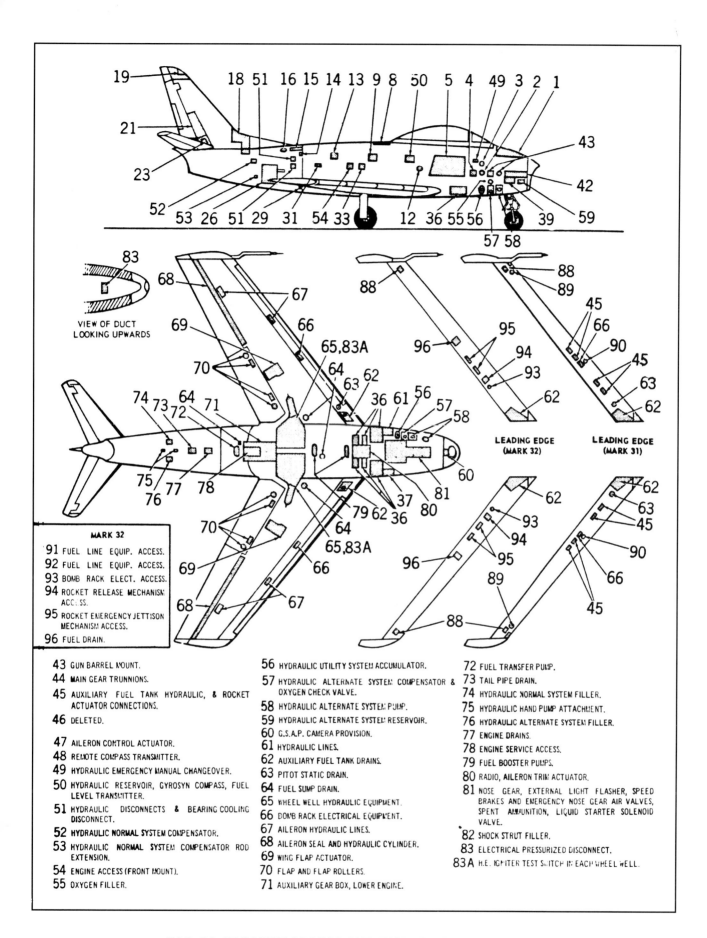

VIEW OF DUCT
LOOKING UPWARDS

LEADING EDGE
(MARK 32)

LEADING EDGE
(MARK 31)

MARK 32

91 FUEL LINE EQUIP. ACCESS.
92 FUEL LINE EQUIP. ACCESS.
93 BOMB RACK ELECT. ACCESS.
94 ROCKET RELEASE MECHANISM ACCESS.
95 ROCKET EMERGENCY JETTISON MECHANISM ACCESS.
96 FUEL DRAIN.

43 GUN BARREL MOUNT.
44 MAIN GEAR TRUNNIONS.
45 AUXILIARY FUEL TANK HYDRAULIC, & ROCKET ACTUATOR CONNECTIONS.
46 DELETED.

47 AILERON CONTROL ACTUATOR.
48 REMOTE COMPASS TRANSMITTER.
49 HYDRAULIC EMERGENCY MANUAL CHANGEOVER.
50 HYDRAULIC RESERVOIR, GYROSYN COMPASS, FUEL LEVEL TRANSMITTER.
51 HYDRAULIC DISCONNECTS & BEARING COOLING DISCONNECT.
52 HYDRAULIC NORMAL SYSTEM COMPENSATOR.
53 HYDRAULIC NORMAL SYSTEM COMPENSATOR ROD EXTENSION.
54 ENGINE ACCESS (FRONT MOUNT).
55 OXYGEN FILLER.

56 HYDRAULIC UTILITY SYSTEM ACCUMULATOR.
57 HYDRAULIC ALTERNATE SYSTEM COMPENSATOR & OXYGEN CHECK VALVE.
58 HYDRAULIC ALTERNATE SYSTEM PUMP.
59 HYDRAULIC ALTERNATE SYSTEM RESERVOIR.
60 G.S.A.P. CAMERA PROVISION.
61 HYDRAULIC LINES.
62 AUXILIARY FUEL TANK DRAINS.
63 PITOT STATIC DRAIN.
64 FUEL SUMP DRAIN.
65 WHEEL WELL HYDRAULIC EQUIPMENT.
66 BOMB RACK ELECTRICAL EQUIPMENT.
67 AILERON HYDRAULIC LINES.
68 AILERON SEAL AND HYDRAULIC CYLINDER.
69 WING FLAP ACTUATOR.
70 FLAP AND FLAP ROLLERS.
71 AUXILIARY GEAR BOX, LOWER ENGINE.

72 FUEL TRANSFER PUMP.
73 TAIL PIPE DRAIN.
74 HYDRAULIC NORMAL SYSTEM FILLER.
75 HYDRAULIC HAND PUMP ATTACHMENT.
76 HYDRAULIC ALTERNATE SYSTEM FILLER.
77 ENGINE DRAINS.
78 ENGINE SERVICE ACCESS.
79 FUEL BOOSTER PUMPS.
80 RADIO, AILERON TRIM ACTUATOR.
81 NOSE GEAR, EXTERNAL LIGHT FLASHER, SPEED BRAKES AND EMERGENCY NOSE GEAR AIR VALVES, SPENT AMMUNITION, LIQUID STARTER SOLENOID VALVE.
82 SHOCK STRUT FILLER.
83 ELECTRICAL PRESSURIZED DISCONNECT.
83A H.E. IGNITER TEST SWITCH IN EACH WHEEL WELL.

CAC CA-27 SABRE ACCESS AND INSPECTION PROVISIONS

lons (1,600 litres), but the leading edge tanks each carried an extra 35 gallons (159 litres) increasing the total by a useful 20 per cent to 422 Imperial gallons (1,918 litres).

The final CAC Sabre was the Mk.32 and to many analysts, this aircraft represented the ultimate and most capable day fighter variant of North American Aviation's original design. A total of 69 Sabre 32s was manufactured between December 1955 and July 1961 in three batches. The first 28 aircraft (A94-943 to 970) completed the RAAF's initial order, while further batches of 20 (A94-971 to 990) and 21 (A94-351 to 371) were ordered in 1955 and 1957. The final batch was built at the modest rate of one per month until the last aircraft was flown in August 1961 and delivered to the RAAF the following December. At this stage the unit cost of the CAC Sabre was put at £A526,044 ($A1,052,088).

The Sabre Mk.32 differed from its predecessors in several important areas. Among them was the installation of the improved (and locally built) Avon 26 engine with much better handling characteristics including totally surge free operation; the introduction of the 'dual store' wing and the ability (from 1960) to carry a pair of AIM-9B Sidewinder air-to-air missiles under the wings.

The structural changes necessary to incorporate the extra underwing hardpoints resulted in a slight reduction in the Sabre 32's leading edge fuel tank capacity, the bottom line being a total internal fuel load of 412imp gal (1,873 litres).

Several proposed versions of the CAC Sabre never saw the light of day. Perhaps the most interesting of them was a plan to improve performance by installing a 10,000lb (44.8kN) thrust RA.14 Avon as installed in later versions of the Hawker Hunter. This engine would have required another major redesign of the Sabre's fuselage but the estimated performance gains were substantial and included an initial climb rate of 16,200ft/min (up nearly 40 per cent), a time to height figure of eight minutes to 50,000 feet (instead of 11.1 minutes) and a notable reduction in turning radius.

No newly built CAC Sabres were exported, but the Indonesian and Malaysian air forces received second hand aircraft as part of Australia's commitment to provide military aid to its regional allies.

CA-27 SABRE Mk.32

Powerplant: One 7,500lb (33.6kN) thrust Rolls-Royce/CAC RA.7 Avon Mk.26 axial flow turbojet; internal fuel capacity 412imp gal (1,873 l), provision for 100imp gal (454 l) or 167imp gal (759 l) underwing drop tanks.

Dimensions: Wing span 37ft 1in (11.30m); length 37ft 6in (11.43m); height 14ft 5in (4.39m); wing area 302.3sq ft (28.1m²).

Weights: Empty 12,000lb (5,443kg); normal loaded 17,720lb (8,038kg), maximum 21,210lb (9,621kg).

Armament: Two 30mm Aden cannon in nose with 162 rounds per gun; two AIM-9B Sidewinder AAMs; up to 24 air-to-ground rockets, two 500 or 1,000lb (227 or 454kg) bombs or eight practice bombs.

Performance: Max speed 609kt (1,126km/h) at sea level, 584kt (1,081km/h) at 10,000ft, 528kt (977km/h) at 38,000ft; typical cruise speed 478kt (885km/h); initial climb 12,000ft (3,658m)/min; time to 50,000ft 11.1min; service ceiling 52,000ft (15,850m); ferry range (external fuel) 1,000nm (1,850km).

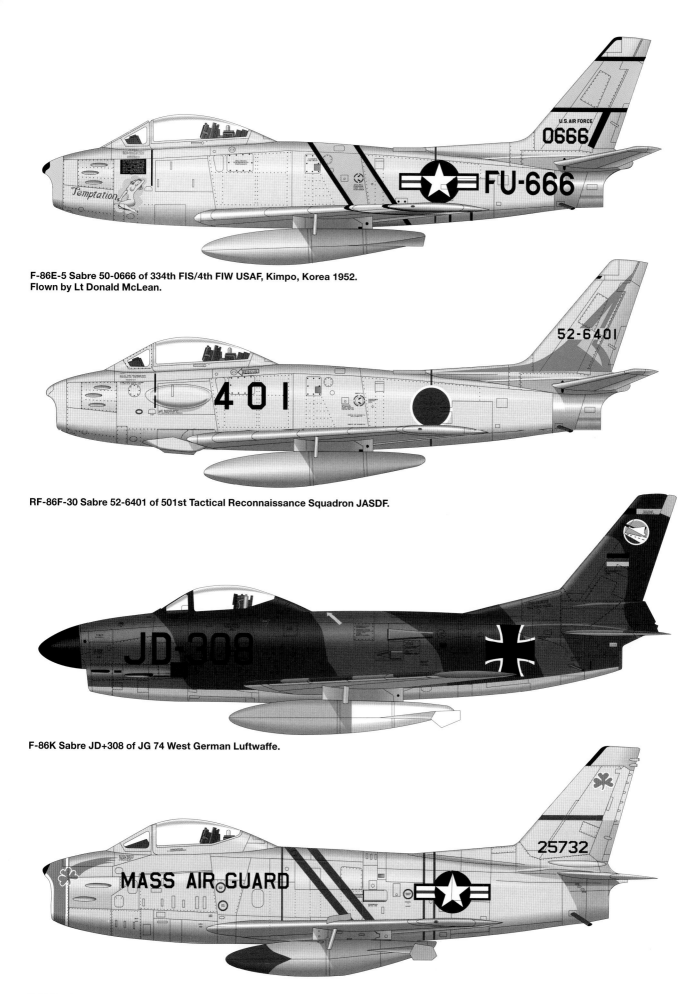

F-86E-5 Sabre 50-0666 of 334th FIS/4th FIW USAF, Kimpo, Korea 1952.
Flown by Lt Donald McLean.

RF-86F-30 Sabre 52-6401 of 501st Tactical Reconnaissance Squadron JASDF.

F-86K Sabre JD+308 of JG 74 West German Luftwaffe.

F-86H-5 Sabre 52-5732 of 101st TFS/104th TFG Massachusetts Air National Guard.

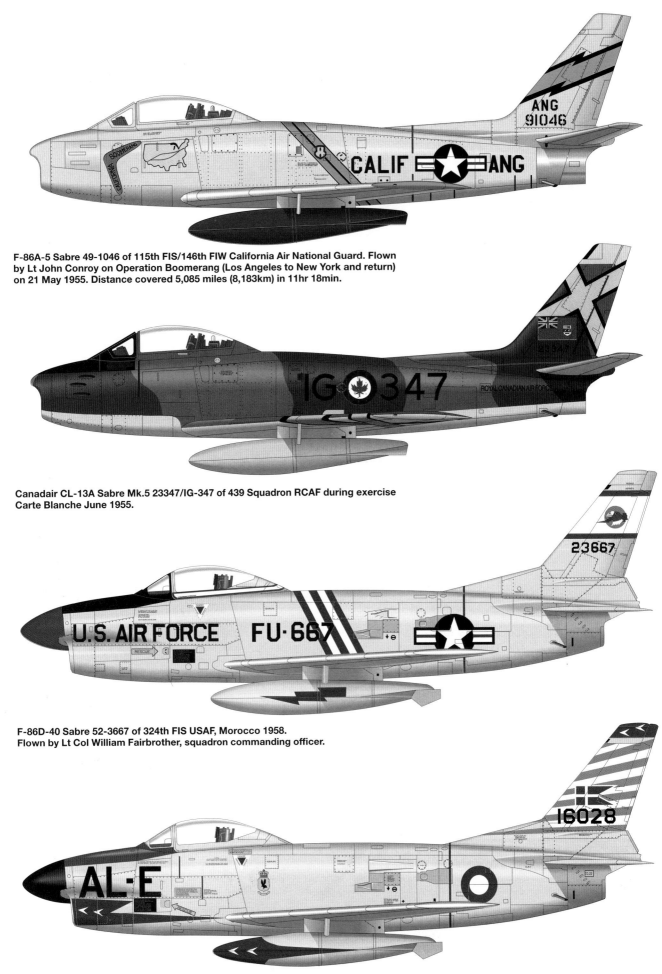

F-86A-5 Sabre 49-1046 of 115th FIS/146th FIW California Air National Guard. Flown by Lt John Conroy on Operation Boomerang (Los Angeles to New York and return) on 21 May 1955. Distance covered 5,085 miles (8,183km) in 11hr 18min.

Canadair CL-13A Sabre Mk.5 23347/IG-347 of 439 Squadron RCAF during exercise Carte Blanche June 1955.

F-86D-40 Sabre 52-3667 of 324th FIS USAF, Morocco 1958.
Flown by Lt Col William Fairbrother, squadron commanding officer.

F-86D-30 Sabre 51-6028 of 726 Squadron Royal Danish Air Force.

F-86L Sabre 53-0573 of 125th FIS Oklahoma Air National Guard.

Commonwealth CA-27 Sabre Mk.32 A94-352 of 76 Squadron Royal Australian Air Force 'Black Panthers' aerobatic team. Note smoke pipe along the fuselage side.

F-86F-1 Sabre 51-2910 'Beauteous Butch II' of 39th FIS/51st FIW USAF, Korea 1953. Aircraft of Capt Joseph McConnell, top scoring Korean War ace.

F-86K Sabre 54822/13-QG of 13th Escadre French Air Force 1960.

USAF

Yalu River

★ Pyongyang

★ Seoul

F-86F

Miss Tena

1 0   5 M
0   5   10   15   FT

U.S. AIR FORCE
24877
Col.W.B.Wilmet
Miss Tena
FU-877

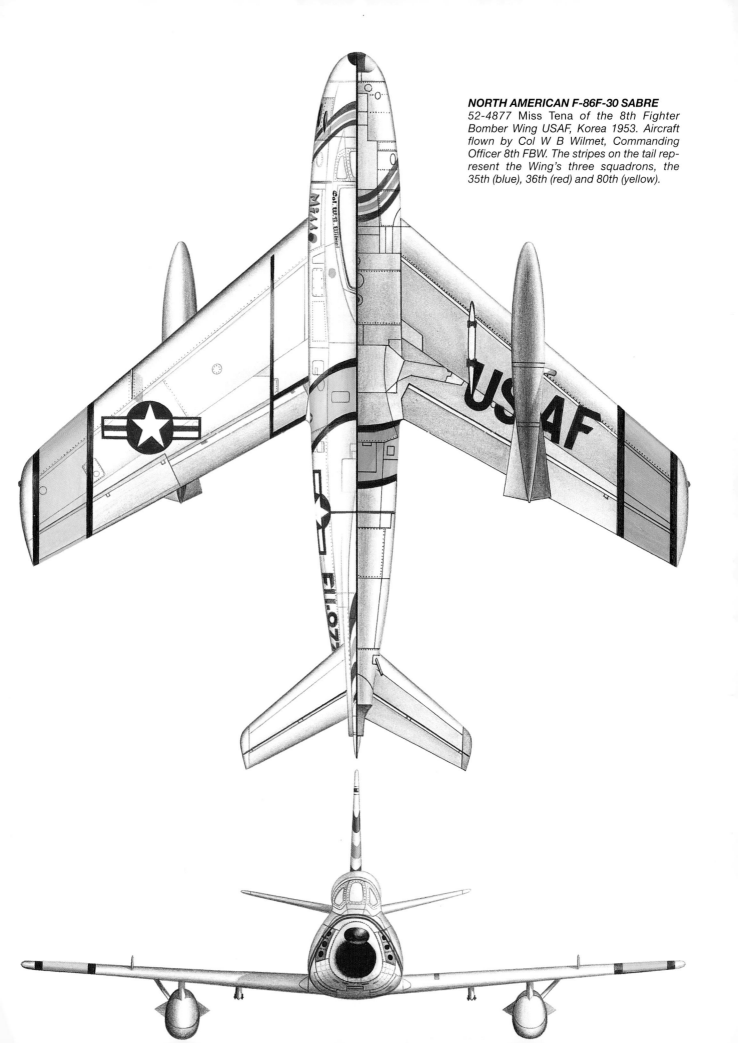

NORTH AMERICAN F-86F-30 SABRE
52-4877 Miss Tena of the 8th Fighter Bomber Wing USAF, Korea 1953. Aircraft flown by Col W B Wilmet, Commanding Officer 8th FBW. The stripes on the tail represent the Wing's three squadrons, the 35th (blue), 36th (red) and 80th (yellow).

SABRE OPERATORS

The following is a brief summary of Sabre operations by all 37 nations which have operated the F-86, CL-13 and CA-27 over the years. At the time of writing in late 1994, only one air arm – Bolivia's *Fuerza Aerea Bolivano* – still operated the Sabre as a front line operational aircraft.

Most of the countries listed purchased their Sabres second hand from several sources including from the large stock of aircraft which became available when the US Air Force, Royal Canadian Air Force and others began retiring the fighter from front line service. Other nations purchased their Sabres 'third hand' while many countries received ex USAF aircraft – mainly F-86Fs and to a lesser extent F-86Ds – under the US Mutual Defence Assistance Programme (MDAP).

New Sabres were delivered from production in the USA, Canada and Australia (the latter only to the Royal Australian Air Force) and from the assembly lines established by Fiat in Italy and Mitsubishi in Japan. While Fiat supplied new aircraft to several European countries, Mitsubishi Sabres were built exclusively for Japan's own needs. Canadair was a major exporter of new Sabres with more than half of its production run of 1,815 aircraft going to foreign air forces.

The following tables summarise the countries which operated Sabres at three 'snapshot' times over the years – 1961, 1977 and 1986. They show the steady decline in the number of operators as more modern types took over, particularly in the gap between 1961 and 1977, the latter list revealing with one exception a lack of night fighter variants and one or two new operators who had purchased second or third hand aircraft during the intervening years.

SABRE OPERATORS – 1961

Argentina (F-86F)
Australia (CA-27)
Canada (CL-13)
Colombia (CL-13)
Denmark (F-86D)
Ethiopia (F-86F)
France (F-86K)
Greece (F-86D/CL-13)
Italy (F-86K/CL-13)
Japan (F-86D/F-86F)
Netherlands (F-86K)
Norway (F-86K/CL-13)
Pakistan (F-86F)
Peru (F-86F)
Philippines (F-86D/F-86F)

A quartet of Royal Australian Air Force Avon-Sabres from 78 Wing practising a display routine over Kedah Peak, Malaysia (then Malaya), near their Butterworth base. The team was rehearsing for the 1959 Philippine Aviation Week air display. (RAAF)

An RAAF Sabre Mk.30 used for trials of the de Havilland Blue Jay (later Firestreak) air-to-air missile.

Portugal (F-86F)
Saudi Arabia (F-86F)
South Africa (CL-13)
South Korea (F-86D/F-86F)
Spain (F-86F)
Taiwan (F-86F)
Thailand (F-86F)
USA (F-86D/F-86L)
West Germany (CL-13)
Yugoslavia (CL-13)

SABRE OPERATORS – 1977

Argentina (F-86F)
Bolivia (F-86F)
Burma (F-86F)
Ethiopia (F-86F)
Honduras (F-86F/CL-13)
Indonesia (CA-27)
Japan (F-86F)
Malayasia (CA-27)
Pakistan (F-86F/CL-13)
Peru (F-86F)
Philippines (F-86F)
Portugal (F-86F)
South Africa (CL-13)
South Korea (F-86F)
Tunisia (F-86F)
Venezuela (F-86F)
Yugoslavia (CL-13/F-86D)

SABRE OPERATORS – 1986

Argentina (F-86F)
Bolivia (F-86F)
Honduras (F-86F/CL-13)

Argentina

The *Fuerza Aerea Argentina* (FAA) had attempted to purchase new Canadair Sabres in the mid 1950s but was thwarted by a lack of finance. The Sabre finally entered Argentine service in 1960 when 28 refurbished F-86F-30s were purchased from the USA. As part of their upgrading, the Sabres were fitted with the F-86F-40's lengthened and slatted wing.

The aircraft equipped the fighter-bomber Groups I, II and IV of Air Brigada IV and saw some brief but unfortunate action in 1962 when they were used to help put down an attempted coup. The FAA's Sabre numbers declined during the 1970s but some were temporarily returned to operational readiness in 1982 at the time of the Falklands War, the intention being for them to provide reinforcement for the other FAA types operating in the conflict. They were not used.

Eleven F-86Fs remained in Argentine service by 1986 for tactical training, but all were withdrawn during the same year after one was lost due to a fatigue failure of the wing.

Australia

All 111 production CAC Avon-Sabres were delivered to the RAAF from late 1954 through to 1961. The Sabre remained the RAAF's front line fighter until 1965 when the Mirage IIIO began to replace it.

The first RAAF Sabre squadron was No 75 which became operational in April 1955. Other squadrons using the aircraft were Nos 3, 76, 77 and 79, along with Operational Conversion Units. The RAAF's Sabres were able to carry a pair of AIM-9B Sidewinder air-to-air missiles from 1960.

Overseas service saw the aircraft operating from Malaya (where some operations were flown against communist terrorists) and Thailand, 79 Squadron's aircraft flying from there during a period of great tension with the Vietnam War raging just across

the border. The Sabre was officially retired from RAAF service in July 1971.

Bangladesh

The December 1971 war between India and Pakistan saw five abandoned Pakistani Canadair Sabre Mk.6s fall into the hands of the newly established Bangladesh Defence Forces. These were operated by Bangladesh for only two years until a lack of spare parts forced their withdrawal from service.

Bolivia

The *Fuerza Aerea Bolivana* (FAB) received nine third hand F-86F-30s (modified to F-40 standards) from Venezuela in October 1973, these aircraft entering service with Air Group 32. A lack of finances has meant that four of the Sabres remained in service in 1994 with no replacement in sight. The other survivors are used as a source of spares. Two were lost in 1984 when a Cessna light aircraft crashed into their hangar at their Santa Cruz base.

Bolivia has the honour of being the last nation in the world to operate the Sabre as a front line fighter, and the aircraft is the FAB's only fighter.

Burma

The *Tamdaw Lay* operated a number of F-86Fs from 1968, the exact quantity being unknown but informed estimates putting the number at 12. The source of the aircraft is usually listed as Thailand. The number in service had reduced to about six by the mid 1970s and the aircraft were effectively out of service by 1981.

Canadair Sabre Mk.6 23757, one of 390 of this mark delivered to the RCAF.

Canadair Sabre Mk.5 23314 of the RCAF's Central Experimental & Proving Establishment.

Columbia received six Canadair Sabre Mk.6s and two F-86Fs in the 1950s and '60s. (MAP)

Canada

The Royal Canadian Air Force was the first export customer for the Sabre and Canada the first country to build the aircraft under licence. As described in more detail in the previous chapter, Canadair built 1,815 CL-13 Sabres in several versions, including two powered by the Avro Canada Orenda engine. More than half of the Sabres were built for export and subsequent resales have seen many air forces operating the type.

The RCAF received its first Sabres in April 1951, entering service with No 1 Fighter Wing's 410 and 411 Squadrons. The type was eventually operated by 13 front line and six reserve squadrons. Of these, 12 front line squadrons were committed to NATO in the 1950s and 1960s, operating mainly from bases in Germany but also from Britain and France. By 1961, eight squadrons (Nos 421, 422, 427, 430, 434, 439, 441 and 444) were based in Europe.

The Sabre was retired from RCAF service in November 1968 and many aircraft were subsequently sold to other nations.

Columbia

The *Fuerza Aerea Colombiana* (FAC) took delivery of six new Canadair Sabre Mk.6s in June 1956 to replace the P-47D Thunderbolts of No 1 *Escuadron de Caza Bombardero* in the fighter-bomber role. The Canadair Sabres were supplemented by two attrition replacement F-86Fs purchased from Spain in 1963. The arrival of Dassault Mirages from 1971 saw the retirement of Colombia's Sabres.

Denmark

The Royal Danish Air Force received 59 F-86D Sabres for use as all weather fighters between 1958 and 1960, the aircraft coming from US Air Force stocks. A further three were delivered in 1962 but these were used for spare parts only.

The F-86Ds served with the RDAF's Nos 723, 726 and 728 Squadrons until 1966 when they were replaced by F-104 Starfighters. The Danish 'Sabre Dogs' were modified to be fitted with Martin Baker ejection seats in place of the standard North American unit, this modification being common among European operators of the aircraft.

The RDAF had an interesting mix of fighters at the time the F-86D was in service, with the Hawker Hunter used for day interception duties, the F-100 Super Sabre as a fighter-bomber and the Republic RF-84F Thunderflash for photo-reconnaissance.

Ethiopia

The Imperial Ethiopian Air Force (IEAF) obtained 12 F-86F Sabres in July 1960 as its first jet fighter equipment following a visit to Ethiopia by a USAF Training Mission. A further 13 F-86Fs were acquired – possibly from Iran – later on. Some reports indicate that some of the Sabres remained in service until as late as 1986, but four or five years earlier than that is probably a more realistic estimate.

It is known that a dozen Sabres remained in Ethiopian service at the time of the country's *coup* in 1977, when a war with Somalia over territorial rights began and allegiances turned to the Soviet Union. Ethiopia quickly became a Soviet puppet and the Sabres fought alongside ever increasing numbers of MiG-21s flown mainly by Russian and Cuban pilots.

France

The *Armee de l'Air* received 60 Fiat built F-86K all weather fighters in 1956-57, supplied under the Mutual Defence Assistance Programme. These were operated by three *Escadre* between then and August 1962 when they were replaced by Mirage IIIs. Twenty-two of the F-86Ks were returned to Italy in the same year, while most of the others were scrapped in France.

Greece

The Royal Hellenic Air Force operated two versions of the Sabre, the Canadair Mk.2 day fighter and the F-86D all weather fighter. The Canadair Sabres were ex RCAF and 106 were delivered from 1954, equipping three squadrons, Nos 341, 342 and 343. The aircraft remained in service

Denmark received 59 F-86D all weather fighters in 1959-60 plus a further three for spares in 1962. (MAP)

Only one Armee de l'Air Sabre remains in France, this Fiat built F-86K in the Musee de l'Air at Le Bourget. (MAP)

Canadair Sabres Mk.2s of the Royal Hellenic Air Force's display team line up on the runway before takeoff. (MAP)

until 1966 by which time they had been replaced by Lockheed F-104G Starfighters and Northrop F-5s.

Greece's 35 ex USAF F-86Ds began arriving in 1960 were operated by Nos 337 and 343 Squadrons. The last of them was retired in 1967.

Honduras

Like so many South and Central American nations, Honduras has been cash starved and therefore unable to purchase modern equipment for its air force. The *Fuerza Aerea Hondurena* (FAH) began receiving Sabres in 1976 from a variety of sources including eight Canadair Mk.4s from Yugoslavia (these being ex RAF before that), four F-86Fs and five F-86Ks from Venezuela, these in turn being former West German aircraft.

All the Sabres were operated by *Escuadron Sabre* and the survivors were retired in approximately 1988 but not before seeing action in the various ongoing wars between Nicaragua's ruling Somozo family and the Sandanista rebels plus the intertwined disagreements between El Salvadore's rulers and the Contra rebels. One El Salvadorean Mil helicopter was probably shot down by an FAH Sabre in 1985 whilst operating in support of the Contra rebels.

Indonesia

The easing of tensions between Australia and Indonesia and the latter's denunciation of communism led to the supply of 18 ex RAAF CAC Sabre Mk.32s to the Indonesian Air Force (TNI-AU) in 1973 under Australia's generous foreign aid policies. One of the Sabres was a non flying training aid.

The Sabres were operated by No

Honduran Sabres were all obtained from second hand sources. The survivors were retired in the late 1980s. (MAP)

14 Squadron and were joined by five ex Malaysian Sabre 32s (also originally provided by Australia) in 1976 as attrition replacements. The Sabres served the TNI-AU until the early 1980s.

Iran

Little is known about Sabre operations by the Imperial Iranian Air Force (IIAF) between the mid 1960s and early 1970s except that a quantity of F-86Fs were acquired and used before being replaced by Northrop F-5s.

Iran's major claim to fame as regards the Sabre was the 1966 episode in which 90 former *Luftwaffe* Canadair Sabres were illegally sold to Pakistan (then subject to a United Nations arms embargo) with Iran acting as the sales agent. The *Luftwaffe* was told the Sabres were for the IIAF, but the intention was always to pass them on to Pakistan.

Iraq

Just five F-86Fs were briefly operated by the Iraqi Air Force from 1958, further deliveries being stopped by a US arms embargo following the overthrow of King Faisal II in July of the same year. Hawker Hunters were also received before the revolution and more were delivered afterwards, while French and Soviet manufacturers were only too happy to see their equipment in Iraqi service following the US ban.

Italy

Italy became a major production source for the F-86K Sabre, not just for the *Aeronautica Militare Italiano* (AMI), but for the air forces of France and West Germany also. Fiat obtained a licence to build the F-86K in 1953 and 221 were assembled by the company mainly from US supplied kits between 1955 and 1957.

Italian F-86K of the 51st Aerobrigada, one of 221 assembled by Fiat for home and export use. (MAP)

A Japanese Air Self Defence Force F-86F-40 built by Mitsubishi. This aircraft is in the colours of the 'Blue Impulse' aerobatic team which flew Sabres for 21 years from 1960. (MAP)

The AMI's association with the Sabre began in 1956 when 180 ex RAF Canadair Mk.4s began arriving. These served with seven *Gruppi* (a unit of about 25 aircraft) but began to be replaced by Fiat G.91s and F-86K Sabres from 1960. The AMI received 93 Fiat built F-86Ks and these were subsequently supplemented by US built F-86Ks perviously operated by the Netherlands and Italian built aircraft which had originally been delivered to France.

The F-86K was operated by four *Gruppi* (three at any one time) and the type was retired from service in 1973.

Japan

The Japanese Air Self Defence Force (JASDF) was a major operator of the Sabre over many years, a total of 435 F-86Fs and 122 F-86Ds being taken on charge. The F-86F total comprises eight F86F-25s, 22 -30s and 105 -40s from the USA and 300 -40s which were assembled under licence in Japan by Mitsubishi. The JASDF's US built F-86Fs were delivered between 1955 and 1957 and 180 were actually supplied. Due to a shortage of pilots, 45 of these were returned to the USA leaving the F-86F total at 135.

The first Mitsubishi built F-86F-40 was flown in August 1956 and the 300th and last handed over in February 1961. Eighteen American supplied F-86F-25s and -30s were converted to RF-86F photo reconnaissance aircraft by Mitsubishi in 1961.

The JASDF's 114 F-86D all weather interceptors were delivered from USAF stocks from January 1958.

At their peak in the early 1960s, F-86Fs flew with three JASDF day interceptor wings, each nominally comprising three squadrons of 25 aircraft. The aircraft in fact served with ten squadrons, Nos 1 to 10, plus the Headquarters Squadron. In addition, there was a single RF-86F squadron (No 501) and one wing equipped with the F-86D, this variant being withdrawn from service in 1968.

The F-86F soldiered on in Japanese service for some time after that, despite the arrival of much more modern aircraft. As late as 1977 there were still 180 on strength, equipping six fighter squadrons and the Headquarters Squadron. The Sabre was finally withdrawn from JASDF service in 1982 and many were returned to the USA for use in the US Navy's QF-86 drone programme.

Malaysia

The Royal Malaysian Air Force (RMAF) received an initial batch of 10 surplus RAAF CAC Sabre Mk.32s in April 1969 as part of an aid package which included two additional airframes for parts, a simulator and training. The RMAF's No 14 Squadron was formed to operate the aircraft and six more were delivered from RAAF stocks in 1971. Five Malaysian Sabres were acquired by Indonesia in 1976 by which time the RMAF's aircraft were being replaced by Northrop F-5E Tiger IIs.

An RF-86F Sabre of the Japanese Air Self Defence Force's 501st Tactical Reconnaissance Squadron. (MAP)

Malaysia received 16 ex RAAF CAC Sabres between 1969 and 1971. This particular aircraft now flies with the RAAF Historic Flight in its original Australian markings.

Netherlands

The *Koninklijke Nederlandse Luchtmacht* (Klu – Royal Netherlands Air Force) received 56 US built F-86Ks in the 1955-57 period plus six Fiat built aircraft in 1957. The Sabres formed the all weather fighter element of the air force for the relatively brief period of seven years, flying with Nos 700, 701 and 702 Squadrons before they were retired in 1964 as F-104G Starfighters began to replace them and the RNAF's other fighter types, the Hawker Hunter, Republic F-84F Thunderstreak and RF-84F Thunderflash.

Norway

Another European recipient of US assistance under the Mutual Defence Assistance Programme, the Royal Norwegian Air Force (RNoAF) operated both F-86Fs and F-86Ks, the latter being the first to enter service in 1955 with 60 US built examples being delivered. One of these was lost during acceptance trials. The F-86Ks served with four Norwegian squadrons – Nos 332, 334, 337 and 339 – although three were normally operational at any one time. Five attrition replacement F-86Ks were later delivered from Fiat's production line and the last F-86K was retired in 1968.

The RNoAF also received 115 F-86Fs from 1957, these aircraft equipping Nos 331, 332, 334, 336 and 338 Squadrons and with the F-86Ks, taking responsibility for Norway's air defences until the mid 1960s when F-104 Starfighters and Northrop F-5s began to take over. The F-86F was retired from Norwegian service in 1966.

Pakistan

A major and long time user of the Sabre, the Pakistan Air Force (PAF) also put its F-86s to extensive combat use in the 1965 and 1971 wars with India. Pakistan operated day fighter versions of the Sabre, 120 F-86F-40s from 1956 and 90 ex *Luftwaffe* Canadair Sabre Mk.6s which were illegally purchased via Iran in 1966.

At the time of the '17 Day War' with India in September 1965, the

Norway operated both F-86K (top) and F-86F (bottom) Sabres from 1955, the last of them retiring in 1968. (MAP)

One of the Philippine Air Force's 40 F-86F Sabres 'up a pole' after retirement. The PAF also operated 20 F-86Ds. (MAP)

PAF had eight squadrons of F-86Fs on its order of battle, Nos 5, 11, 14, 15, 16, 17, 18 and 19, making up a total of about 100 operational aircraft. Of these, about 25 were equipped with Sidewinder air-to-air missiles.

The war was fought over the integration of Kashmir into the Indian Union eight years earlier, an act which was followed by a period of tension and unsuccessful talks to settle the matter.

The PAF's Sabres were extensively used when hostilities began (prompted by a Pakistani artillery barrage across the border into India), using the aircraft for combat air patrols, strikes against airfields and close support missions. Several air battles between Pakistani and Indian aircraft took place, the Sabre's pilots ultimately claiming numerous kills, Hunters (including five in a single action by one pilot), Gnats, Vampires, Mysteres and a Canberra among them.

By the time of the 1971 war with India, the PAF had six Sabre squadrons (Nos 14, 15, 16, 17, 18 and 19) comprising a mixture of F-86Fs and the Canadair Mk.6s which had been delivered in 1966. This time the argument was over the East and West Pakistan issue, the former having declared itself independent as Bangladesh in March 1971. India sided with East Pakistan/Bangladesh and hostilities between the old enemies began in October 1971 and lasted for two months.

The losses for the PAF were heavy and included 54 Sabres (11 of which were deliberately destroyed to avoid capture), although Sabre pilots once again made their mark and despite the age of their aircraft claimed Hunters, Su-7s, Gnats and even a pair of MiG-21s.

The Sabre remained in Pakistan Air Force service until 1980.

Peru

The *Fuerza Aerea del Peru* acquired 14 ex USAF F-86F-25s in 1955 for operation by *Gruppo* 12 which also had a squadron of Hawker Hunters and one of Lockheed F-80C Shooting Stars on its strength. The surviving Sabres were withdrawn in 1979, by which time the FAP had taken delivery of Dassault Mirages and Sukhoi Su-22s.

Philippines

The Philippine Air Force operated a total of 60 Sabres, comprising 40 F-86F-30s (mostly ex Taiwanese aircraft) and 20 F-86Ds delivered in 1957 and 1958, respectively. The Fs equipped three Tactical Fighter Squadrons (Nos 6, 7 and 8) and the Ds flew with a single all weather fighter squadron, No 9. The F-86Ds were retired in 1968 but the last three F-86Fs soldiered on until 1984, by which time they had been long relegated to the training role.

Portugal

The *Forca Aerea Portuguesa* (FAP) received 65 F-86F Sabres from 1958, using them to equip two squadrons, Nos 10 and 11 of Intercept Group No 1. Some FAP Sabres saw action during the Portuguese Guinea guerilla uprisings of 1963-64 flying close support missions and although suffering hits from ground fire, none was lost. The last six Portuguese Sabres were retired in 1980.

Some Portuguese F-86Fs saw action during the Guinea guerilla uprisings of 1963-64. (MAP)

Saudi Arabia

Sixteen F-86Fs were taken on Royal Saudi Air Force (RSAF) strength in 1958, equipping No 7 Squadron. Some other airframes were subsequently delivered for spares and the RSAF's use of the Sabre was very low key although 7 Squadron kept its aircraft until 1977 when they were replaced by Northrop F-5Fs. The Sabres had been used as trainers for some years before that.

South Africa

The South African Air Force (SAAF) had two distinct periods of Sabre operation, the first of them during the Korean War when No 2 'Cheetah' Squadron began equipping with 22 F-86Fs (replacing P-51 Mustangs) from January 1953 and operating them until the end of the war the following July. The Sabres were attached to the USAF's 18th Fighter Bomber Wing and were used for close support, combat air patrol and interdiction operations, flying 1,470 sorties for the loss of six aircraft. After the war had ended, most of the Sabres used by the South Africans were allocated to Taiwan.

The second part of the SAAF's Sabre story involves the acquisition of 34 new Canadair Sabre Mk.6s in 1956 for operation at home. The Sabres served with Nos 1 and 2 Squadrons in their front line days and with 85 Advanced Flying School in later times, ending their SAAF service with that unit in 1980.

South Korea

The Republic of Korea Air Force (ROKAF) received some 150 F-86Fs and 40 F-86Ds. The first batch of 90 F-86Fs was received from the USAF in 1955 with a further 27 following in

South Africa received 34 new Canadair Sabres in 1956. (MAP)

1958. Others were subsequently also delivered. The F-86Fs were used to equip two day fighter wings, each comprising three squadrons.

The F-86Ds gave the ROKAF its first all weather fighter capability. These aircraft were also ex USAF and

were delivered in 1960 to equip a single squadron. The F-86Ds were retired in 1978-79, and while most of the remaining Fs were withdrawn at around the same time, it has been reported that a few were kept flying until as late as 1987.

The Republic of Korea Air Force's 40 F-86Ds gave South Korea its first all weather fighter capability. (MAP)

Spanish F-86Fs were used to replace the Hispano Buchon, a licence built version of the wartime Messerschmitt Bf 109. (MAP)

Spain

Spain's *Ejercito del Aire* (EdA) was extensively reorganised from 1953 with the signing of the Spanish-American Defence Treaty, part of the deal being an arrangement by which the USAF could use bases in Spain.

For Spain there was the supply of equipment including F-86F Sabres to replace the previous front line fighter, the Hispano Buchon, a licence built version of the WWII Messerschmitt Bf109. The EdA received 244 F-86Fs to equip five day fighter wings, the Sabre remaining Spain's premier fighter until F-104G Starfighters began to take over in 1965. The last Sabres were retired at the end of 1972.

Taiwan

The Chinese Nationalist Air Force (CNAF) received no fewer than 320 F-86F and seven RF-86F Sabres between 1954 and 1958, many of the early aircraft being examples which had seen action in USAF during the Korean War. One of them was an aircraft which had been flown by the USAF's top ace in Korea, Joseph McConnell's *Beautious Butch*.

The Sabres were operated by two wings which were maintained on constant alert against close neighbour communist China, and the aircraft saw action in August and September 1958 when China attempted to blockade two small islands in the Straits of Formosa (Quemoy and Matsu) which were held by the Nationalists. Sabres were used to provide air cover for the islands and soon found themselves in combat with Chinese MiG-15s and MiG-17s.

Sidewinder air-to-air missiles were added to the Sabres' armoury during the course of the conflict and this had a marked effect, the Nationalists

claiming 31 MiG kills for the loss of just two Sabres. On one day alone, 10 MiG kills were claimed by the Sabre pilots of which four were by Sidewinder.

The fighting died down after six weeks, but another skirmish took

place in July 1959 and five MiG-17s were claimed destroyed by the Nationalist Sabre pilots.

The CNAF continued using its Sabres well into the 1970s and some sources say as many as 100 were still in service as late as 1977.

Thailand

The Royal Thai Air Force received 40 F-86Fs from 1960 to equip one combat wing comprising two squadrons, Nos 13 and 43. It also received 20 F-86Ls in 1964 (operated by 12 Squadron) and was the only air force outside the USAF to fly this upgraded conversion of the F-86D all weather fighter.

The RTAF's Sabres were replaced by Northrop F-5s from 1975.

Tunisia

The *Armee de l'Air Tunisienne* obtained 12 F-86Fs from the USA in 1969 and operated them until 1978 when they were replaced by Aermacchi MB-326KTs. While they were operating, the Sabres equipped Tunisia's one and only combat squadron.

One of 20 F-86L Sabres operated by Thailand from 1964 and flown by 12 Squadron. (Philip J Birtles)

A Royal Thai Air Force F-86F Sabre on display in Bangkok after retirement. (MAP)

Turkey

The *Turk Hava Kuvvetleri* (THK) operated a mixture of day and all weather fighter Sabres, starting in 1954 with the delivery of the first of 105 ex Royal Canadian Air Force Canadair Sabre Mks. 2 and 4 which equipped Nos 141, 142 and 143 Squadrons. These were subsequently supplemented by 12 ex USAF F-86Fs.

About 50 F-86Ds were supplied by the USA in 1962 but both these and the day fighter Sabres had been retired by 1969.

United Kingdom

The Royal Air Force was a major user of the Sabre but only for a very brief period, large numbers of Canadair Sabres being taken on strength from late 1952 as a stop gap measure pending the sorting out of problems with Britain's two new swept wing fighters, the Hawker Hunter and Supermarine Swift. The Sabre therefore became the RAF's first operational swept wing aircraft.

The need to temporarily use the Sabre came from the RAF's commitments to NATO, particularly in Ger-

Turkey received 105 ex RCAF Sabre Mks 2 and 4 from 1954 and a dozen ex USAF F-86Fs later on. (MAP)

many where the existing Vampires and Meteors would be clearly outclassed by the MiG-15 if the need to fight came. As a result, a total of 431 Canadair Sabres was delivered to the RAF, comprising three Mk.2s and 428 Mk.4s. The Mk.2s were returned to Canada when deliveries of the later mark got underway.

The Sabres equipped Nos 3, 4, 20, 26, 67, 71, 93, 112, 130 and 234 Squadrons with the 2nd Tactical Air Force in West Germany, while two home based squadrons – Nos 66 and 92 – also operated the aircraft. Their period of service was very short and by the end of 1956 all the squadrons were equipped with Hunters.

Most British Canadair Sabres served with squadrons with the 2nd Tactical Air Force in Germany. These aircraft were photographed in May 1953. (via Philip J Birtles)

Sabre F.4s of 112 Squadron RAF. Britain's Sabres remained in service only until 1956 by which time they had been replaced by Hunters. (via Philip J Birtles)

United States of America

The major operator of the Sabre, the USAF took delivery of more than 5,800 Sabres, regular service beginning in March 1949 when the 1st Fighter Group's 94th Fighter Interceptor Squadron at March AFB, California, received its first F-86A.

Sabres subsequently flew with 150 front line squadrons plus 57 Air National Guard (ANG) units. The final operational flight by the aircraft was recorded in September 1970 by an F-86H of the 138th Tactical Fighter Squadron, New York ANG.

The USAF's major combat experience with the Sabre was during the Korean War, and this is discussed elsewhere in this book. There were other 'incidents' involving USAF Sabres, a potentially serious one being the Berlin Wall crisis of 1961 when the Soviet Union sealed some 80 entry points from East to West Berlin and construction of a physical barrier between the two halves of the city – the Berlin Wall – was begun.

Tensions between east and west were high and among the many USAF aircraft standing by in the area in case of trouble were three F-86H Tactical Fighter Squadrons, the 101st, 131st and 138th, part of the 102nd Tactical Fighter Wing, Massachusetts Air National Guard. The squadrons were activated and their Sabres deployed to Phalsbourg in France in October 1961 and remained there until August 1962 by which time the crisis had passed.

The US Navy also operated some Sabres, taking a number of F-86Hs when their USAF/ANG service had ended and using some as target drones and others as aggressor aircraft – simulating MiG-17s which were being encountered over North Vietnam – in the Top Gun training programme. The drones were used as targets in the testing of air-to-air missiles.

It is in the role of target drone that the Sabre continued in US service until the mid 1990s with the Navy. An initial batch of 32 F-86Hs was obtained, the first of these entering service in 1970. Some were operated by US Navy squadron VX-4 at Point Magu, California, for Top Gun training, but most were converted to QF-86H drones for use as Full Scale Aerial Targets (FSAT) in missile trials. These aircraft were operated by the Pacific Missile test Centre at Point Magu and the Naval Weapons Centre at China Lake, California. Other

F-86Hs were subsequently obtained and the last of them was shot down at the end of the 1970s.

To replace the QF-86Hs, the USN obtained stocks of F-86Fs, mainly from Japan (whose aircraft had to be either scrapped or returned to the USA under the terms of MDAP) and also from Korea and Taiwan. Some 140 aircraft were procured for conversion to QF-86F drones at a cost of about $US350,000 each. The first QF-86F conversion flew in 1978 with service at China Lake starting the following year. Like the QF-86H before it, the QF-86F could be flown either by remote control or with a pilot on board.

As an aside, it's interesting to note that these aircraft had to be obtained from overseas as the vast majority of ex USAF/ANG Sabres which were not exported had their main spars cut to ensure they did not fly again.

Another user of drone Sabres was civilian operator Flight Systems Inc,

which converted and operated F-86Es and Canadair Sabre Mk.5s (all as QF-86Es) on behalf of the USA Army Missile Readiness Command. Flight Systems' first two conversions were F-86Es but the bulk were ex Royal Canadian Air Force Mk.5s, some 55 of which were acquired.

Venezuela

The *Fuerzas Aerea Venezolanos* (FAV) received 30 F-86F Sabres between 1955 and 1960 to equip two day interceptor squadrons, some of them becoming involved in the January 1958 attempted *coup* against the government of Brig Gen Marcos Perez Jimenez. The Sabres were used to strafe several buildings in the capital, Caracas, including the Presidential Palace, the Ministry of Defence building and the National Security headquarters.

There was more drama associated with the FAV's next Sabre procurement in 1967-68 when 47 F-86Ks were purchased from the *Luftwaffe*. The aircraft were surplus to West German requirements and the sale generated loud protests from the USA. Many of the F-86Ks were in effect new, having never been removed from their crates after delivery to Germany. The F-86Ks equipped two squadrons but most were never flown and along with the F-86Fs, were retired in the early 1970s. Four were sold to Honduras in 1969 at a very large profit.

West Germany

The Federal German *Deutsche Luftwaffe* was reformed in 1956 and a large proportion of its initial equipment comprised Canadair Sabres. Seventy-five ex RCAF Mk.5s were delivered in 1957 followed by 225 new Mk.6s from 1959, the last Sabres to come off Canadair's produc-

tion line. These Sabres equipped three interceptor fighter wings (each comprising two squadrons with 18 aircraft) and remained in service until 1966.

The *Luftwaffe* also received 88 Fiat built F-86Ks in 1957-58, although they didn't enter service with their two squadrons until 1960. More than 30 never even flew in *Luftwaffe* colours, remaining in their delivery boxes and stored. Germany's controversial sale of 47 F-86Ks to Venezuela in 1967 included these unflown aircraft. The F-86K was formally retired from *Luftwaffe* service in 1966.

Controversy also surrounded the sale of 60 ex *Luftwaffe* Mk.6s to Pakistan in 1966. The aircraft were intended for Iran, but that country was acting as agent for Pakistan which was subject to a United Nations arms embargo at the time.

Yugoslavia

The *Jugoslovensko Ratno Vazduhoplovstvo* (JRV) obtained 121 former RAF Canadair Sabre Mk.4s from 1956 to equip two day interceptor Air Divisions. The JRV also obtained a large number of ex USAF F-86Ds, some 130 being delivered in 1961. While the Canadair Sabres had been retired by 1975, at least some F-86Ds are reported to have remained in service until 1980, making Yugoslavia one of the last operators of the Sabre.

Federal Germany operated both day and all weather fighter versions of the Sabre, the Canadair version (top) and (below) the Fiat built F-86K. (MAP)

One of about 130 ex USAF F-86D Sabres delivered to Yugoslavia in 1961. (MAP)

FLYING THE SABRE

The place is the Royal Australian Air Force base at Williamtown near Newcastle, New South Wales on the east coast of Australia in the late 1950s. The mission is a ground attack gunnery exercise at the nearby Saltash firing range ... about 40 minutes of intense activity for the pilot of a CAC Avon Sabre.

With considerable help from Wing Commander Noel Kruse RAAF (retired), a former RAAF pilot with more than 1,600 hours on Sabres, we are flying the lead aircraft of a flight of four Sabres on the sortie, starting in the briefing room and progressing through the pre flight checks, the mission itself and afterwards.

It is important to note that the checks and procedures mentioned below are by no means complete; the following is intended to give an indication of what was required to fly a mission in a Sabre while pointing out some of the relevant aspects.

★   ★   ★

Prior to each sortie there would be a roughly 30 minute briefing with your team. In this case we're using four aircraft on the range for maximum effect and talking from the point of view of the leader of the whole thing. First, there'd be the leader's briefing. Even though each one of the pilots had heard it all 50 or 100 times before we still went over it carefully because there's always the odd change and it was not good to get complacent. We'd go through the standard thing: start, taxi, takeoff, first heading then departure, the runway, the rejoin procedure, run in, pitch out and so on, working our way right through the sortie.

A 40 minute flight would involve the entire afternoon. Normally we'd get two flights a day, maybe doing the same thing, once in the morning and once in the afternoon. A pilot might fly as a leader on one of them and then as number three or whatever on the next one.

Having briefed the sortie, the next thing to do would be to go into the safety equipment section to kit up, collecting parachute, 'bonedome' and G-suit. One thing people don't realise with the Sabre was that the North American ejection seat didn't have the parachute installed in it, so it was worn on the pilot's back as he walked out to the aeroplane and back again. He'd sit in just this seat which was a 'catapult' only, unlike the Martin-Baker which had, and still does

have, everything included. The seat kicked the pilot out once he'd ejected and at whatever height it happened to be, so he'd free fall until either the chord to open the 'chute was pulled or the automatic barostatic device opened it at around 14,000 feet.

After putting the G-suit and Mae West on and the parachute over that, it was time to go out to the aeroplane via the flight office where the pilots were assigned aircraft for the flight, check the unserviceabilities and sign the necessary forms. Even though some aeroplanes had pilots' names painted on the side, that was mainly a PR exercise and they by no means ended up in 'their' aeroplane, even though it may well have been involved in his particular flight.

By the time the pilot reached his aircraft the ground power units were plugged in and working. These were great big old Diesel driven things called a Deutz which used to chug away throwing out large quantities of black smoke. There would be at least one airman there to help with the strap in.

After placing parachute and helmet on the port wing it was time for the walkaround, starting at the front fuselage near the port wing root leading edge and walking around the aeroplane checking everything in general and some things in particular.

In both the gun panels there was a little slot in which a red flag should *not* have been seen if the guns were live or which would be there if they were safe. If live gunnery was the day's mission, then it shouldn't have been there.

Walking around the front of the aeroplane you checked the nosewheel steering mechanism was engaged. It's a hydraulically actuated mechanism but when they towed the aeroplane they could physically disconnect the wheel from the upper part of the leg so it fully castored, so you had to check that that was tightened properly. Checking up inside the nosewheel bay there were a couple of gauges which indicated the pressure of the hydraulic reservoirs for the nosewheel and speedbrake emergency extension accumulators – about 1200psi was what we were looking for. Of course there was the other things to check like strut extension, tyre condition and so on.

Walking around to the right wing you checked all the retraction mechanism because the Sabre had one particular possible malfunction which if it

occurred the emergency system wouldn't work. This was a matter of checking a weld but of course there were several other things that could go wrong. In the well was a 'door closed' switch which had to be flipped to the closed position. Nothing happened because at this stage there was no hydraulic power to the aeroplane. When it arrived, all the flipper doors would close automatically.

Then it was the wing, just checking its general condition and that of the control surfaces, the filler caps and so on while trying not to do yourself an injury by walking into the pitot tube! The ailerons were rigid – you couldn't wiggle them up and down like your average light aeroplane – because they were all hydraulic and irreversible. In fact if they did move you had a problem. The flaps were electrically actuated and hydraulically driven so they were usually in the down position. They only went down 30 degrees so they were really for lift only.

Standing at the trailing edge of the wing there were a couple of louvres in the fuselage which were dump valves for the compressor. Below a certain rpm the compressor delivered too much air to the engine so it would come out through these louvres. Of course you had to check they were clear. Immediately behind that was the right hand speed brake and near there was an another accumulator for this which also had a pressure valve which had to be checked for pressure.

Then it was down to the tail. Some taller people could just reach up, grab the elevators and make sure they were also rigid but most couldn't reach so they didn't bother. One thing well worth checking was that the tailpipe inside the rear fuselage did have a bit of movement in it because when it got hot it expanded and would lock solid. If it was too tight you'd get this rubbing between it and the main fuselage and a very disconcerting vibration in the airframe.

Then it was down the left hand side to the speedbrake and another compressor dump valve to check the left hand wing and control surfaces and back to the left hand undercarriage. Apart from checking all the normal things in the undercarriage well there were a couple of switches which had to be in the 'on' position as they were associated with the starting cycle. Also the exhaust from

RAAF CAC Sabre Mk.32 of the type flown in this description of a gunnery training sortie.

the starter motor came out through the left hand wheel well and you had to ensure the undercarriage flipper door was flipped up manually because there was a little hole in it which came up and engaged the exhaust pipe. Otherwise this red hot exhaust would play on the inside and probably melt the flipper door. But there was a microswitch in the well which wouldn't allow you start the engine if the door wasn't closed.

This walkaround took about five minutes to perform once you knew what to look for. At this point you walked out to the front of the aircraft and waited for the other guys in your formation to do the same thing because there was no point in getting into the cockpit only to sweat to death if somebody had a problem which delayed them. When everyone gave the thumbs up – so far so good – you'd get into the aeroplane after clipping on your parachute.

The strapping in process was a little involved. First you'd have to attach your dinghy lanyard to the left hand side of the Mae West, then connect the G-suit hose which came out of your left hand hip into another hose which came up through the floor in the centre, then do up your harness which was just a lapstrap and shoulder harness – there was no negative 'g' strap – which was a bit unfortunate because the lack of it meant that many pilots were never as firmly attached to the seat as they'd have liked despite pulling the lapstrap as tight as possible.

As part of connecting the buckle, you had to insert what they called the 'carrot'. This was a spring loaded cable which clipped into the top of the

buckle. If you needed to eject, this cable would remain attached and reel itself out to about five feet and then pull out the switch which activated the barostatic device which was supposed to automatically open the parachute at 14,000 feet. Before starting the cockpit checks the last thing to do was put the helmet on and attach and check the oxygen system.

Down To Business

The cockpit check was in a left to right sequence starting from the side console on the left, then the main and centre panels and the right hand console. The throttle quadrant was on the left side and it had an emergency speedbrake dump valve, the throttle, the flap lever and the high pressure cock arranged in priority by size with the throttle the biggest. Forward of that was the Sidewinder panel and a fuel dip switch, a device which retarded the throttle by around 300rpm when a Sidewinder was launched. This was to avoid engine compressor surge as the missile hurtled past the intake sending a shockwave down the engine air intake. This operated automatically and under deceleration the engine wouldn't surge. It would pick up again after about five seconds.

The main flight panel had all the standard things plus a hydraulic valve with a selector switch for the three separate hydraulic systems – the normal and alternate systems which only powered the flight controls and a utility system which drove everything else. 'Alternate' was the one selected at this stage. There was also a single radio with preset frequencies.

Next was the centre console with the weapons switching with switches for bombs, rockets guns and camera. There was a switch down there which was 'sight/camera/radar' in the down position and 'sight/camera/radar/ guns' in the up position. There were bomb selectors, rocket selector – you could select whether you wanted to fire them singly or in ripple fashion – and a gunsight depression device on which you could set the depression of the sight to suit various bombing or gunnery functions. These were set in advance, in this case for air to ground gunnery.

The right hand panel contained all the engine switches with low pressure cock, engine master switch, fuel transfer switches. On the right hand side was a radio compass and a circuit breaker panel which couldn't be seen despite the lovely labels on them! If anything went wrong all you could do was slide your hand along the panel and if anything was sticking out, push it back in!

Now it's time to start the engine. The ground crewman would switch the 'ground/flight/off' switch to 'ground' which gave the aircraft a power supply – remember you're hooked up to the Deutz – and then the warning lights and so could be tested.

Turn the radio on, look across at the other pilots and check they're ready to go. Radio calls might be 'Stingray Blue check' and you'd hear 'Blue Two, Three, Four'. Then it was simply 'Stingray Blue start engines'. Starting was simple – hit the starter button and at the same time advance the HP cock and sit back and let it all happen. The engine would spin to

1800-2000 revs on the starter motor, then the fuel would be injected automatically at the appropriate moment, the engine would catch and wind up to about 3000rpm.

As soon as the motor started to wind up the aircraft's main hydraulic pumps were operational and what had to be done very quickly during this initial run up stage was check out the automatic transfer system on the hydraulics. If the system selected system failed it would automatically change over to the other flight controls system. The 'alternate' was electrically powered, the 'normal' system was engine driven. The first check – before you start – is that alternate hydraulic pressure was OK and as soon the engine started and before the hydraulics had fully built up you'd flick a little switch on the side which would change the system from 'alternate' to 'normal'.

Then you'd immediately grab the stick and furiously wobble it around the cockpit. The aim was to exercise the controls so dramatically that the hydraulic pressure dropped to a level low enough to make the system automatically switch to the other system. In other words you were checking the automatic changeover was working properly. It must have looked strange, all these Sabres in a neat row on the flight line with their control surfaces moving up and down with gay abandon!

After completing the remainder of the after start checks which included

setting up the sight for the mission and then caging for the taxi and take-off, the ground crew was given the thumbs up at which point they changed the external 'ground/flight/off' switch to 'flight', unplugged the ground power, closed the panel and you're away on aircraft internal power.

Another look along the line and another radio check on the squadron frequency that everyone in the flight was ready then it was onto the tower frequency and another check that everyone was OK. It was standard procedure to check everyone was on line after a frequency change.

After taxi clearance had been given the flight moved off. With the engine idling at 3000rpm the taxi was quite fast so constant jabs on the brakes were necessary. The nose-wheel steering was connected to the rudder pedals but it had to be engaged by pressing a button on the front of the control column grip which had to be held in the whole time.

While taxying in staggered pairs the pre takeoff checks were performed. The mnemonic was TAFFIOH – Trim: just short of fully aft; Air-brakes: cycle them once to make sure they're working; Fuel: quantity, HP cock on, booster pump on, check that the pressurisation warning light had gone out if you were carrying tanks; Flaps: down; Instruments: standard checks plus making sure the gyro compass was synchronised; Oxygen: recheck the indication blink-

ers and everything else was working; Harness, Hydraulics (pressure, alternate light out, 'normal' selected) and of course a check that the controls were free and in the correct sense.

Upon lining up on the runway you'd set the air conditioning and close the canopy, remembering to duck because the frame was at about eye height!

Airborne!

The leader would pull up on the extreme left hand side of the runway, number two would be just to the right of the centreline, number three would fit in between which left room for number four on the right hand side. A quick nod from one pilot to the others to indicate 'ready' would be followed by a wind up signal from the leader. The engine would be run up to about 7600rpm which would take six to eight seconds to achieve. At that number of revs you had to check your jet pipe temperature (JPT) was in the correct 580-680°C range, there were no fire warning lights, the generator light was out and the oil pressure was at a minimum of 15psi. Then it was another quick look around to make sure everyone was OK, a nod of the head by the leader and a simultaneous brake release for a formation takeoff with the rear pair starting a few seconds later.

The nosewheel was lifted off at 90 knots and if it wasn't up by about 100 you'd never get off the ground due to the nose down stance of the

An RAAF Sabre Mk.32 of 75 Squadron shows of its weapon carrying capabilities including Sidewinder air-to-air missiles.

Sabre. At that speed negative lift was generated if the angle of attack hadn't been raised to the correct level. If for some reason the nose hadn't come off you had to shove the stick sharply forward and back again to bounce the aircraft off the nosewheel and up into the correct attitude. If that didn't work the takeoff had to be aborted there and then because the runway was fast disappearing behind you.

By the time the nosewheel came fully up there was about 115 knots on the clock and the aeroplane just flew itself off about ten knots later. You'd hold that very flat attitude for some time to build up speed. The Sabre's best climb speed was about 350 to 400 knots which explains why you never saw them doing steep climbs immediately after takeoff.

When the aircraft left the ground the undercarriage had to be retracted immediately because the gear limiting speed of 180 knots came up very quickly with the aircraft accelerating rapidly. The flaps had to be quickly retracted for the same reason. It looked all very 'gung ho' retracting the wheels so soon but it was an operational necessity as they took quite a few seconds to go up and it was very easy to exceed that limiting speed.

As this flight's going to the nearby Saltash range you'd restrict your speed to around 300 knots to allow numbers three and four to catch up. As the range was only five miles north of the airfield you had to fly a dumbbell pattern out to sea to allow the

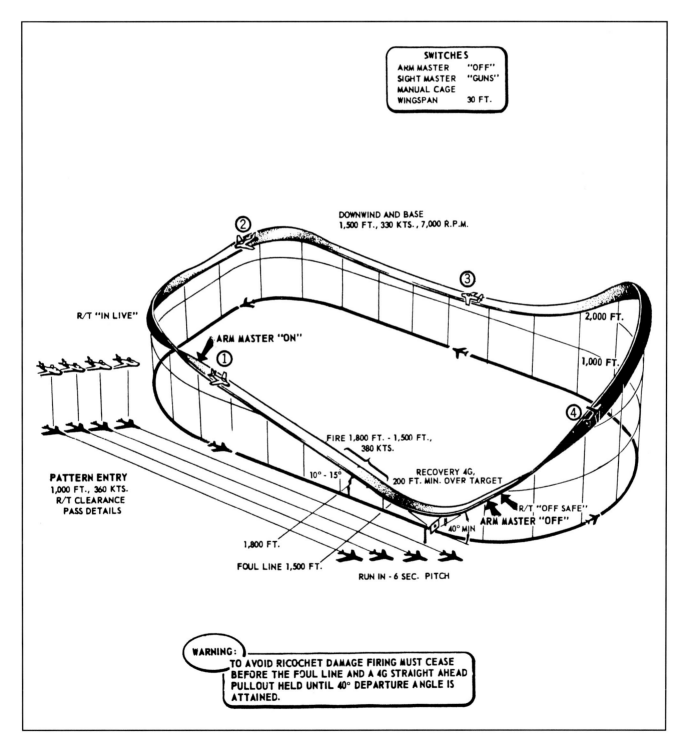

The gunnery exercise described in this chapter in diagrammatic form with the required heights and speeds shown.

RAAF Sabre Mk.32 (A94-982) with a pair of 167imp gal (759 l) drop tanks under the wings.

formation to get set and speed and height to be established. By the time you made the final 90 degrees turn to run into the range across the beach you were established at the correct height – 1500 feet in the case of a gunnery exercise – and at the release speed and in an echelon right formation. Another frequency change – to the range frequency – and another check in followed, then it was onto the range: 'Stingray Blue five miles out with four chicks' and they'd reply 'clear on'.

The run into the pattern would be along the attack direction and then there would be a pitch out into the circuit [refer the diagram reproduced here] at six second intervals. In those days it was a left hand pattern.

The gunnery pattern was flown at 1500 feet, the attack speed was around 400 knots and the dive angle was 15 degrees.

The circuit pattern was much the same size as you'd do in a Piper Tomahawk or Cessna 152 except it was somewhat faster which meant that 4-4.5g was being pulled on the corners as you stood the Sabre on its wingtips.

'Blue One in live' was the phrase used as the leader turned onto base leg and the Range Safety Officer's responsibility was to clear each aeroplane in on each pass. Meanwhile the pilot had already selected 'sight/camera/radar/guns' on the armament master selector while the master switch providing power to the circuit was not turned on until the aircraft was well into its attack run just in case the pilot inadvertently pulled the trigger while moving the control column.

The range was judged purely by estimation and a two second burst was the normal for this kind of exer-

cise. The target was a very course mesh like a stiff hessian bag about 15 feet square strung up between telephone poles. It was black with a big orange circle in the middle.

The one thing that helped in assessing the range was that they told you how big the circle was and the pipper on the gunsight was the same size at firing range. So we're in the gunnery pass and the slope range of about 1500 feet has to be assessed with a cease fire no closer than 600 feet from the target which is pretty close when you're going 400 knots. The fall of shot could be seen straight away, and you'd see dust hopefully behind the target.

At this stage, coming towards the target in a 15 degree dive at 400 knots you are destined to fly over the target at low altitude unless something fairly dramatic was done. There was a real danger of picking up ricochets, no so much from your shells but from the guy behind you, whose shell might hit another one already embedded in the sand behind the target. This happened to a Sabre, hit by a round fired by a Meteor ten years earlier!

The sequence was this: as soon as you'd fired it was a 5g pull into a 60 degree nose up pitch which puts the aircraft into a rate of climb somewhere in the region of 12,000 feet per minute. Of course the circuit height is only 1500 feet, so something's got to be done quickly to stay within reasonable height limits. You rolled on 90 degrees of bank, keeping the 'g' on, pulled it onto its back pointing about 30 degrees down and rolled it out at 1500 feet on downwind. The aircraft would reach a peak height of about 3500-4000 feet before dropping back to the correct height.

It was lots of fun! There was the

odd occasion when you were feeling really exuberant when you'd roll the other way and do a Derry turn back onto the straight and level! While all this was going on you had to flip the armament master switch to off, call 'off safe' and commence the next run.

Eight runs would be the normal number and it all got a bit hectic with four aeroplanes screaming around in this very tight pattern at relatively high speed. They were going over the target about once every ten seconds, a fair old rate.

On the way into the final pass the leader would call 'in live, last pass' and after firing, the flight would recover straight ahead rather than flying back into the pattern and set course for home.

The pilots wouldn't know how good their shooting had been until they were back at base after the targets had been pulled down, examined, and the results telephoned through. Each aircraft had its rounds dipped in a different coloured thick gooey paint which left a stain on the target so they could tell who'd done what.

Over the aerodrome the flight was settled into echelon right and would then make an upwind run at circuit height – 1500 feet – and as it ran down the runway they would simply pitch out at four second intervals. The aim of the pitch was to slow down. In a fighter the best way to lose airspeed was in a turn while pulling a high angle of attack so it was a 60 degree, 2g turn with power back to about 5500rpm and speed brakes out. This would bring the speed back from 360 to about 185 knots as the aircraft rolled out downwind.

Then it was down with the gear, and if you'd judged the turn correctly your wingtips were tracking down the runway. The reason for maintaining not less than 5500rpm was simply that below that it took a long time to spool up again, which could be embarrassing if you needed to go around.

Onto base leg it was time to put the flaps down to 30 degrees. With everything down and speed brakes out about 6200rpm would see the aircraft come down on a constant turning approach from 1500 feet at around 160 knots and would slowly be bleeding speed off until it was down to 150 knots when you rolled out of the turn and 130 over the threshold. The approach was fairly flat in the latter stages because the nose had to be gradually eased up in the last quarter of a mile to get rid of airspeed.

Once over the threshold you were virtually committed to land so it was off with the power and aim to touchdown on the piano keys at around 120 knots. Wasting as little runway as possible was important because the Sabre was one of the worst stopping aeroplanes ever built!

The trouble was, the brakes were too powerful and all too easy to lock up, blow a tyre and have a nasty accident off the runway somewhere. As a result, they couldn't be used very much which in turn lengthened the landing roll. In the wet the aeroplane would aquaplane very easily with its high pressure tyres until it got down to about 90 knots. Remember, we're touching down at 120 or so, so a fair bit of speed had to be knocked off before the tyres would provide any grip and allow the brakes to be used. This took half the runway to achieve using correct aerodynamic braking technique.

The trick was to use the flaps. The aim was to raise the nose and stall the wings on the ground, but having just touched down the aeroplane was still well above its stalling speed with flaps down and would tend to takeoff again if the stick was pulled back. So the moment the aircraft touched down you'd raise the flaps – which would increase the stalling speed and help pitch the nose up – hold the nose well up and when the stall was

felt put the flaps back down again even if they hadn't cycled fully up yet.

You could feel the aircraft dig right in – it was like hitting a brick wall – and the speed could be brought back to 70 knots after which the nose-wheel could be lowered and the brakes gently applied. Of course as soon as everything was nicely under control it was standard procedure to move to the exit side of the runway just in case the guy behind hadn't been so successful in slowing it all down!

After taxying back to dispersal and shutting down, the pilots went to the flight hut to sign off the aeroplane and note any unserviceabilities, then it was back to the crew room via the safety equipment section to return parachutes, Mae Wests and helmets. A debrief followed, at which the newest pilot who the leader had just bagged for not keeping up with the formation properly or similar minor misdemeanours, inevitably returned the highest score on the gunnery range!

RAAF Sabres of 5 Operational Training Unit on the flightline at their Williamtown base.

MIKOYAN-GUREVICH MiG-15

More than four decades after its first appearance in Korea, the MiG-15 is finding popularity in the West as a jet warbird.

Mikoyan-Gurevich MiG-15

By October 1950, the Korean War was going well for the western nations which had rushed to defend democratic South Korea from invasion by the communist North. It appeared the war was as good as won after only four months of fighting. United Nations forces had pushed far into North Korea, had captured the capital, Pyongyang, and were pushing towards the Yalu River which formed the border between North Korea and Manchuria. It really looked as if the UN troops would be 'home by Christmas', as the politicians like to say.

All this changed the following month when the communist Chinese committed their army and air force to the battle. Suddenly, the UN forces found themselves heavily outnumbered and not only unable to continue their advance but also forced to withdraw.

In the air, the situation also changed dramatically. With the Chinese came a shock to the United Nations air forces – a new Soviet jet fighter called the MiG-15.

Until then, the allied air forces had enjoyed almost complete air superiority in the skies over Korea with tactical and strategic bombing missions able to be flown without hindrance. There was an air of complacency which could almost be interpreted as arrogance as US Air Force Boeing B-29 Superfortress heavy bombers roamed over North Korea at will, destroying railway marshalling yards, steel factories, harbour facilities, oil depots and other industrial targets which presented themselves. It got to the point where the B-29s were being used as ground attack aircraft, even strafing targets with their guns.

Then the MiG-15 appeared and this all changed, as suddenly, air superiority could not be guaranteed any longer. The appearance of this hitherto unknown jet fighter changed the equation completely as here was an aircraft at least equal to anything the Americans could offer. In a flash, the word 'MiG' became synonymous with Soviet fighter aircraft, and would remain so for the duration of the Cold War and beyond.

Forced to respond to the threat, the USAF quickly sent F-86 Sabres to Korea to combat the MiGs, setting the stage for the first war involving sustained combat between jet powered fighters.

The MiG-15 went on to become the standard day fighter with nearly 40 Soviet aligned nations, some of them still operating the type well into the 1990s. Production amounted to at least 7,500 aircraft (some estimates go much higher than that) with variants coming from production lines in the Soviet Union plus Czechoslovakia, Poland and China.

The North Atlantic Treaty Organisation (NATO) introduced an identification system for Soviet aircraft in 1954, giving them names followed by a suffix letter to identify a particular variant. Fighters were all given names starting with 'F' (bombers were 'B', transports 'C', trainers 'M' and so on), and the MiG-15 was allocated 'Fagot'. For the record, a fagot (or faggot, sometimes) is – according to the Oxford Dictionary – a "bundle of sticks or twigs for fuel; bundle of steel rods; dash of liver chopped, seasoned and baked".

The Soviet System

The Soviet Union's aircraft design and manufacturing system differed greatly from that of the West, where an aircraft company usually combines both functions within its organisation, exceptions occurring when other manufacturers are sometimes subcontracted to build components or even whole aircraft.

The Soviet system worked on the basis of centralised control with design, testing and research and manufacturing facilities operating separately. The various design bureaux (OKB – *Opytno-konstruktorskoe Biuro*) have become associated with particular types of aircraft over the years. Mikoyan-Gurevich (MiG) for example, is traditionally associated with fighters – as is Sukhoi – while Antonov is regarded as a designer of large transports, Ilyushin and Tupolev with transports and bombers, Beriev with flying boats and Kamov and Mil with helicopters. The most diverse of the OKB's has been Yakolev, which

A former Polish MiG-15UTI/SBLim-2 now operated as a civilian warbird.

The first product from the Mikoyan-Gurevich Design Bureau to attain production, the MiG-1 fighter.

has designed fighters, bombers, transports, trainers, light aircraft and helicopters over the years.

All these design bureaux came under the control of the TsKB (Central Constructor Bureau) and controlling the whole question of military aircraft procurement was the MAP (Ministry of Aircraft Industry). All elements of business of obtaining aircraft for the Soviet Air Forces (VVS) was controlled by the MAP, including organising production in one of the many state owned factories.

The TsKB had no direct equivalent in the West's procurement system, equating more closely to a manufacturer's advanced design department.

While the Western military aircraft 'free enterprise' acquisition system can sometimes be accused of leaving the door open for cost overruns, delays and even political corruption from time to time, the Soviet system was far from perfect with sweeping central decisions being made, often to detrimental effect as its basic inflexibility came to the fore. There were also some advantages, notably a lack of interference from elected Members of Parliament or Congressmen who know little or nothing about aircraft or the military but insist on putting their opinions forward!

The Soviet doctrine was all-important through all of this, and its enforcement was always ruthlessly applied. There was no such thing as failure, and of course all good ideas came from within the Union and never from the West. A classic example of this is a history of the Tupolev Tu-4 bomber written by a Russian. The Tu-4 was a direct, unlicensed copy of the Boeing B-29 Superfortress but the book fails to mention the American aircraft even once!

The Stalin years were particularly difficult with 'Uncle Joe' responsible for the deaths of countless thousands of his countrymen if they showed the slightest sign of dissent, real or imagined. Even the higher levels of influence were not immune,

several OKBs which fell out of Stalin's favour for various reasons being disbanded or 'disrated', Lavochkin and Myasischev among them. Even Sukhoi, today a major designer of combat aircraft, was disrated in 1949 but had its position reinstated after Stalin's death in 1953.

Joseph Stalin died in 1953, his last years in power covering the period during which the MiG-15 was developed, manufactured and proven in combat.

Mikoyan and Gurevich

The Mikoyan-Gurevich OKB was the only Soviet design bureau to honour two designers in its title, their surnames contracted and combined to form the name 'MiG'.

The men behind the appellation which became synonymous with Soviet jet fighters were Anushavan Ivanovich ('Artyom') Mikoyan and Mikhail Iosifovich Gurevich. The two men had completely different backgrounds: Mikoyan born in 1905 in the small Armenian village of Sanain, the son of a poor carpenter; the 12 years older Gurevich was from a fairly wealthy family in the Ukrainian village of Rubanhchin.

Mikoyan received a good education and gradually moved towards his ultimate career as an aircraft designer and OKB head via factory work, a period of service with the Red Army infantry, study at the prestigious Zhukovsky Academy in Moscow (the centre of Soviet aviation technical learning) and a heavy involvement with the Bolshevik Party. Mikoyan's time at Zhukovsky saw him develop as an organiser, engineer and 'aviation person' generally.

He learned to fly and in company with fellow students designed and built his first aircraft, a quite advanced ultralight aircraft called the *Oktyabrenok*, a cantilever monoplane with the pusher engine mounted behind the cockpit and with full span flaps and leading edge slats. The aircraft successfully flew in November 1937 (one month after Mikoyan's graduation from Zhukovsky as a Red Army Air Force Mechanical Engineer) and at one stage was mooted for series production.

Mikoyan acquired tuberculosis in the 1920s and although he partially recovered, the illness affected him for the remainder of his life. He died in 1970 at the age of 65, while Gurevich passed away six years later at 83.

It was during his factory working stint that Mikoyan picked up the nickname 'Artyom' and this stuck to such an extent that it soon became in effect his real name, even appearing on official documents and in his signature.

Mikoyan was a dedicated Bolshevik and communist, a situation which helped his career growth. Another factor which cannot be overlooked is the influence of his older brother, Anastas, who gradually worked his way into the upper echelons of the Communist Party. By 1946 he was deputy premier of the Soviet Union and a favourite of Stalin's. Anastas'

MiG's first massed produced fighter, the MiG-3, built in 1941 and 1942.

The MiG designed I-250 mixed powerplant experimental fighter was capable of a top speed of 513mph (825km/h), some 60mph (96km/h) faster than the best conventional piston engined fighters of the day.

influence continued under Krushchev, and he was possibly that leader's closest advisor.

With hindsight it has become clear that Anastas Mikoyan was a great help to OKB MiG during the Stalin years when purges were common and design bureaux with much better records than MiG's were downgraded or eliminated. The elder Mikoyan's influence also helped in the areas of funding and production allocation. None of this is to suggest that MiG's successes were entirely down to the very influential Anastas, but in Stalin's time when the purges followed no logical course and were likely to involve the most loyal Soviet citizens, this influence was invaluable. After Stalin came Krushchev, with a continuation of Anastas Mikoyan's influence and the continued growth of OKB MiG.

OKB MiG

Mikoyan's time at Zhukovsky led to a job with the Polikarpov design bureau, at that time the leading Soviet fighter OKB. Mikoyan's first task was to prepare the I-153 biplane fighter (with retractable undercarriage) for series production. There he met Nikolai Polikarpov's deputy chief designer, the very experienced Mikhail Gurevich, a friendship and working partnership soon developing.

Polikarpov's star was waning at the time due to his reluctance to embrace the new monoplane fighter concept at a time when the world was turning that way. Polikarpov was undecided about which path to take and was still designing biplanes as late as 1938. As the Soviet Union's premier fighter designer it was to him that everyone looked. When it was realised that Soviet fighter design had fallen well behind the rest of the world, Polikarpov came under scrutiny and quickly produced the I-180 monoplane in 1938, but the crash of all three prototypes resulted in a purge of the Polikarpov design bu-

reau, although the once great man survived as he personally retained Stalin's loyalty.

These events provided Mikoyan and Gurevich with an immense opportunity and the pair decided in 1939 to enter a competition for a new monoplane fighter. They formed a small design bureau (with the motto 'Speed and Altitude') and came up with what would go into production as the MiG-1, the prototype of which was flown in April 1940. The new fighter reached a speed of 402mph (648km/h), the fastest achieved by any Soviet aircraft to that point.

The MiG-1 had a steel tube forward fuselage and wooden rear fuselage and was powered by a 1,350hp (1,005kW) Mikulin AM-35A 12 cylinder piston engine. The MiG-1 entered VVS service in early 1941, at which time the MiG design bureau was formally recognised by the Soviet Authorities with Artyom Mikoyan as director and chief designer.

Only about 100 MiG-1s were built and these were quickly followed by the improved MiG-3 on the production line, entering service by mid 1941. This aircraft had the distinction of being the first to be tested in Russia's first full scale wind tunnel. Compared with its predecessor, the MiG-3 featured an improved canopy design

and increased wing dihedral but like the earlier aircraft suffered from inadequate armament (one 12.7mm and two 7.62mm machine guns), poor manoeuvrability at low and medium altitudes and a high landing speed. Production ended in 1942 after 3,200 had been built due mainly to the AM-35 engine being cancelled. The MiG-3 was effectively out of front line service by the middle of 1943 and although by no means a 'great' fighter, it was available when needed and did a good enough job.

OKB MiG's primary task during the remainder of the war was to operate as an experimental design centre, an activity which meant it was well placed to take advantage of the design skills associated with the jet engine when it came along.

Among the types developed by MiG during the war were the I-220/221/222/224 and 225 prototypes, all of them piston engined fighters. The I-224 was notable for featuring a pressurised cockpit, while the I-225 with 2,200hp (1,640kW) Mikulin AM-42FB V12 engine reached a maximum speed of 451mph (726km/h) in level flight in early 1945.

Mikoyan's interest in mixed powerplant designs led to the I-250 which featured a 1,450hp (1,080kW) Klimov VK-107 piston engine in the nose and a 660lb (2.96kN) thrust Khalshchevnikov air reaction compressor (jet) in the truncated rear fuselage. This diminutive aircraft (span 30ft 6in/9.5m and length 26ft 3in/8.2m) was developed in late 1944 and reached a top speed of 513mph (825km/h). It is believed that 50 production examples were built as the MiG-13, equipped with cannon and machine gun armament and flying with the Soviet Navy for testing until 1950.

A remarkable experimental design was the Utka, a piston engined (110hp/80kW Shvetsov radial) pusher type with a high mounted swept wing over a three seat cabin, canard surfaces on the nose, wing mounted vertical tail surfaces, no horizontal

The first indigenous Soviet jet aircraft, the MiG-9 of 1946.

The prototype for the MiG-15, the S-01, first flown on 30 December 1947.

tailplane and fixed undercarriage. The Utka was built as a research vehicle into the stability characteristics of the canard design and how it could be applied to jet fighters.

The First MiG Jets

The mixed powerplant configuration of the I-250 was the first step in the journey which took Mikoyan and Gurevich to the MiG-15 and beyond. Two designs preceded it: the rocket powered I-270 which was based on the German Messerschmitt Me 263 but with unswept wings and conventional tail surfaces (albeit with a T-tail arrangement), and the MiG-9, initially powered by a pair of 1,760lb (7.88kN) thrust BMW 003A turbojets mounted side by side in the fuselage. More powerful local derivatives of German engines were subsequently fitted.

The Soviets had gained something of a windfall in late 1944 when crates of BMW 003 and Junkers Jumo 004 jet engines were captured and immediately shipped back to experimental establishments for examination. At the same time, the decision was taken to copy them and put them into production, incorporating improvements as necessary and when the available expertise allowed it.

Once German research facilities had been captured by the Allies, much data on high speed aerodynamics and hardware became available to the USA, Britain, the Soviet Union and others, all of which would be put to good use in the years immediately following the war. Among the German aircraft secured by Soviet Forces was a prototype Me 263 rocket fighter, which was examined in great detail by several OKBs including MiG. From this came the I-270, only two of which were built in 1947.

MiG's first real jet fighter was developed as the I-300 and went into production as the MiG-9. Initial studies for this twin engined fighter centred around a configuration very similar to the Messerschmitt Me 262 with underwing jets, an example of

which had been captured by the Soviets in late 1944. MiG dropped this concept during 1945 and went with the definitive engines-in-fuselage design instead with the exhausts exiting under the fuselage below the trailing edge wing root. An unswept, tapered wing was fitted, engine air entered through a split nose intake and cannon armament was installed in the nose.

The first I-300/MiG-9 was flown in April 1946 and therefore officially became the first indigenous Soviet jet aircraft to do so. The competing Yak-15 was also ready to fly at the same time, so a coin was tossed to see which aircraft would make history!

The MiG-9 was developed through several production versions (including a two seat trainer) and about 550 were built between 1946 and 1948. Its top speed of 565mph (909km/h) and good rate of climb made it a useful performer for its day although it was soon eclipsed by later designs. The MiG-9 had its problems including nosewheel oscillation and airframe vibration at high speeds. Another problem was a tendency for the engines to flame out when the guns were fired. This characteristic was

traced to ingestion of the guns' gases, and here the Soviets were not alone as the designers and operators of several other first and second generation jet fighters – notably the Hawker Hunter – would soon discover!

Towards MiG-15

The next step in the evolution of Soviet jet fighter design was obviously the incorporation of a swept wing to exploit the performance potential offered by the jet engine. Like other designers around the world, Mikoyan and Gurevich closely studied the research into high speed aerodynamics which had been carried out by German scientists but which had not been able to be put into practice.

The catalyst for what would become the MiG-15 was provided by a meeting at the Kremlin in March 1946 at which Stalin ordered the development of a new high altitude day fighter capable of a speed of more than 1,000km/h (621mph) and a ceiling in excess of 14,000m (45,930ft). It was assumed the new fighter would have swept wings, an ejection seat for the pilot, ground attack capability, an endurance of at least one hour and the ability to operate from rough airstrips.

The MiG, Lavochkin and Yakovlev OKBs were issued the specification and all set about designing an aircraft which if successful, would be subject to production in large numbers. The design bureaux were instructed to work closely with the Central Aero-Hydrodynamics Institute (TsAGI) which had been studying swept wings since the mid 1930s and now had access to vast amounts of captured German data.

Design work under the designation Project S proceeded with input from the TsAGI, and from German data in

Another view of the S-01 prototype on the ground. The following prototypes and production aircraft had revised canopy framing and airbrakes fitted.

particular, some of Kurt Tank's work having influence on the new fighter's characteristics. One of Tank's design studies combined the main features of the MiG aircraft in its early design stages: a short, circular fuselage with nose intake and rear jetpipe, a mid mounted wing swept at 35 degrees and large vertical tail surfaces with a T-tail arrangement for the tailplane and elevators. Project S's tail would eventually appear in a cruciform layout with the horizontal surfaces placed not quite halfway down from the top of the fin and rudder. All tail surfaces would be swept.

The experimental programme to discover the best combination of wing sweep, anhedral, thickness, chord and so on took some time to complete, such were the possible combinations available. Many configurations were tested in TsAGI's wind tunnel, some of them only very slightly different from others as the search for the correct combination went on.

Manna From Heaven

While development of the new fighter's airframe and systems went ahead quickly, the major problem facing the designers of all Soviet jet aircraft at the time was the lack of a suitable engine. All that Soviet engineers had to work with at the time were the German BMW 003 and Junkers 004 axial flow turbojets which produced not much more than 2,000lb (8.96kN) thrust, less than half what was estimated would be required for the Project S fighter. There was some knowledge of the Rolls-Royce Nene centrifugal flow engine (much of it from studying photographs in aviation magazines!) and

The Lavochkin La-15 was the MiG-15's major rival and was ordered into production but axed after about 500 had been built.

more information on this was sought by whatever means possible.

At this point Soviet engine technology was lagging well behind the West but a saviour was at hand in the form of the postwar socialist British government of Clement Attlee. This government solved the Soviet design teams' problems at a stroke by not only inviting some leading engineers to Britain to inspect the Rolls-Royce Nene and Derwent engines in detail but following this up by sending 25 Nenes and 40 Derwents to the Soviet Union as part of a September 1946 trade agreement. The first engines were dispatched immediately.

This misguided act was the result of some in the British government applying the false reasoning that if you arm your enemy he won't attack you, while others simply wanted to look after their in many ways like minded 'comrades' in Moscow. Just four years later, MiG-15s powered by

Nene copies would be shooting down British, American, Australian and other allied pilots over Korea ...

Needless to say, both engines were quickly copied and put into unlicenced production (the first drawings were issued as early as October 1946!), the 5,000lb (22.4kN) thrust Nene proving ideal for the Project S fighter, which had to have its fuselage redesigned to accommodate the greater diameter of the centrifugal flow engine.

The Nene went into production in the Soviet Union as the RD-45, named after State Aviation Factory (GAZ) No 45 in Moscow where it would be built. Most of the previous 'reverse engineering' work and production of drawings work had been performed at GAZ-117 in Leningrad, home of the Klimov design office.

Towards First Flight

By now known internally as the I-310, the new MiG fighter's design was pretty much settled by mid 1947 and apart from detail changes, the prototypes differed little from production MiG-15s including the installation of a single 37mm NS-37 (with 40 rounds) and two 23mm NS-23 (80 rounds each) cannon in the nose. This relatively heavy armament later caused the Americans some concern in Korea as it had much greater hitting power than the six 50-calibre machine guns installed in the F-86 Sabre, forcing the USAF to experimentally fit cannon in that aircraft.

The wings were swept at 35 degrees and featured 2 degrees anhedral while the fin featured a 56 degrees sweep and the fixed tailplane 35 degrees (initially) and then 42 degrees. The wing featured outboard ailerons, inboard Fowler flaps, a simple leading edge with no slats, was of laminar flow section and had two fences over the full chord inboard of the ailerons.

Flight controls were initially manual

The Yakovlev Yak-30 was another rival for the MiG-15 but was not ordered into production.

S-02 (top) and S-03, the second and third prototypes for the MiG-15. These aircraft were close to the initial production standard. Note the anti spin rockets under S-02's wings.

but boosted ailerons were fitted to production aircraft; the hydraulically actuated tricycle undercarriage was of wide track levered suspension design with low pressure tyres for operation from rough fields and the gun armament was housed in a demountable pack which was raised and lowered by a winch and cables system for a quick turnaround. Like the F-86 Sabre, the MiG had a 'break point' for the detachment of the entire rear fuselage for easy access to the engine. The pilot sat in a pressurised cockpit under a rear sliding bubble canopy on a locally designed ejection seat.

The RD-45 engine was mounted in the fuselage aft of the cockpit and fed by a plain nose inlet with bifurcated ducting which passed on either side of the cockpit and then above and below the unbroken wing centre section before entering the engine's plenum chamber behind the wing. The total fuel capacity of 275imp gal (1,249 l) was housed entirely in non self sealing fuselage tanks, the main one of 231imp gal (1,049 l) between the cockpit and engine supplemented by a 44imp gal (201 l) tank under the jet pipe in the rear fuselage. Structural provision was made for two underwing hardpoints which would later carry drop tanks and other stores.

A compact design, the I-310 was about 10 per cent smaller than the XP-86 Sabre and its 'clean' takeoff weight some 25 per cent less.

Although the first flight of the prototype I-310 is generally reckoned to have taken place in December 1947, a bit of MiG mythology persists which says a prototype with *dihedral* rather than anhedral wings flew on 2 July 1947 and crashed. Reputable sources have dealt with this in different ways, some presenting it as fact, some as rumour and others ignoring it all together.

Even such respected scribes as Roy Braybrook and Bill Gunston don't agree on the issue, Braybrook presenting it as fact and Gunston describing reports of the incident as "certainly untrue". Considering the amount of research data available to the aircraft's designers, it seems highly unlikely that the extremely dangerous combination of swept wings and dihedral would have been tested on a real aircraft.

Regardless of all this, the first I-310 (S-01) in a form very close to the production MiG-15 was first flown on 30 December 1947 from Ramenskoye airfield in the hands of test pilot Viktor Yuganov. The MiG's future rival, the North American Sabre, recorded its first flight just under three months earlier on 1 October.

Testing and Evaluation

Initial testing revealed some minor problems which resulted in the length of the jet pipe being reduced by just over one foot (32cm) to eliminate a thrust loss caused by the pipe being too long, and the sweep of the horizontal tail surfaces increased from the original 35 degrees to 42 degrees.

The I-310's handling was found to be generally satisfactory but at high Mach numbers (above 0.86) yaw stability became poor and the aircraft tended to flick out of high-g turns into a high speed stall and spin, as did many Western aircraft of the time. Severe buffeting was encountered at high Mach numbers, resulting in the incorporation of a pneumatic air brake on either side of the rear fuselage which opened automatically at Mach 0.92.

S-01 was retained for factory tests while the second and third aircraft (S-02 and S-03) were delivered to the LII (Flight Research Institute) in May and June 1948. These aircraft differed from the first one only in detail, changes including the incorporation of air brakes and modified canopy framing.

The I-310's main rivals for a production order were the Lavochkin La-15 and Yakovlev Yak-30, both of which first flew during 1948. The La-15 (with shoulder mounted wings and undercarriage mounted on the fuselage) quickly emerged as the most serious rival and comparison testing by the Soviet Air Force Scientific Test Institute revealed advantages in both. The La-15 demonstrated better stability at high Mach numbers, generally superior handling and no speed limitations. On the debit side, the La-15's short-coupled and narrow track undercarriage made crosswind landings difficult and its complex structure made mass production complicated and labour intensive.

The I-310 had better firepower, range and rate of climb and its simpler manufacturing processes plus easier maintenance in the field counted strongly in its favour. As it happened, both types were ordered into production but service experience quickly confirmed the MiG's overall superiority and that combined with the logistical problems associated with having two different types performing the same job resulted in the La-15 being axed after about 500 had been built.

Confirmation that the I-310 would be put into production was received in March 1948, the aircraft henceforth being referred to as the MiG-15.

On a historical note, it was mentioned earlier that the name MiG came from a combination of Mikoyan and Gurevich. Artyom Mikoyan became the dominant force from about 1950 as Gurevich's health began to fail. Although the design bureau retained the name 'MiG', its full form became known as simply 'Mikoyan' from the MiG-19 of 1953 and onwards.

Many restored MiG-15s are now appearing in warbirds fleets around the world. These two examples were restored in Australia. (Jim Thorn/Gerard Frawley)

Many Eastern European countries have their retired MiG-15s in museums, often stored outdoors with obvious effects on their condition. This Hungarian MiG-15bis (top) and Polish MiG-15UTI/SBLim demonstrate. (MAP)

A warbird MiG-15UTI (top) taxies out during an air show. Nicely preserved (bottom) is this East German MiG-17F Fresco C. (Jim Thorn/MAP)

MiG-15

The first production version of the MiG-15 (later codenamed *Fagot* by NATO and then *Fagot A* when other versions were identified) made its first flight exactly one year after the prototype, on 30 December 1948. Once again, test pilot Viktor Yuganov was at the controls.

Production aircraft were very similar to the second and third prototypes with revised canopy framing and shorter tail pipe. Small triangular air brakes were added to the rear fuselage (operating automatically to restrict speed to Mach 0.92), a gun camera was installed in a small lip on the top of the air intake and the aircraft received a slightly wider chord rudder with trim tab.

The Klimov RD-45 (Nene copy) centrifugal flow turbojet was rated at 5,000lb (22.26kN) thrust, providing a maximum level speed of 567 knots (1,050km/h) at sea level, initial climb rate of 8,260ft (2,520m) per minute, service ceiling of 49,870 feet (15,200m) and a range with standard internal fuel of 766nm (1,419km) or 1,036nm (1,919km) with a pair of 55imp gal (250 l) underwing slipper tanks. Slipper tanks of 66imp gal (300 l) subsequently became available, as did drop tanks of 87imp gal (398 l) capacity.

MiG-15s from the production line only ever had two underwing hardpoints, these carrying a variety of loads ranging from the fuel tanks mentioned above to rockets or a single 550lb (250kg) bomb.

The aircraft's gun armament was modified during the course of its production run. The big hitting single 37mm N-37 cannon remained but the relatively slow firing pair of Nudelmann-Suranov 23mm NS-23s were eventually replaced by NR-23s of the same calibre and muzzle velocity (690m/sec) but with a 50 per cent greater rate of fire of 850 rounds per minute. The N-37 fired at only 400 rounds per minute but its muzzle velocity of 900m/sec was high. This fire power was considerably greater than that offered by the F-86 Sabre's six 50-calibre machine guns and proved to be source of real concern for the Americans during the Korean War.

Early MiG-15s were equipped with only basic avionics including HF and LF radio, a gyroscopic gunsight and radio compass, with items such as Identification Friend or Foe (IFF) equipment, radio altimeter and marker beacon receiver incorporated later in the production run.

Product Improvement

Early service revealed several shortcomings with the basic MiG-15, among them poor fuel consumption, reliability, overhaul life and low thrust from the RD-45 engine plus the potentially dangerous tendency to flick out of a tight turn and loss of directional stability at high Mach numbers. The engine problems were gradually overcome as Klimov's experience and knowledge began to climb the 'learning curve' and a much improved but similarly rated version – the RD-45F – was introduced relatively early in the production run.

Many of the MiG-15's aerodynamic problems stemmed from a very poor build quality at first in addition to any fundamental design problems which existed. The directional instability resulted in a speed limit of Mach 0.88 being applied until things were sorted out, investigations revealing that poor adherence to manufacturing tolerances were to blame. In the wing, for example, deviations of up to 0.15in (4mm) were found in the aerofoil dimensions, with obvious results. The problems were difficult to find because of the large variation in manufacturing tolerances found in different aircraft, even from within the same production batch.

This was eventually rectified to a satisfactory level, although manufacturing quality throughout the Soviet Union and its Eastern European allies continued to leave something to be desired. A 'quick fix' for any wing asymmetry caused by manufacturing defects appeared in the form of a ground adjustable trim tab on the starboard wing. Once this was under control, the Mach 0.88 speed limit was increased to the previous Mach 0.92, controlled by the automatically opening speed brakes on the rear fuselage.

MiG-15 with 66imp gal (300 l) underwing slipper tanks. These increased the aircraft's fuel capacity by nearly one quarter.

An early production MiG-15 with unreliable and thirsty RD-45 engine. Production quality was a major problem with the MiG-15 early in its life, widely varying manufacturing tolerances – particularly in the wings – contributing to handling difficulties.

Despite its faults and limitations, the MiG-15 quickly became appreciated by its users as a simple, robust and reliable combat aircraft and was given the nickname *Samoljot-Soldat*, 'aircraft-soldier'.

The basic MiG-15 received other detailed improvements and equipment upgrades during its relatively brief production run before the more powerful MiG-15bis was introduced in 1950. Among them were revised elevator balance, improved instrument panel design, updated and more extensive avionics fits including an ILS system, external fuel tanks, an engine air starting system, improved pilot protection armour, a thickened windscreen, a gunsight designed to minimise injury to the pilot during an accident by automatically sliding forward and the major improvements (NR-23 guns and RD-45F engine) mentioned earlier.

Experimental and limited production versions of the basic MiG-15 included the **MiG-15U** (*Ustanovka* – swivelling device) ground attack variant with a pair of 30mm cannon mounted under the forward fuselage on vertically swivelling mounts capable of moving through a range of -55 degrees to +5 degrees. The single prototype was tested in 1951 but the idea was found to be impractical although a MiG-17 was later similarly modified for trials.

An interesting variation was the **MiG-15LL** (*Letayushchye Laboratorii* – flying laboratory) for high speed testing with the primary aim of achieving supersonic flight in a dive, something which a normal MiG-15 had and could not achieve as its stability problems limited it to Mach 0.92.

The MiG-15LL initially looked similar to the standard aircraft but was equipped with special test instrumentation. It first flew in September 1949, a series of dives resulting in a speed of Mach 0.985 which revealed the need for a larger vertical tail surfaces and powered controls, as control forces were exceptionally high.

The aircraft was then reconfigured to incorporate a larger fin of completely new design, a ventral fin, increased chord horizontal tail and powered controls. The result was a claimed speed of Mach 1.01 in October 1949 when test pilot Anatoliy Tyuteryev dived the MiG-15LL from 41,000 feet (12,500m). The LL's main contribution was the lessons learned in the areas of boosted controls and the development of yaw damper all flying horizontal tail surfaces, lessons which would be applied to future MiG jet fighters.

MiG-15 (Fagot A)
Powerplant: One 5,000lb (22.26kN) thrust Klimov RD-45 or RD-45F (Rolls-Royce Nene) centrifugal flow turbojet; internal fuel capacity 275imp gal (1,250 l); provision for two 55imp gal (250 l), 66imp gal (300 l) or 87imp gal (396 l) underwing tanks.
Dimensions: Wing span 33ft 3in (10.13m); length 33ft 4in (10.16m); height 11ft 1.7in (3.39m); wing area 221.8sq ft (20.6m²).
Weights: Empty 7,456lb (3,382kg); loaded (clean) 10,595lb (4,806kg); loaded (with 55imp gal underwing tanks) 11,596lb (5,260kg).
Armament: One 37mm NS-37 (with 40 rounds) and two 23mm NS-23 or NR-23 (80 rounds each) cannon in lower forward fuselage.
Performance: Max speed 567kt (1,050km/h) at sea level, 557kt (1,033km/h) at 16,400ft; initial climb (clean) 8,260ft (2,520m)/min; time to 16,400ft (5,000m) 2.3min, time to 32,800ft (10,000m) 7.1min; service ceiling 49,870ft (15,200m); range (internal fuel) 766nm (1,419km), range with 55imp gal external tanks 1,036nm (1,919km); max endurance 3hr 13min.

MiG-15bis

The definitive and most produced MiG-15 single seat fighter variant, the MiG-15bis offered notably improved performance over its predecessor thanks to the efforts of Vladimir Klimov and his design team, which developed the basic RD-45/Nene copy into a more powerful and ultimately more reliable engine with reasonable times between overhaul. Designated the VK-1 in honour of its designer, the new engine produced 5,950lb (26.6kN) thrust (a nearly 20 per cent improvement on the original) and incorporated several hundred detail design changes over the earlier engine.

The VK-1 featured redesigned combustion chambers, tailpipe and turbine blades and was only slightly physically larger than its predecessor although with a dry weight of 1,950lb (885kg) it was some 350lb (160kg) heavier. When it first entered service the VK-1 had an overhaul life of just 25 hours, this figure improving to the much better but still modest (by Western standards) 150 hours with the developed VK-1A. One of the problems contributing to the low

The MiG-15LL flying laboratory for high speed testing with modified tail surfaces and powered controls. It reached a claimed Mach 1.01 in October 1949.

overhaul life of Soviet engines was the use of poor quality materials in their construction, a result of availability and the fact that in the late 1940s/early 1950s, engineers were still learning about the metallurgical and other technical aspects of the jet engine.

The airframe which would accommodate the VK-1 engine was developed in 1949 under the project code SD and put into production as the MiG-15bis. The first Project SD aircraft was flown in July 1949 and mass production was initiated early in 1950. Early aircraft were not very different from the original MiG-15 including the installation of the less powerful RD-45F engine but the intended improvements were quickly incorporated on the production line.

With the VK-1 engine installed the MiG-15bis demonstrated speeds some 16-20mph (26-32km/h) faster than the original aircraft (depending on height), an initial rate of climb of over 10,000 feet per minute (3,050m/min) or more than 20 per cent better than before and improved service ceiling. Range was slightly down due to the VK-1's greater fuel consumption, despite an increase in the aircraft's fuel capacity.

Many Improvements

The modifications applied to the MiG-15bis were many and varied, resulting in a considerably more capable combat aircraft than before. The fundamental changes were: the more powerful engine; an extensive weight reduction effort which resulted in a basic airframe which was 200lb (90kg) lighter; increased internal fuel capacity of 322imp gal (1,462 l); larger airbrakes with their hinge point moved slightly forward; wider chord ailerons; revised internal structure to accommodate the slightly larger VK-1 engine; perforated flaps (part of the weight reduction programme); modified wing spars; increased elevator balance; the incorporation of narrow trim tabs on the wing trailing edges; and improved aileron boost.

Also fitted was the improved N-37 37mm cannon (in place of the NS-37) in later aircraft as well as two 23mm NR-23s, although some of the early aircraft had slower firing NS-23s. This armament further widened the 'hitting power' gap between the MiG-15 and the F-86 Sabre. It was calculated that only two N-37 or eight NR-23 rounds would be sufficient to bring down a large bomber such as the B-29 Superfortress while a single N-37 or two NR-23 rounds would deal with a Sabre. This was a marked contrast to the reverse situation in which it was reckoned that 1,024 rounds of 50-calibre were required to shoot down

The first Project SD fighter, prototype for the improved MiG-15bis and first flown in July 1949. The MiG-15bis had more power, increased internal fuel, improved flying controls and uprated armament.

Maintenance work on an East German MiG-15bis with the open forward equipment hatch revealing the battery (at front) and VHF radios behind.

An early production MiG-15bis. Production of this major MiG-15 single seat variant began in early 1950.

a MiG-15, or nearly two-thirds of the Sabre's ammunition supply!

The MiG-15bis also had numerous equipment and detail changes, most of which were progressively incorporated on the production line. Radio and operational equipment was improved over the original aircraft with the standard fit eventually including VHF, marker beacon, IFF on some aircraft, a radio compass and radio altimeter.

The MiG-15bis retained the single hardpoint under each wing, but more external fuel tank options were available, choices including 55imp gal (250 l), 66imp gal (300 l), 87imp gal (396 l) or 132imp gal (600 l) units, the latter increasing the maximum range to 1,360nm (2,520km). Aircraft equipped with the large tanks were originally dubbed the MiG-15bisS (*Soprovozhdeniye* – accompaniment/escort), but this designation was dropped when they became a standard option. Two

110lb (50kg), 220lb (100kg) or 550lb (250kg) bombs could be carried underwing when fuel tanks were not, or two rocket pods.

Subvariants

Numerous MiG-15bis subvariants were developed, many of them not progressing beyond the testing stage. Some of these are listed below:

MiG-15bis SD-UPB: (*Uvelichnenyye Podvesnyi Bakami* – enlarged underwing tanks). Developed for escort fighter duties and fitted with two large 257imp gal (1,170 l) underwing tanks. First tested in June 1950 but not produced, 132imp gal (600 l) tanks adopted instead (see above).

MiG-15bisR: (*Rasvedtchik* – reconnaissance). Photo reconnaissance variant with two vertical cameras in the lower fuselage under the cockpit, replacing the N-37 cannon and one of the NR-23 guns. Internal fuel capacity was slightly reduced. The pro-

totype (a conversion) was flown in 1950 and production began the following year.

MiG-15bisF: Also a reconnaissance variant but with a single camera mounted in a pod under the nose. Guns removed, production limited.

MiG-15bisISh: (*Istrebityel Shturmovik* – fighter-assault aircraft). An attempt to produce more heavily armed close air support version of the aircraft, the ISh featured a strengthened wing and upgraded weapons pylons capable of carrying three bomb racks for 110lb (50kg) or 220lb (100kg) bombs or rockets. The standard gun armament was retained. The MiG-15bisISh was tested but not put into production, dedicated close support types being developed instead, notably by Sukhoi.

MiG-15bis Burlaki: Various methods to increase the operational range of the MiG-15 were attempted, particularly to provide an escort for the VVS's Tupolev Tu-4 *Bull* (Boeing B-29 copy) bombers. The Burlaki system was based on the Tu-4 towing its own escorting MiG-15 on a mission, the fighter then starting its engine and disengaging from the bomber when needed.

The towing system was developed by Yakovlev and although mechanically feasible when tested, the pilots of the MiGs could not endure the extreme cold they were subjected to while under tow, because without the engine running, the fighter's cockpit could not be heated. Even if the pilot could function properly after the long tow, his chances of returning safely were virtually nil as the MiG-15 would have insufficient fuel to return to a friendly base.

A preserved example of the MiG-15bisISh fighter-assault aircraft with large multi purpose weapons pylon inboard of the drop tank. (MAP)

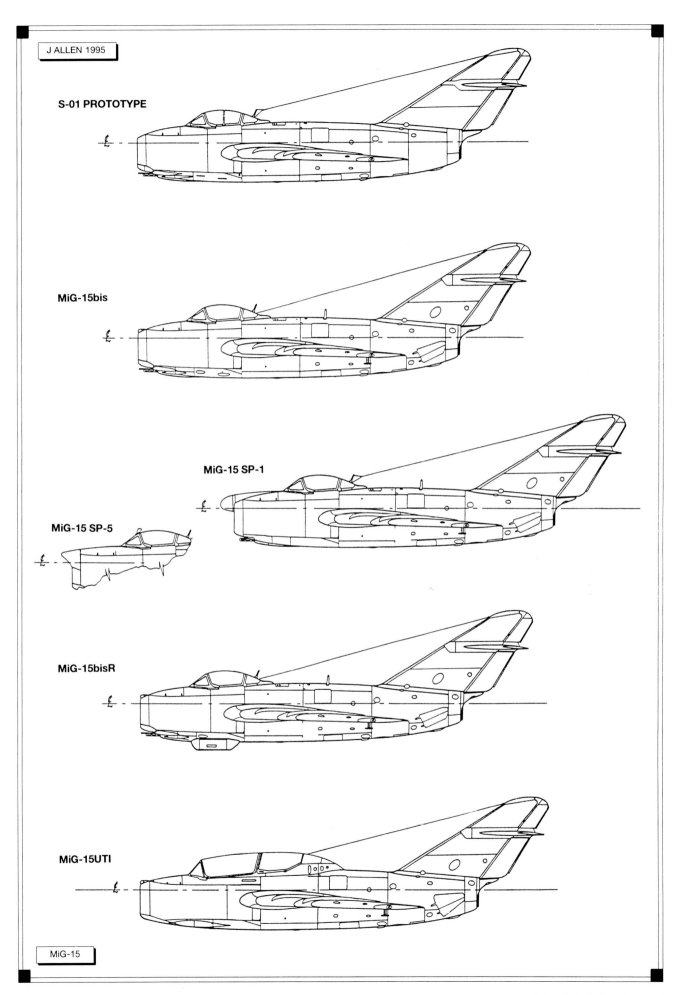

J ALLEN 1995

S-01 PROTOTYPE

MiG-15bis

MiG-15 SP-1

MiG-15 SP-5

MiG-15bisR

MiG-15UTI

MiG-15

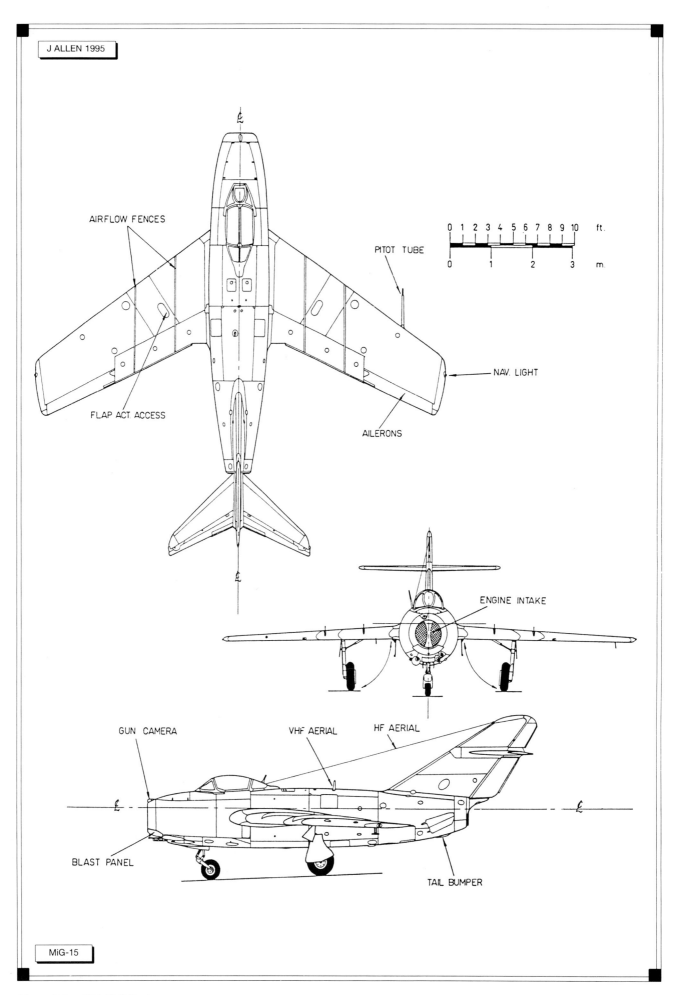

AIRFLOW FENCES

PITOT TUBE

NAV. LIGHT

FLAP ACT ACCESS

AILERONS

ENGINE INTAKE

GUN CAMERA

VHF AERIAL

HF AERIAL

BLAST PANEL

TAIL BUMPER

MiG-15

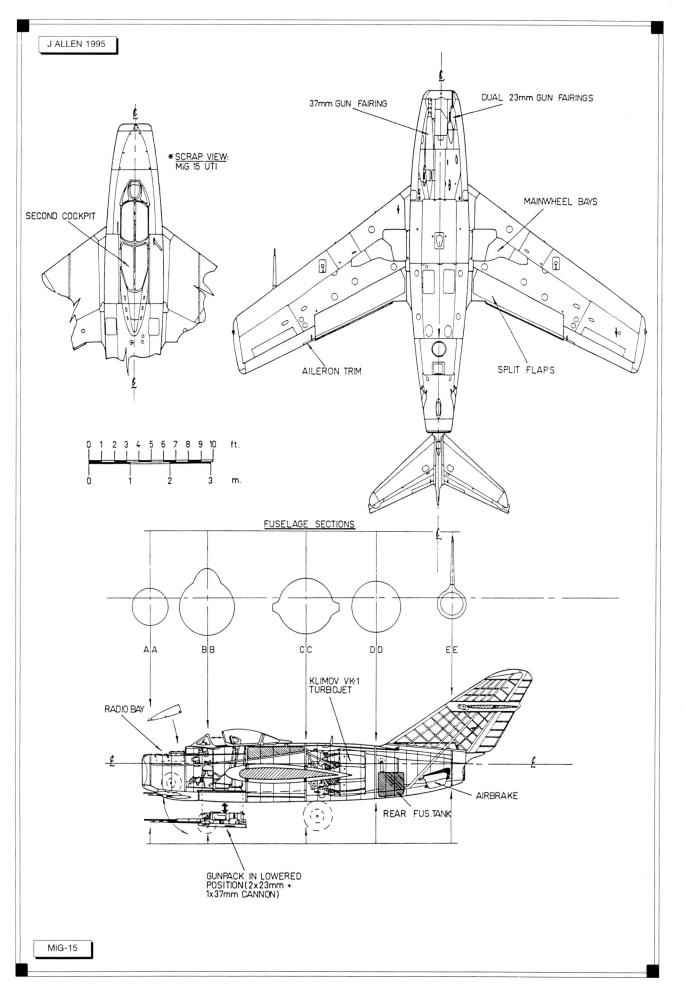

J ALLEN 1995

* SCRAP VIEW:
MiG 15 UTI

SECOND COCKPIT

37mm GUN FAIRING

DUAL 23mm GUN FAIRINGS

MAINWHEEL BAYS

AILERON TRIM

SPLIT FLAPS

0 1 2 3 4 5 6 7 8 9 10 ft.

0 1 2 3 m.

FUSELAGE SECTIONS

A A   B B   C C   D D   E E

KLIMOV VK-1
TURBOJET

RADIO BAY

AIRBRAKE

REAR FUS.TANK

GUNPACK IN LOWERED
POSITION (2 x 23mm +
1 x 37mm CANNON)

MiG-15

Aerial refuelling techniques were tested using the hose and drogue system and Tupolev Tu-4 (Boeing B-29 copy) tanker aircraft.

MiG-15bis Aerial Refuelling: A more practical approach to extending the MiG-15's range was the use of aerial refuelling. Tests on the MiG-15 began in 1951 using a Tu-4 as the tanker aircraft. The hose and drogue system (as used by the British and the US Navy) was adopted, the fighter being fitted with a refuelling probe mounted on the port side of the nose. There were many problems, most of them stemming from the hoses oscillating and breaking the MiG's refuelling probe. As a result, operational service was at best extremely limited and largely experimental.

MiG-15bisSB: (*Stihaci-Bombard-ovaci* – fighter-bomber). Conversion of MiG-15bis optimised for fighter bomber role with six position hardpoint under the wings capable of carrying four unguided 130mm rockets, bombs or rocket pods. Could also be equipped with RATO (rocket assisted takeoff) equipment and braking parachute. The first conversion appeared in 1958 and many aircraft were subsequently remanufactured to SB standards, including in Czechoslovakia.

MiG-15bisT: (*Tahac* – towing). Conversion of both MiG-15bis and early model MiG-15s (MiG-15T) to target towing aircraft for use in air defence training with winch and tow line equipment installed.

MiG-15bis SP-1: In its standard form, the MiG-15 was very much a day fighter with no radar. The SP-1 was the design bureau's first attempt at an all weather, radar equipped interceptor based on the standard aeroplane. Recognising the need for a fighter which could intercept the new generation of Western jet bombers in all weathers and at night, a specification for such an aircraft was issued in late 1949, along with instructions to develop a suitable airborne intercept radar system.

This was developed by Andrejeja Slepushkin and codenamed *Toriy* (later *Korshun* – vulture) and was of the single antenna type with combined search and tracking functions. Using the radar, the pilot had to manually fly the aircraft to a suitable firing position.

A MiG-15bis was fitted with the radar and called the SP-1. The radar was mounted on a redesigned nose section in a radome above the circular intake in a manner similar to the later F-86D Sabre. The top surface of the nose was recontoured and in order to make space available and to save weight, the two port side 23mm cannon were removed.

The SP-1 first flew in May 1949 and was extensively tested, these tests revealing a very heavy pilot workload which only the most skilful and experienced pilots were capable of handling. Five other aircraft were converted to SP-1 configuration in 1951 but series production was not undertaken.

MiG-15bis SP-5: Developed slightly after the SP-1 described above, the SP-5 followed a similar concept but utilised the Viktor Tikhomirov designed *Izumrud* radar which utilised separate antennae for the search and tracking functions, the latter being performed automatically rather than manually and therefore substantially reducing the pilot's workload. The internal computer calculated the optimum firing position and commanded the pilot when to open fire.

A MiG-15bis was converted to SP-5 standards in 1950, the physical characteristics of the aircraft including the tracking radar antenna housed in a small radome mounted on the splitter plate in the middle of the intake and the search antenna in a protruding 'lip' radome above the intake. Armament was reduced to a pair of 23mm cannon, one on each side of the lower forward fuselage.

Trials of the *Izumrud* radar system proved successful with the result that a small production batch of SP-5s was built as the MiG-15P. The radar went into regular service in 1952 on the MiG-15's successor, the MiG-17.

Despite the introduction of the MiG-17 into production during 1951, the MiG-15bis continued to be manufactured in the Soviet Union until 1952 and later in other countries. The two seat MiG-15UTI (described below) was produced for a longer period and in greater numbers. As

The first radar equipped MiG-15 variant, the SP-1 with Toriy radar. Tests revealed a very heavy workload for the pilot and only the most skilled were able to manage it.

Two views of the MiG-15bis SP-5 of 1950 with Izumrud radar. Note the two scanners, one on the intake splitter (tracking) and the other in the lip above the intake (search).

mentioned earlier, the number of MiG-15s which were built is impossible to accurately assess, but a figure of around 8,000 seems to be a reasonable 'guesstimate', including those built under licence in Poland, Czechoslovakia and China. Of those, about 40 per cent are reckoned to have been single seaters.

> **MiG-15bis (Fagot B)**
> **Powerplant:** *One 5,950lb (26.6kN) thrust Klimov VK-1A centrifugal flow turbojet; internal fuel capacity 322imp gal (1,462 l); provision for two 55imp gal (250 l), 66imp gal (300 l), 87imp gal (396 l) or 132imp gal (600 l) underwing tanks.*
> **Dimensions:** *Wing span 33ft 3in (10.13m); length 33ft 4in (10.16m); height 11ft 1.7in (3.39m); wing area 221.8sq ft (20.6m²).*
> **Weights:** *Empty 8,115lb (3,681kg); loaded (clean) 11,177lb (5,070kg); maximum 13,327lb (6,045kg).*
> **Armament:** *One 37mm N-37 cannon (with 40 rounds) and two 23mm NR-23 cannon (80 rounds each) in lower forward fuselage; provision for two 110lb (50kg), 220lb (100kg) or 250lb (550kg) bombs or two rocket pods under wings.*
> **Performance:** *Max speed 581kt (1,075km/h) at sea level, 565kt (1,046km/h) at 10,000ft; initial climb (clean) 10,100ft (3,078m)/min; time to 16,400ft (5,000m) 1.9min, time to 32,800ft (10,000m) 4.6min; service ceiling 50,855ft (15,500m); range (internal fuel) 718nm (1,329km), range with 132imp gal (600 l) external tanks 1,360nm (2,519km); max endurance 2hr 57min.*

MiG-15UTI

A two seat advanced trainer variant of the MiG-15 fighter figured early in MiG's thoughts and in April 1949 development of such an aircraft was ordered under the designation ST or I-312. In production form the aircraft

was called the MiG-15UTI (*Uchebno-Trenirovochnyy Istrebitel* – training fighter) and was dubbed *Midget* by NATO. The Soviets gave it a much more homely nickname – *Babushka* (grandmother) or sometimes *Matushka* (good old woman)!

MiG was already well advanced with its design for a two seat MiG-15 by the time the development order

was issued, this variant in fact beating the definitive single seater (MiG-15bis) into the air, first flying in June 1949. The UTI went on to become the most built and longest serving MiG-15 variant with many countries still operating it well into the 1990s. Production outlasted the single seaters by several years and was undertaken in China, Poland and Czechoslovakia

The first MiG-15UTI was flown in June 1949, this variant going on to account for more than half of the overall MiG-15 production total.

A warbird MiG-15UTI, this shot clearly showing the canopy arrangement in which the forward section hinged sideways and the rear part slid aft. (Alan Scoot)

as well the Soviet Union. In addition, many single seaters were subsequently converted to trainers.

The MiG-15UTI differed from the standard aircraft in having its forward fuselage stretched by 3ft 3in (1m), providing accommodation for two seats in tandem with the two crew sitting under a new two piece canopy, the forward portion of which

was hinged to starboard. The rear section slid backwards to open. Both pilots had ejection seats and the two cockpits were duplicated except that the rear (instructor's) position lacked a gunsight.

The need to accommodate an extra seat necessitated a redesign of the fuel system, internal capacity reducing to 243imp gal (1,106 l) housed

in a smaller main fuselage tank, a rear fuselage tank and a new, small tank mounted under the front cockpit. Two 55imp gal (250 l) or 66imp gal (300 l) underwing tanks could be carried.

The MiG-15UTI's armament was substantially reduced from the fighter, usually comprising a single NR-23 23mm cannon (with 80 rounds) or one 12.7mm UBK-E machine gun

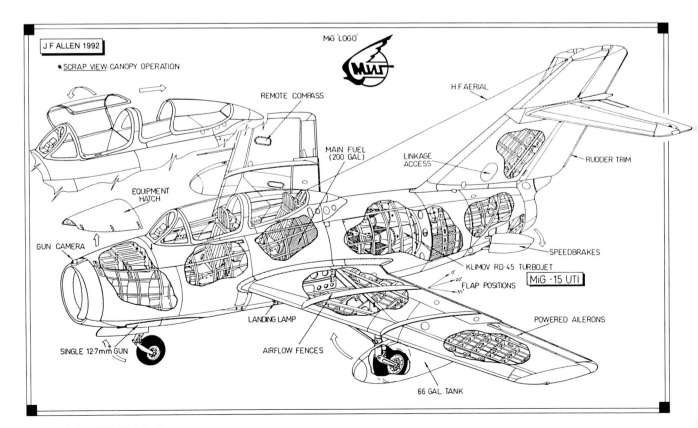

(150 rounds) mounted in the lower port side nose. Some later UTIs had an improved 12.7mm machine gun and the first prototype was the only example to be fitted with both a single cannon and machine gun.

The UTI was otherwise similar to the initial MiG-15 *Fagot A*, including use of the 5,000lb thrust RD-45F engine. Its longevity has largely been a function of necessity as no trainer versions of the following MiG-17 and MiG-19 were produced. This has resulted in the UTI having to serve as the conversion trainer for these aircraft as well over a career which by the mid 1990s was well into its fifth decade. The UTI remained even in Soviet service as a conversion trainer until the 1970s when the MiG-21U *Mongol* finally replaced it.

Midget Variants

The basic MiG-15UTI remained much the same throughout its production life, which in the Soviet Union continued for a few years after the single seat models had been replaced by the MiG-17. The aircraft was subject to numerous avionics and equipment upgrades, however, mainly due to its longevity of service and the changing demands placed on it as it was used to convert pilots onto newer generation fighters.

There were some experimental and trials UTIs flown under the general designation MiG-15UTI-LL (flying laboratory), these aircraft used for ejection seat trials, mainly designed to minimise the risk of injury to pilots when they 'punched out'. Various capsules were tested but the bulk of the work concentrated on developing seats which were stable when used, earlier seats tending to tumble as they left the aircraft

The MiG-15UTI ST-7 and ST-8 were developed to provide pilots with training on the *Izumrud* airborne interception radar which would equip all weather fighter variants of the MiG-17 and other aircraft. Externally, the aircraft modified to incorporate the radar had similar nose arrangements as the MiG-15bis SP-5 single seater described above.

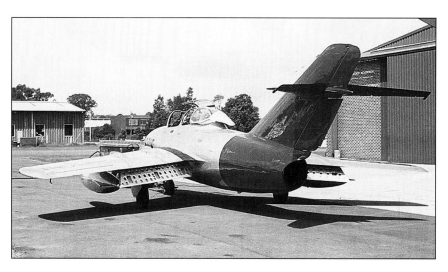
MiG-1515UTI from the rear, showing the perforated flaps, a weight saving device also used on the MiG-15bis.

A MiG-15UTI on display at the Soviet Air Force Museum, Monino. (MAP)

Ejection seat tests from a MiG-15UTI-LL, in this case using a dummy rather than real human being.

MiG-15UTI (Midget)
Powerplant: One 5,000lb (22.26kN) thrust Klimov RD-45F (Rolls-Royce Nene) centrifugal flow turbojet; internal fuel capacity 243imp gal (1,106 l); provision for two 55imp gal (250 l) or 66imp gal (300 l) underwing tanks.
Dimensions: Wing span 33ft 3in (10.13m); length 36ft 7in (11.15m); height 11ft 1.7in (3.39m); wing area 221.8sq ft (20.6m²).
Weights: Empty 8,200lb (3,720kg); max loaded 11,938lb (5,415kg).
Armament: Either one 23mm NR-23 cannon (with 80 rounds) or one 12.4mm UBK-E machine gun (150 rounds) or one 12.7mm A-12.7 machine gun.
Performance: Max speed 549kt (1,015km/h) at sea level, 547kt (1,010km/h) at 9,600ft; time to 16,400ft (5,000m) 2.6min, time to 32,800ft (10,000m) 6.8min; service ceiling 48,640ft (14,825m); range (internal fuel) 513nm (949km), max range (external fuel) 770nm (1,425km); max endurance 2hr 31min.

Radar equipped MiG-15UTI ST-7, developed to provide training on the Izumrud airborne interception radar.

Czechoslovakia built the basic MiG-15 under licence as the S-102 and the MiG-15bis as the S-103. Total Czech single seater production amounted to 1,473 aircraft.

The unique Czechoslovakian UTI-MiG-15P with Izumrud-5 radar in a redesigned nose. (Peter R March)

A Czech S-103 (foreground) and Polish Lim-2 (both locally built MiG-15bis) during a Warsaw Pact exercise.

FOREIGN PRODUCTION

Czechoslovakia

It was decided to manufacture the MiG-15 under licence in Czechoslovakia in 1950, the first aircraft coming from the Letova factory in Prague the following year. The first few aircraft were assembled from mainly Soviet components and in Czech service the aircraft was known as the S-102, the 'S' standing for *Stihac* (fighter).

Production of the S-102 amounted to 853 aircraft until the S-103 (MiG-15bis) came on line in 1954, adding a further 620 to the tally. Production was switched to the Aero Vodochody plant in Prague during 1953.

The two seat MiG-15UTI replaced the S-103 on the Czech production lines in 1956. Called the CS-102 (*Cvicini Stihac* – training fighter), no fewer than 2,012 were built bringing the Czech MiG-15 total to 3,485, the largest number outside the Soviet Union.

The MiG-15's RD-45 and VK-1 powerplants were also manufactured in Czechoslovakia, Motorlet building some 5,000 of these engines under the designations M-05 and M-06, respectively.

Czech built MiG-15s were widely exported, overseas customers including Egypt and Syria (MiG-15bis/S-103) and most Soviet *Bloc* countries plus Iraq and Indonesia (UTI/CS-102). Many were also used by the Soviet air forces.

Several Czech subvariants were produced, the most important of which was the MiG-15SB fighter-bomber, many of which were converted from the standard MiG-15/S-103 from 1958. The conversion involved fitting six pylons instead of the normal two, creating considerably greater offensive armament options. RATO gear could also be fitted, as could a braking parachute.

A similar conversion (but without RATO and braking parachute) to the more capable MiG-15bis/S-103 became available from 1968, with one aircraft further modified at the request of North Vietnam to carry two K-13 Atoll air-to-air-missiles (a copy of the American AIM-9B Sidewinder) under the wings. The 37mm cannon was replaced by an infrared target detection system but trials of the installation proved disappointing and the idea was abandoned.

Other Czech conversions resulted in the MiG-15T target towing aircraft, and the one-off UTI-MiG-15P of 1959 which was similar to the Soviet UTI SP-7 and 8 radar trainers but with later *Izumrud-5* equipment installed.

The MiG-15UTI was built in China as the JJ-2, and export versions were designated FT-2. (MAP)

China

Communist China decided in 1950 that it should establish an industry building modern jet aircraft and naturally turned to the Soviet Union for assistance. An agreement was reached in October 1951 which would eventually see MiGs built at China's Shenyang industrial complex and no fewer than 847 Soviet advisors and experts were despatched to help the Chinese prepare the MiG-15bis and its VK-1A engine for local production in what now would be termed a 'technology transfer' arrangement.

The project progressed slowly and by the time the Chinese were ready to start manufacturing aircraft in 1956 it was realised it would be better to skip the by now obsolete MiG-15 completely and go straight into producing the MiG-17. The first Chinese built MiG-17F (called the J-5) was flown in August 1956.

Although complete MiG-15 fighters were not officially built in China, spare parts and assemblies were manufactured to support the large numbers in Chinese service, known as the J-2. It is known that some complete aircraft were built up from Soviet and local parts. Complete MiG-15UTIs were built, however (as the JJ-2) and many were exported to Albania, Bangladesh, North Korea, North Vietnam, Pakistan and elsewhere as the FT-2.

A large repair and refurbishment programme was established at Shenyang for China's J-2s, more than 500 passing through this organisation between 1951 and 1953 alone mainly as a result of Korean War action. Second hand Chinese MiG-15bis/J-2s were subsequently refurbished and exported to several other nations as the F-2.

Poland built the MiG-15 under licence as the Lim-1 and Lim-2, the latter equivalent to the MiG-15bis.

Polish Lim-2s on patrol.

Poland did not build new MiG-15UTIs but converted some single seaters to trainers as the SBLim-1 and -2. (Bill Lines)

Hungary

Following deliveries of the first Soviet built MiG-15s (as the Jaguar) to Hungary in 1953, it was decided to build the aircraft in that country. Preliminary production was well underway and the first aircraft close to completion when the October 1956 uprising brought an end to the project before any Hungarian built MiG-15s had been flown.

Poland

Preparations for production of the MiG-15 in Poland began in 1951, a total of 727 aircraft emerging from the WSK plant at Mielec between 1951 and 1956. The first six aircraft were assembled from Soviet built components, the first aircraft flying in July 1952. Full Polish production followed these early aircraft, the first locally built aircraft flying in January 1953.

The first 227 aircraft were built to the basic MiG-15 standard and were called Lim-1 (*Licencyjny Mys'liwiek* – licence fighter). These were succeeded on the production line in September 1954 by the Lim-2, equivalent to the MiG-15bis. Deliveries of Soviet built Lim-2s had begun the previous year. A total of 500 Lim-2s was manufactured, the last of them handed over in November 1956.

A subvariant was created when many Lim-1s were brought up to Lim-2 equipment and avionics standards but retaining the original lower powered RD-45 engine and the small airbrakes. These aircraft were dubbed the Lim-1.5 (one-and-a-half). Other Polish subvariants created by conversion included the Lim-2R reconnaissance version.

The aircraft's engines were also built under licence in Poland, the RD-45F becoming known as the Lis-1 and the VK-1A as the Lis-2.

Although Poland did not manufacture new MiG-15UTI two seaters (these were imported from the Soviet Union and Czechoslovakia), many Lim-1s were converted to UTI configuration by the Polish Aviation Repair Factory as the SBLim-1 (*Szkolno Bojowy* – combat training). A shortage of RD-45 (Lis-1) engines in the 1970s resulted in a training variant unique to Poland – the SBLim-2 – which featured the more powerful engine of the MiG-15bis/Lim-2 married to the UTI airframe.

Most Polish converted trainers featured a single 23mm cannon gun, but two other conversion marks resulted in the SBLim-1A and -2A variants for reconnaissance and artillery spotting duties armed with two 23mm cannon and cameras. These variants first appeared in 1968 but some of the SBLim-2As were subsequently reconverted to trainers and given the designation SBLim-2M.

THE MiG-17

Although outside the main scope of this volume, the MiG-15's successor – the MiG-17 – requires a brief description because it was a close relative of the earlier aircraft incorporating new features intended to correct some of the problems encountered with the MiG-15 and provide improved performance and capability. The new fighter was dubbed *Fresco* by NATO.

Studies into what eventually became the MiG-17 began in early 1949 under the Soviet military designation I-330 and Project SI by the MiG design bureau. The main objective was to cure the MiG-15's handling prob-

The SI-2, first flying prototype for the MiG-17.

MiG-17F Fresco C of North Vietnamese ace Colonel Toon, responsible for shooting down 13 American aircraft in the Vietnam War.

lems, particularly at high Mach numbers where directional control remained a serious problem, limiting the aircraft to a speed of Mach 0.92 as a result. Other matters which required attention included the MiG-15's behaviour in tight turns and its rate of roll.

The major advance in the MiG-17 was the incorporation of a completely new wing of longer span, thinner thickness/chord ratio (the wing was the same thickness as its predecessor's but the chord was wider) and greater sweep – 45 degrees inboard and 42 degrees outboard – compared with the MiG-15's constant 35 degrees sweep. The wing's anhedral was increased from -2 to -3 degrees and the trailing edge was revised with a new wider inboard section. A third chord-wise fence was added to each wing, outboard of the two original units.

The tail surfaces were also redesigned, despite looking similar to the MiG-15's. The fin was taller, the rudder longer with reduced chord and the horizontal surfaces were fixed and of greater span and sweep than the earlier aircraft's. Armament was initially the same as the MiG-15bis – one 37mm N-37 and two 23mm NR-23 cannon – while the first production model retained the MiG-15bis's 5,950lb (26.6kN) thrust Klimov VK-1A centrifugal flow turbojet based on the Rolls-Royce Nene. The rear fuselage was lengthened by 35.4in (90cm) and internal fuel capacity increased.

The first two Project SI prototypes were conversions of MiG-15 airframes, the first (SI-1) initially being used as a static test airframe (for wind tunnel work and so on), leaving SI-2 as the first aircraft to fly. This milestone was achieved on 1 Febru-

ary 1950 with Ivan Ivashchenko at the controls. Within a few weeks it was claimed that Ivashchenko had reached Mach 1.03 in a dive but the programme suffered a setback the following month when SI-1 failed to recover from a high speed dive and hit the ground at high speed, killing Ivashchenko.

No technical reason was found for this accident but other problems came to the fore as testing of new prototypes continued. The most serious of these were aileron flutter and a phenomenon known as 'aeroleastic divergence' in which a lack of wing rigidity causes the ailerons to make the aircraft roll in the opposite direction to the control input. Fixing these problems resulted in a substantial redesign of the wing, but trials were successfully completed by June 1951 and the aircraft was ordered into production as the MiG-17 two months later.

MiG-17s For The World

The MiG-17 was manufactured in four major versions (described below) and numerous subvariants in the Soviet Union, China and Poland, production amounting to at least 8,000 examples from all sources. Soviet production ended in 1958.

The MiG-17 has flown in the colours of no fewer than 38 nations and even in the mid 1990s remains in widespread service. It has been involved in numerous conflicts around the world since the 1950s including Vietnam, Pakistan versus India (twice), Biafra, the various Arab versus Israel wars, Uganda versus Tanzania, Mozambique, Afghanistan and many other local conflicts.

The Vietnam war provided several North Vietnamese 'aces' in MiG-17s, including the legendary Colonel Toon, who shot down 13 American aircraft before being killed in an engagement against a US Navy F-4J Phantom

Early production MiG-17 Fresco As.

J ALLEN 1995

PROTOTYPE

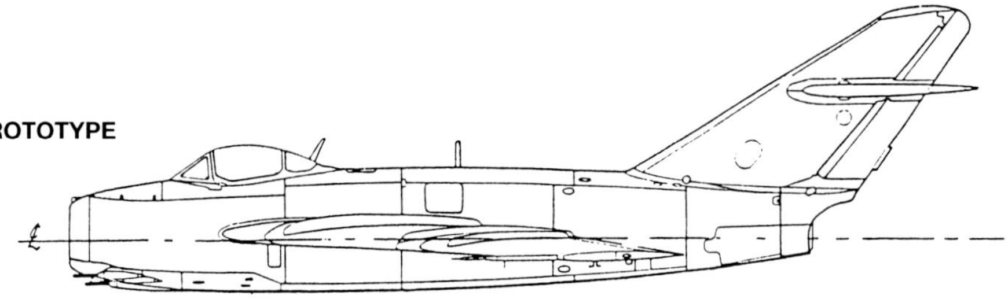

MiG-17

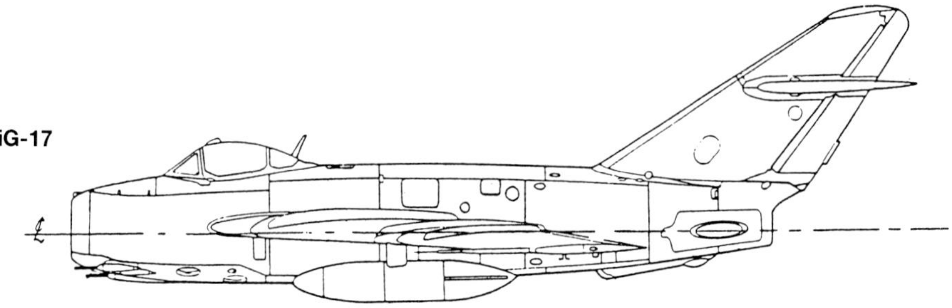

MiG-17F

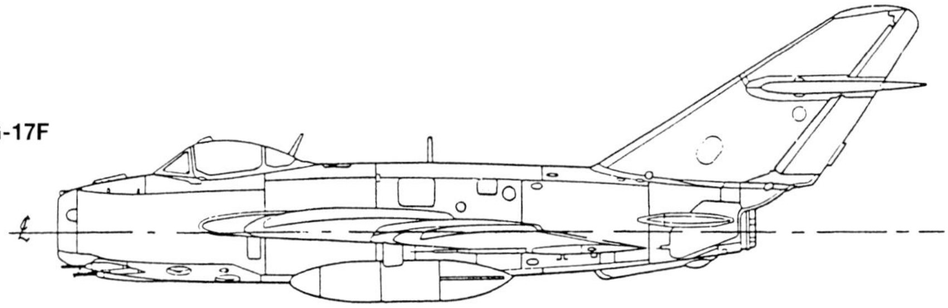

MiG-17PF

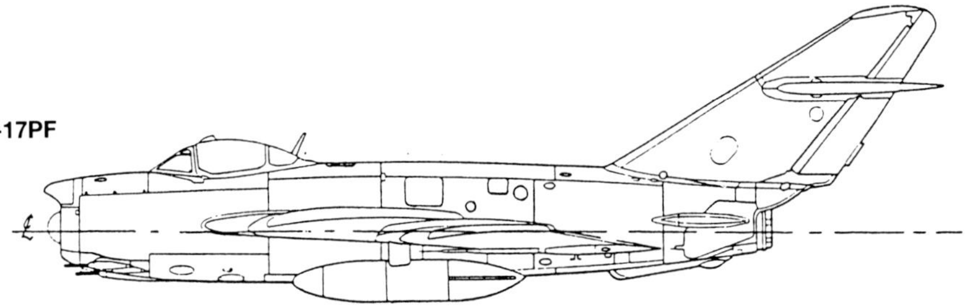

MiG-17PFU

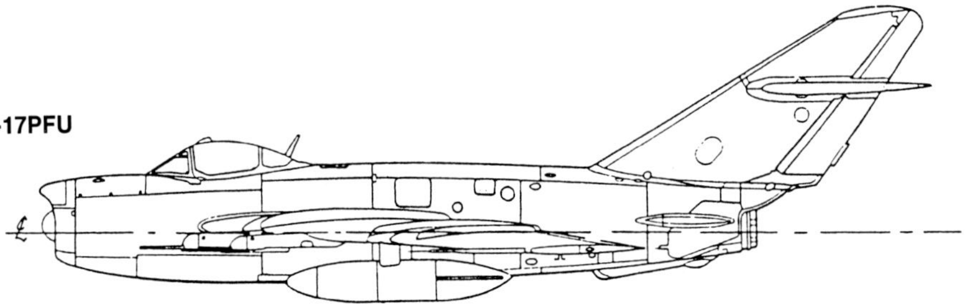

MiG-17

A MiG-17F Fresco C with afterburning engine, the main production version of the aircraft.

flown another ace, Lt Randy Cunningham. It could be said that North Vietnam's often successful use of the technically obsolete but nimble and gun equipped MiG-17 had some influence on future US policy, as the great power quickly realised that ever larger supersonic fighters armed only with less flexible missiles were not necessarily ideal in typical air-to-air combat where the fight got progressively lower and slower. Soon, Phantoms would have a gun and American manufacturers would be developing lighter fighters with an emphasis on dogfight ability like the F-16.

No two seat trainer version of the MiG-17 was designed and produced in the Soviet Union, with the result that the MiG-15UTI had to serve as the conversion trainer for it and the later MiG-19. The only two seat 'MiG-17' was developed by China and this was very much a MiG-15/17 hybrid. Called the JJ-5, it combined the cockpit/forward fuselage and powerplant/rear fuselage of the MiG-15UTI with the wings and tail surfaces of the MiG-17. China built over 1,000 JJ-5s, including export FT-5s.

MiG-17 Major Variants:

The following briefly describes the characteristics of the four major production versions of the MiG-17 Fresco. Although some of the aircraft's subvariants are mentioned, the one-offs and minor versions are not as the intention is to describe the broad picture only.

MiG-17 *(Fresco A)*: The initial production version of the MiG-17 had the major physical characteristics described above but with some detail changes including the addition of a small ventral fin, revised canopy framing, a small trim tab on the rudder and enlarged and repositioned airbrakes on the rear fuselage.

A single hardpoint under each wing was capable of carrying a drop tank, bomb of various sizes up to 550lb (250kg), unguided rockets or rocket pods. Regarded as an interim model, the *Fresco A* was relegated to training duties with the arrival of later variants. Production ended in early 1953.

MiG-17F *(Fresco C)*: The main production version of the aircraft from late 1952, the MiG-17F featured an afterburning development of the basic VK-1 engine designated the VK-1F *(Forsirovanyy* – boosted). It was otherwise similar to the original *Fresco A* apart from the physical changes associated with the afterburner tail pipe. The airbrakes were also redesigned and the pilot received a much improved ejection seat.

Rated at 7,450lb (33.4kN) thrust with afterburner, the VK-1F gave the MiG-17F superior performance compared with its predecessor, notably in the areas of rate of climb and airfield performance. The disadvantages included increased fuel consumption (necessitating the carriage of external tanks most of the time) and strict limitations on the use of the afterburner in early aircraft due to the engine tending to burst into flames. The MiG-17F was afforded priority production status and forced the single seat versions of the MiG-15 out of production. Manufacture continued until the end of the Soviet MiG-17 line in 1958.

The MiG-17F was also built in Poland at the WSK-Mielec factory as the Lim-5 and in China as the Shenyang J-5, 767 aircraft coming from this production line between 1956 and 1959. Poland contributed about 1,000 MiG-17s to the overall tally including the locally improved Lim-6 variants.

The MiG-17F was built in Poland as the Lim-5. (MAP)

An Egyptian MiG-17F in action during one of the Middle East wars against Israel.

MiG-17PFU *(Fresco E)*: Although built only in relatively small numbers, the MiG-17PFU was an important aircraft because it was the Soviet Union's (and Europe's) first fighter armed solely with air-to-air missiles, in its case four AA-1 *Alkari* beam riding weapons. The guns were deleted.

The MiG-17PFU entered production in 1954 and featured the same powerplant as the MiG-17PF but had *Izumrud-2* radar and a semi active radar guidance system. The missiles were mounted on underwing rails and the existing hardpoints was retained for the carriage of drop tanks.

MiG-17PF *(Fresco D)*: An all weather fighter development of the MiG-17F fitted *Izumrud-1* radar in the nose and the fixed armament of three 23mm cannon, the 37mm gun being deleted. The MiG-17PF was developed via the earlier MiG-17P with non-afterburning VK-1A engine. Only a few -17Ps were built (it had mediocre performance) but the PF became the Soviet Union's first fully operational all weather fighter.

Production was undertaken in Poland as the Lim-5P (the last example was delivered in 1960) while China's J-5A equivalent incorporated some redesign. Production deliveries began in 1956.

MiG-17F (Fresco C)
Powerplant: *One 5,950lb (26.6kN) dry and 7,450lb (33.4kN) afterburning thrust Klimov VK-1F centrifugal flow turbojet; internal fuel capacity 312imp gal (1,415 l); normally two 88imp gal (400 l) underwing drop tanks.*
Dimensions: *Wing span 30ft 10in (9.40m); length 36ft 5in (11.10m); height 12ft 3in (3.73m); wing area 243.2sq ft (22.6m^2).*
Weights: *Empty 8,664lb (3,930kg); loaded (clean) 11,800lb (5,352kg); maximum 13,858lb (6,286kg).*
Armament: *One 37mm N-37 cannon (with 40 rounds) and two 23mm NR-23 cannon (80 rounds each); provision on two underwing hardpoints for bombs, rockets and rocket pods.*
Performance: *Max speed 618kt (1,144km/h) at 9,800ft, 611kt (1,130km/h) at 16,400ft; max climb 12,795ft (3,900m)/min; time to 16,400ft (5,000m) 2.5min with afterburner, 4.0min dry; service ceiling (dry) 49,540ft (15,100m), service ceiling (afterburner) 54,460ft (16,600m); range (internal fuel) 367nm (679km), range with drop tanks 557nm (1,030km); max ferry range 903nm (1,670km).*

(left and bottom) Two preserved East German MiG-17PF Fresco Ds with Izumrud radar in the nose. (MAP)

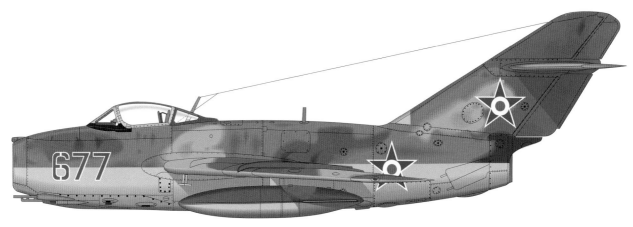

MiG-15bis '677' of Hungarian Air Force in late service.

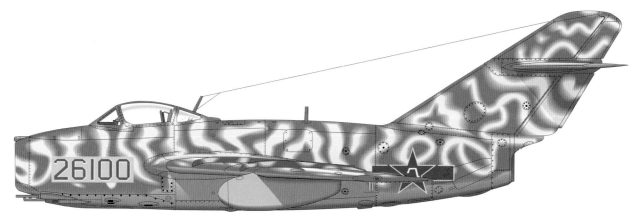

MiG-15bis '26100' of Chinese People's Liberation Army Air Force, Korean War period.

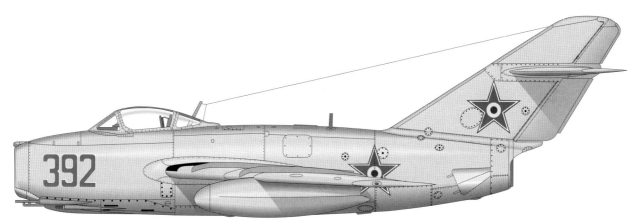

MiG-15 '392' of Romanian Air Force early 1960s.

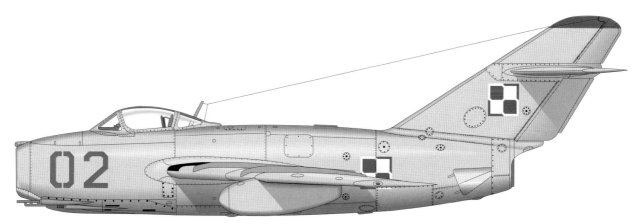

MiG-15 '02' of 1 PLM Warzsawa Polish Air Force.

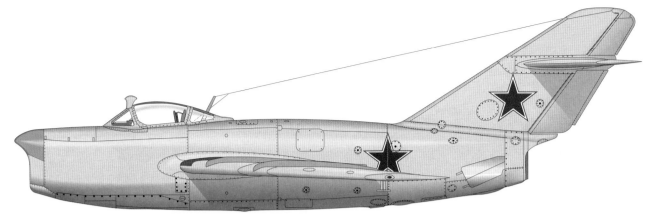

MiG-15bis SP-5 all weather fighter prototype 1950.

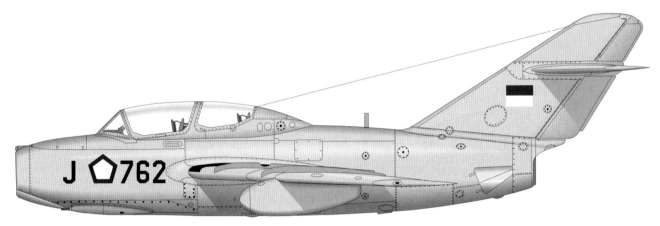

MiG-15UTI J-762 of Indonesian Air Force 1960s.

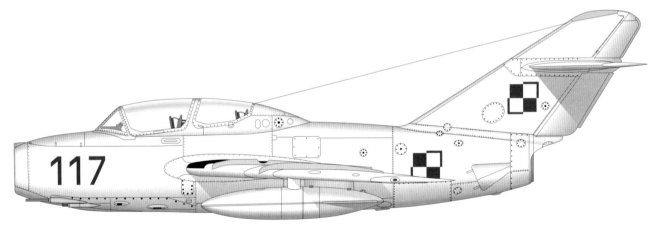

SBLim-2 '117' of 45 Ground Attack Training Regiment, Polish Air Force 1990.

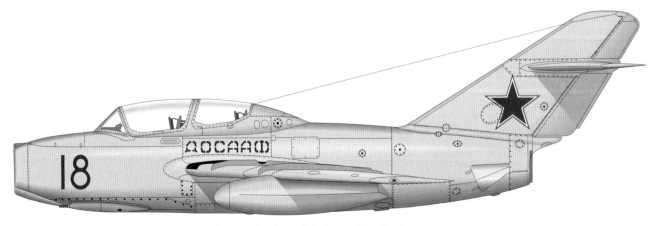

MiG-15UTI '18' of Soviet Volunteer Society to Support the Army, Aviation and the Fleet.

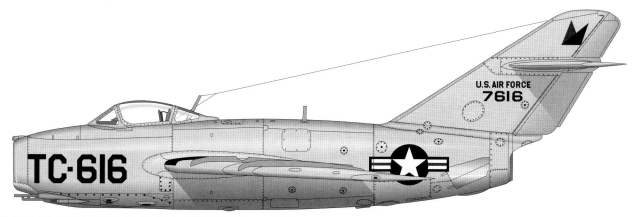

MiG-15bis TC-7616 USAF during testing at Wright-Patterson AFB.
Ex North Korean aircraft delivered by defecting pilot September 1953.

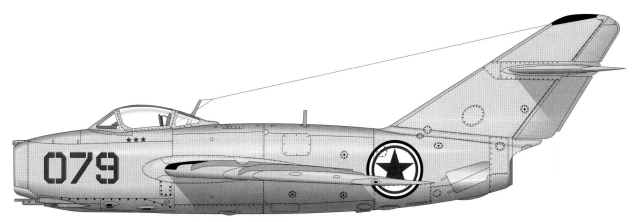

MiG-15bis '079' of North Korean People's Air Force, Korean War.

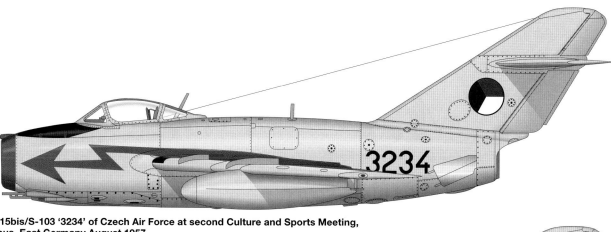

MiG-15bis/S-103 '3234' of Czech Air Force at second Culture and Sports Meeting,
Cottbus, East Germany August 1957.

Former People's Republic of China Navy J-2 (MiG-15bis) restored in USA 1988 as
'15' of Soviet Volunteer Group in Korean War. US civil registration N15PE.

DDR
Luftstreitkräfte

Rostock
Hannover
Berlin
Magdeburg
Bonn
Dessau
Leipzig
Dresden
Frankfurt

МиГ-15
УТИ

1   0   5   M

0   5   10   15   FT

118

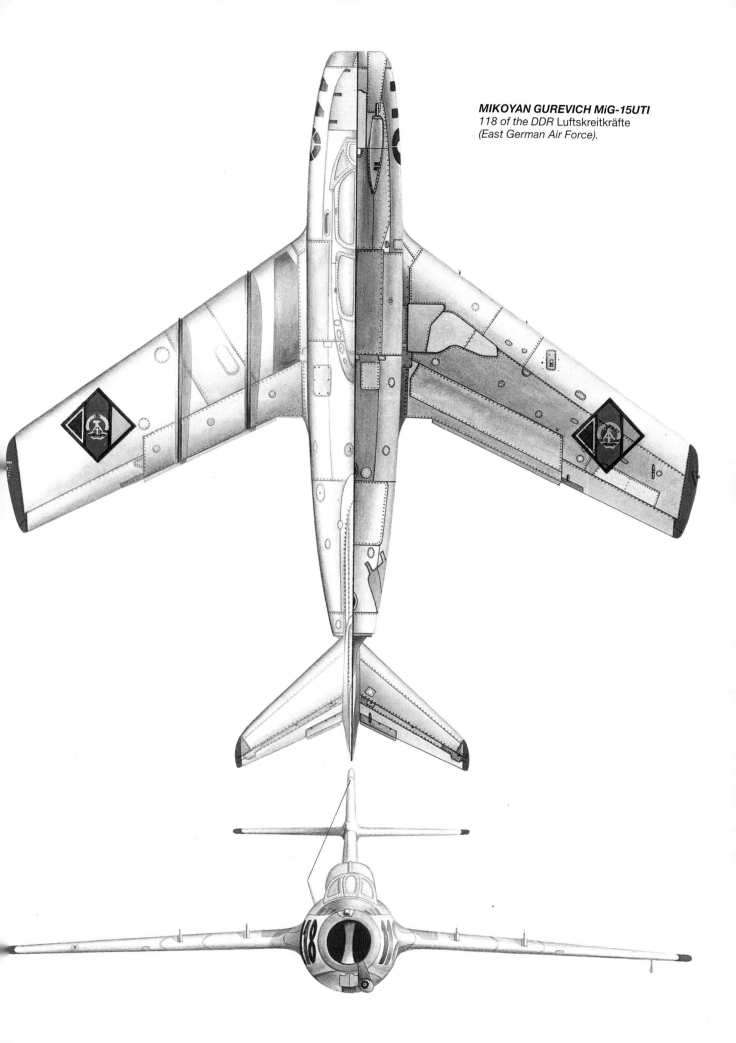

MIKOYAN GUREVICH MiG-15UTI
118 of the DDR Luftskreitkräfte
(East German Air Force).

MiG-15 Around the World

Some 40 nations have operated the MiG-15 and/or its licence built derivatives since it entered Soviet service in 1949. A brief summary of these countries' use of the aircraft follows, starting with a description of the Soviet military organisation as it stood in the late 1950s when use of the MiG-15 was at its peak.

Soviet Union

The Soviet Union's *Voenno-Vozdushnye Sily* (VVS – Military Aviation Forces) represented what was numerically the largest air arm in the world in the late 1950s and early 1960s. It was divided into four main components: *Istrebitelnya Aviastiia Protivovozdushnoi Oborony* (IA-PVO – Fighter Air Armies of the Defence Forces); *Dalnaya Aviatsiya* (DA – long range aviation); *Frontovai* (FA – Frontal Aviation); and *Aviatsiya-Voenno Morskikh Flota* (A-VMF – Naval Air Fleet).

The MiG-15 was mainly operated by the IA-PVO, whose activities embraced every component of the air defence system including anti aircraft artillery, surface-to-air missiles, early warning systems and interceptor fighters. The IA-PVO's Moscow headquarters assigned its forces according to the importance attached to a particular specified Defence District. In the late 1950s these districts included Moscow, Stalingrad, Baku, Kiev, Gorki, Leningrad, Kharkov and Khabarovsk.

The MiG-15 entered service with the Soviet Air Force in 1949.

The IA-PVO's forces were divided into Air Divisions, each of which had a statutory strength of three Air Regiments comprising a force of 37 aircraft. These were in turn divided between three squadrons. The IA-PVO accounted for about 20 per cent of the VVS's operational aircraft strength in 1960.

Long Range Aviation (DA) provided the strategic bombing forces comprising medium and long range bombers plus aerial refuelling tankers and transport aircraft. Frontal Aviation (FA) was numerically the largest of the Soviet air forces with some 60 per cent of the Soviet Union's operational aircraft in 1960. The FA's role was tactical support of the armies and protection of the country's frontiers. It had its own force of interceptors which were responsible for

defending the entire zone which surrounds the Soviet Union and the controlled corridors which provided the only air lanes of entry.

The Naval Air Fleet (A-VMF) was a shore based force for the direct support of the Soviet Navy, bearing in mind there were no Soviet aircraft carriers at the time of the MiG-15 and for a considerable time afterwards. The A-VMF was generally equipped with the same aircraft types as the other air arms and aircraft were distributed between the five Soviet fleets.

The Cold War period saw great tension between the Soviet Union and the West. Reconnaissance flights by mainly American but also British aircraft often operated behind the Iron Curtain and over countries sympathetic to the Soviet cause in Europe

A preserved Soviet Air Force MiG-15. Most served with the IA-PVO – Fighter Air Armies of the Defence Forces. (MAP)

and Asia. Numerous interceptions of these aircraft were made by Soviet fighters, some of them resulting in combat. Between 1946 and 1977 at least 40 American aircraft were shot down during the course of these activities, the MiG-15 being responsible for some of the early ones.

Known victims of the MiG-15 during this period include a USAF Boeing RB-50 reconnaissance bomber over the Sea of Japan in July 1953, an RB-29 Superfortress also over the Sea of Japan in November 1954 and a US Navy P2V Neptune which was forced down after a MiG-15 attack over the Bering Straits in June 1955. There were many cases of aircraft being 'buzzed' by MiG-15s and several where gunfire was exchanged. In one of these a USAF F-86 Sabre shot down a MiG-15 over the Sea of Japan in February 1955 while another MiG was lost a year earlier when an escorted reconnaissance aircraft was intercepted.

MiG-15UTI in Soviet service. (MAP)

Afghanistan

A military air agreement between Afghanistan and the Soviet Union was signed in 1955, resulting in Russian equipment being operated since then. Three MiG-UTIs were among the aircraft provided at the beginning of the programme and more were subsequently delivered. Afghanistan's recent political turmoil and its war with the Soviet Union has left the situation unclear, but in 1994 it was thought that at least 10 UTIs remained in service.

Albania

Two squadrons of MiG-15s supplied by the Soviet Union became operational in 1950 and these remained Albania's sole combat aircraft for more than a decade. They were supplemented by MiG-15UTIs later in the 1950s.

When Albanian relations with Russia declined in the 1960s, China stepped in to provide military equipment including sufficient F-2s (MiG-15s) to equip two squadrons. FT-2s (MiG-15UTIs) were also provided and at least six of each of these Chinese built types remained in service in 1994.

Algeria

Algeria gained independence from France in 1962 and for many years after that was armed by the Soviet Union. MiG-15bis fighters and MiG-15UTI trainers began arriving in 1963 (some via Egypt) to form three squadrons. Two squadrons equipped with 20 MiG-15s were still operational well into the 1980s, but by 1994 the fighters had gone although more than 30 MiG-15UTIs remained in service.

Angola

Angola was a late starter in the acquisition of MiG-15s, this happening only in 1976 after gaining independence from Portugal. After a struggle in which the Marxists gained control, Soviet aircraft began equipping the Angolan Air Force, among them an initial quantity of three MiG-15UTIs for training duties.

The number in service had grown to nine by 1994, by which time some transport and training aircraft plus helicopters had been acquired from the West.

Bulgaria

A member of the Warsaw Pact for many years, Bulgaria received its first MiG-15s in the early 1950s to form two air regiments in which they were used as fighter-bombers.

This was reduced to single regiment in 1957, the other re-equipping with MiG-17s in the interceptor role. MiG-15UTIs followed, these outlasting the single seaters in service by some years.

Bulgaria was thought to still have about 30 MiG-15UTIs in service in 1988 but the last of them was retired in the early 1990s.

Bulgarian MiG-15UTI. (MAP)

A Chinese MiG-15bis/J-2 on display. (MAP)

Cambodia

The confused state of Cambodia's politics over the past three decades has left the country's air force in a general state of disarray, virtually ceasing to exist in 1979 after the Vietnamese invasion. It is known that some MiG-15bis and MiG-15UTIs (Chinese F-2s and FT-2s) were delivered at one stage, but nothing is known of their fate.

China

Plans to build the MiG-15bis in China were changed to the MiG-17 as the 'technology transfer' from the Soviet Union which started in 1950 took some years to complete. China did receive Russian built MiG-15s (as the J-2) and built its own MiG-15UTIs as the JJ-2. When exported, these aircraft were redesignated F-2 and FT-2, respectively.

By 1960 China still had about 200 J-2s operating with front line units in the fighter-bomber role along with large numbers of JJ-2s. Their numbers gradually declined during the 1970s and 1980s, but even in 1994 authoritative listings of air force strengths were still noting more than 100 J-2s and JJ-2s in Chinese service with the single seaters performing ground attack training duties.

China's main combat use of the MiG-15 in combat was in the Korean War, which is discussed in the following chapter.

Congo

The former Belgian Congo achieved independence in 1961 and immediately forged links with the Soviet Union and China, the supply of military aircraft coming with this including MiG-17s and MiG-15UTIs. A single UTI was still in service in 1994.

Cuba

The revolution of 1958 and the accompanying rise to power of Fidel Castro witnessed Cuba becoming a Soviet puppet, although the collapse of the Soviet Union in 1991 and the lack of continued financial and military support which followed has brought hardship to Cuba.

The Soviet influence brought with it military aid, including an initial batch of 12 MiG-15UTIs in 1960. MiG-15bis fighters followed. MiG-17s subsequently took over the interceptor role and by the mid 1970s the *Fuerza Aerea Revolucionaria* had 15 MiG-15s and about 20 UTIs for training. Even by 1994 that number had reduced only slightly to 10 and 15, respectively.

Czechoslovakia

The *Ceskoslovenske Letectvo* received MiG-15s initially from the Soviet Union in 1950 followed by local production of the basic MiG-15 (as the S-102), MiG-15bis (S-103) and MiG-15UTI (CS-102) by Aero Vodochody in Prague. The Czechs contributed 3,485 of the total MiG-15 production tally, the largest number built outside the Soviet Union, and developed several local subvariants. By 1960 the Czech Air Force's MiG-15s had been allocated to ground attack duties, the type equipping three Ground Attack Regiments.

Czech MiG-15s were responsible for the shooting down of a USAF Republic F-84G Thunderjet in March 1953. Two F-84s operating from Germany had penetrated Czech airspace and were intercepted by MiG-15s with one of the American fighters shot down in the ensuing battle. Other intercepts were made in the following years (some resulting in the forcing down of the encroaching aircraft) while Czech MiG-15s were also responsible for the downing of many US Central Intelligence Agency balloons which carried cameras and

Cuba still operates the MiG-15UTI in the mid 1990s. (MAP)

A Czech S-103 photographed from the cockpit of an accompanying aircraft.

propaganda material. The balloons were launched in Germany and were carried eastwards by the prevailing winds. Some 150,000 of these balloons were launched between 1954 and 1965 at the height of the Cold War.

Egypt

Although Egypt broke its ties with the Soviet Union in 1976 and became more inclined towards the West, before that it had been firmly entrenched in the Soviet family, its military equipment reflecting that fact. As such the MiG-15 was an important part of its air force in the 1950s and 1960s, participating in several of the Middle East wars of the period.

The first Egyptian MiG-15s arrived from Czechoslovakia in 1955, just in time to see action in the Suez Crisis the following year. The crisis was precipitated by Egypt's nationalisation of the Suez Canal, thus threatening to deny use of this vital link to other nations. Britain and France prepared to partially invade Egypt and occupy the canal zone, with the help of the Israelis. Egypt had three MiG-15 squadrons at the time and although most were destroyed on the ground, some did participate in successful ground attack sorties. There were several instances of combat between Egyptian MiGs and Israeli Mystere IVAs, the MiGs coming off second best.

By the time of the Six Day War against Israel in 1967, Egypt still had a couple of operational MiG-15 squadrons as did Syria, but again most were destroyed on the ground in Israeli pre-emptive strikes and their combat use was very limited.

The War of Attrition against Israel in 1970 saw the Egyptian Air Force by now equipped with large numbers of supersonic MiG-21s, although a combined force of about 150

MiG-15s and -17s was still in service for air defence and ground attack duties. Once again, losses were heavy.

Egypt had replaced its MiG-15s by the 1973 Yom Kippur war but had previously used them to fight against the British in Yemen between 1962 and 1967. They were used mainly for ground attack missions, although the MiG-17 bore the brunt of this duty.

The two seat MiG-15UTI remained in Egyptian service long after the single seaters had been retired, the last one not being withdrawn until the late 1980s.

East Germany

A Warsaw Pact member and the only one to place its forces entirely under Soviet command in peacetime, East Germany had a surprisingly

small force of MiG-15bis fighters as they were delivered relatively late and were quickly replaced by MiG-17s. The first MiG-15s were delivered in 1956 and they began to be replaced in the front line role just two years later. The remaining interceptor wing which kept its MiG-15s was re-equipped with MiG-21s in 1961.

As was the case with other air forces, the MiG-15UTI trainer lasted rather longer and about 20 were still in service in the late 1980s. The reunification of the two Germanies in 1990 saw them (and the remaining 30 MiG-17s) finally retired.

Finland

Finland utilised a small fleet of MiG-15UTIs for training in the 1960s and 1970s. By 1977 three were still in service.

Guinea Republic

This small West African republic was established in 1958 and its air force formed the following year with Soviet assistance. A small number MiG-17Fs and MiG-15UTIs were initially supplied and although two of the UTIs were still officially on strength in 1994, their serviceability was an unknown.

Guinea-Bissau

The former colony of Portuguese Guinea turned Marxist on its independence in 1974 and the establishment of an air force four years later came with mainly Soviet assistance. The Soviets provided a handful of MiG-17Fs and MiG-15UTIs, only one of the latter having been listed as in service over the past decade.

An East German pilot prepares for another sortie. The MiG-15 was in front line service with East Germany for a short time before being replaced by the MiG-17.

Two of the small fleet of MiG-15UTIs operated by Finland. (MAP)

Hungary

Warsaw Pact member Hungary received its first MiG-15s from Russia in 1953 under the name Jaguar, but well advanced plans to produce the aircraft locally were thwarted with the 1956 uprising.

Before the uprising, Hungary had three Fighter Regiments each with 70 MiG-15s and a fourth Regiment with 30 aircraft. The Hungarian Air Force was re-established after the abortive act of defiance (in which Hungarian MiG-15s strafed Soviet targets) but re-equipment was slow, aircraft gradually coming from both the Soviet Union and Czechoslovakia. The MiG-15bis remained in service throughout the 1960s and the MiG-15UTI remained on strength in small numbers until the early 1990s.

Hungary's plans to build the MiG-15 under licence were interrupted by the 1956 uprising but many were imported from the Soviet Union. (MAP)

Iraq operated its MiG-15UTIs until the late 1980s.

Indonesia

Until 1965 and the arrival of President Suharto, Indonesia had been very much a friend of the Soviet Union and its military equipment inventory reflected that. Among the equipment provided was a number of MiG-15UTIs for pilot training, complete with Soviet instructors. With the withdrawal of Soviet support in 1965, the MiGs and other aircraft which had been provided were fairly quickly grounded due to a lack of spares.

Iraq

The downfall of the Iraqi monarchy in 1958 saw a switch to Soviet sympathies, with the usual inflow of arms and equipment from that source. Iraq received some MiG-17s, MiG-15s and MiG-15UTIs with more than 20 of the latter still in service in 1988 and retirement following soon afterwards.

Libya

Another Arab state with Soviet leanings and a tendency to promote terrorism since the arrival of Colonel Muamer Khaddafi, Libya's air force grew rapidly in the 1970s as Soviet aid poured in. One or two Western nations – notably France – were also happy to sell the Libyans arms. Some MiG-15UTIs which had been previously delivered soldiered on for a few years into the 1970s.

Madagascar/Malagasy Republic

Madagascar gained independence from France in 1958 and established a small air force three years later, equipped mainly with Soviet aircraft. Much of the training was provided by North Korean personnel. It thought that the list of aircraft received included a small number of MiG-15UTIs.

Mali

Another African state which was once a French colony, Mali followed the example set by many other similar countries by turning to the Soviet Union on achieving independence in 1960. Mali subsequently received a single MiG-15UTI, and although it's not clear whether it's the same aircraft, one example remained in service in 1994.

Mongolia

This Soviet satellite's air force was fundamentally run by the Soviet Union until the latter's disintegration but it continues to be administered among Soviet lines. It once operated both MiG-15s and MiG-15UTIs but the single seaters left service in the late 1970s. Three UTIs were on strength in 1994.

Morocco

Morocco achieved independence from France in 1956 and has since obtained military equipment from that country, the Soviet Union and the USA. The period of Soviet influence saw the acquisition of two MiG-15UTIs in 1961, both of which have long been removed from service.

Mozambique

Another in the long list of former colonies in Africa which turned to the Soviet Union after independence, Mozambique once belonged to Belgium and achieved independence in 1975. MiG-21s, MiG-17s and three MiG-15UTIs duly arrived, although the latter were out of service by 1988.

Nigeria

Nigeria was a British colony until 1960 and after independence gained assistance from West Germany and India, although the Soviet Union stepped in with equipment for the air force in 1967 with the outbreak of civil war and the fighting with Biafra. Included were some MiG-15UTIs. The war lasted until 1970 and the last couple of UTIs remained in service until the early 1980s.

North Korea

The North Korean Air Force suffered great losses in the first few months of the Korean War (discussed in the following chapter) but massive re-equipment by the Soviet Union (which also supplied China) with MiG-15s quickly changed the shape of the war and the shape of aerial combat generally, with jets meeting in battle for the first time.

North Korea had several hundred MiG-15s in service by the end of the war, although the single seaters began to be replaced as front line fighters from 1960, when more than 350 were still on strength. North Korean MiG-15UTIs remain in service even in the mid 1990s, with more than 30 (actually Chinese built FT-2s) still serving in 1994.

North Vietnam

The North Vietnamese Air Force had a single combat squadron of MiG-17s before the outbreak of the Vietnam War against the USA and its

The MiG-15bis delivered to the USAF in Korea by defecting North Korean pilot Lt Kum Suk No. He received $US100,000 for his trouble.

A selection of Polish MiGs (top to bottom): Soviet built MiG-15 Fagot As; a Polish built Lim-2; SBLim trainer conversion; and Lim-2. (MAP)

allies, this situation changing markedly over the next few years as military support from both the Soviet Union and China began pouring in.

Although North Vietnam became a major operator of the MiG-17, its use of the MiG-15 fighter was limited and most aircraft were UTI trainers, the type remaining in service after the unification of North and South Vietnam. About 15 were still flying in Vietnamese colours in 1994.

Pakistan

Pakistan established military and trade ties with China in 1966, resulting in the supply of several Chinese built variants of MiG fighters, among them FT-2 (MiG-15UTI) trainers. Six remained in service in 1994.

Poland

A major contributor to the Warsaw Pact, Poland's aircraft industry built more than 700 MiG-15 single seaters under licence between 1951 and 1956 as the Lim-1 (MiG-15) and Lim-2 (MiG-15bis). Two seat MiG-15UTIs were not built as new aircraft in Poland, but many of the fighters were converted to trainers as the SBLim-1 and SBLim-2. The Polish Air Force also received some Soviet built MiG-15s before local production began.

The Lim-1 and -2 had been relegated mainly to the ground attack role by the end of the 1950s but as was the case with most other countries equipped with the aircraft, the two seat versions carried on for many years, although only a handful remained in service in 1994.

Romania

One of the smaller members of the Warsaw Pact, Romania began receiving MiG-15s and MiG-17s in 1956 to equip three Fighter Regiments of 70 aircraft each. MiG-15UTIs were also acquired. The single seaters were subsequently used as fighter-bombers and then for training. About 40 MiG-15s remained in service through the 1970s, that number reducing to 30 by the late 1980s and to 12 (both single and two seaters) in 1994.

Somalia

This African nation achieved independence in 1960 with the ending of Italian trusteeship and received Soviet equipment for its military forces between 1963 and 1977. Among the aircraft received was a quantity of MiG-15bis and UTIs.

The internal turmoil which characterises Somalia in the 1990s began in 1977 with the outbreak of war with Ethiopia, which immediately received help from Somalia's former ally, the Soviet Union. In a case of strange bedfellows, it was later revealed that Israel also supplied equipment to Ethiopia. The war lasted until 1978 with the Somali forces quickly overwhelmed, although Ethiopia did not carry out its threat to invade. Somali MiG-15s were used for ground attack during the conflict.

Somalia has been in a state of disorganisation ever since, despite links with the USA and other nations. Two MiG-15UTIs were listed as being on strength in 1988, but the internal troubles which have been going on since then following the overthrow of the government have made their status in 1994 unclear.

Sri Lanka (Ceylon)

Ceylon (as it was then) received a single MiG-15UTI from the Soviet Union in the mid 1960s. This remained in service until about 1987.

Sudan

Sudan's air force enjoyed a decade of Soviet aid until 1977, during which time it received a variety of aircraft including a small number of MiG-15UTIs. These were out of service by the mid 1970s.

Syria

Syria formed part of the United Arab Republic (along with Egypt and North Yemen) and therefore was supplied with military equipment by the Soviet Union. The first MiG-15s arrived in 1955, but some were lost on the ground during the Suez Crisis the following year. That unfortunate trend continued in the 1967 Six Day and 1973 Yom Kippur Wars with Israel when MiG-15s and other aircraft were destroyed on their airfields before they could take an active part in the battle.

A photograph which pretty well sums up the state of the Somali Air Force in recent times with junked MiG-21s and a MiG-17 left to rot.

Syria also received MiG-15UTIs, of which at least 25 remained in service in 1994.

Tanzania

Formed by the unification of Tanganyika and Zanzibar in 1964, this African state turned to China for its military equipment from 1970, the aircraft supplied including two FT-2s (MiG-15UTIs). These remained in service in 1994.

Uganda

Uganda obtained two MiG-15UTIs in the early 1970s along with a small force of MiG-17s. Other Soviet aircraft were also supplied (including MiG-21s) but the Israeli raid on Entebbe in 1976, the invasion of Uganda by Tanzania in 1979 and the military coup of 1985 all conspired to destroy most of the aircraft.

USA

Once the existence of the MiG-15 had been revealed over Korea in late 1950, the USA and its allies became

very keen to acquire one or more examples for evaluation. The wreckage of an early production aircraft was recovered from shallow water off the coast of Korea by the Royal Navy in July 1951 and transported to the USA for analysis, and although valuable information was gained, a complete and flyable aircraft was still sought.

There was a missed opportunity in March 1953 when a Polish pilot decided to defect to the West and crash landed his MiG-15bis on the Danish Island of Bornholm. Although some examination of the aircraft took place, the Danes returned it to its owner before any detailed analysis could be performed.

The Americans therefore instigated Operation Moolah which offered the then enormous reward of $US100,000 for any pilot prepared to fly a MiG-15 into the base at Kimpo in South Korea. Leaflet drops over North Korea promoted the scheme and on 21 September 1953 – after hostilities had ended – Lt Kum Suk No duly

Evaluation of the captured MiG-15 in the USA – firing the guns (left) and examining the weapons pack (right) which was lowered from under the fuselage by a winch system.

Two shots of the MiG-15 during flight evaluation trials in the USA from Wright-Patterson AFB. Many leading Western fighter pilots flew the aircraft.

obliged, arriving at Kimpo in North Korean MiG-15bis number 2057.

The aircraft was immediately dismantled and transported to the USA where it was reassembled, examined and flown by many Western pilots from the Wright-Patterson AFB. The MiG-15 was given the US identification number TC-7616 and Kum Suk No his $100,000 and political asylum. Later it was claimed that the North Korean pilot knew nothing about the reward, was going to defect anyway and just happened to land at Kimpo as per the leaflet instructions!

Yemen

North Yemen (once part of the United Arab Republic) and South Yemen (the former British Protectorate of Aden) became Soviet allies many years apart (in the early 1960s and early 1980s, respectively) and received aircraft from that source including some MiG-15UTIs. After some tension between the two countries which included military clashes, they amalgamated in 1990 with the resulting almost exclusively Soviet equipped United Yemen Air Force operating four UTIs.

Flying the MiG-15

Air Vice-Marshal Bill Collings, RAAF (ret) is involved in the flying of one of the ever increasing number of MiG-15 warbirds around the world. Here, he presents his impressions of the Soviet fighter from the pilot's seat.

I became involved in flying the MiG-15 purely by accident. In early 1991, an acquaintance in the defence industry field whom I had known while I was serving in the Royal Australian Air Force (RAAF) acquired one of a batch of six MiG-15UTI aircraft imported from Poland. He and his partner were looking for a pilot to carry out the post reassembly test flights and I offered my services. As I had served in Korea I had always had a yen to see what the contemporary Russian aircraft of that era were like, so I took on the task for my friend.

Apart from the difficulties the authorities might have in granting a permit to fly for such an aircraft, for the pilot the greatest difficulty is to obtain the necessary information to operate the aircraft. Anyone with experience in acquiring a foreign aircraft from a non English speaking country, as I myself had on the RAAF Mirage project, will realise the problems of interpreting documents translated into English by a non native speaker of English. In addition, technical documents reflect the national ethos

of the parent country and one has to learn in what context the information is given. Moreover, for those who are used only to the high standard of modern western manuals, to have to use documentation from forty odd years ago is, to say the least, a revelation.

Some aspects of operation of the aircraft had to be learnt by trial and error. For example, the ADF is the Russian version of an American wartime unit with a changeover lever for the various frequency ranges. In the MiG, there is also an electronic frequency range selector in parallel with the manual selector. However, the documentation does not connect the two and it was some time before we sorted that one out.

It was necessary to read a lot and cross refer to make sure that one had all the relevant information. In the description of the fuel system, there is not one complete statement of the operating sequence of the system. One has to use several references to understand the sequence of use of the fuel from the various tanks.

One thing which did help is that the MiG's engine is a developed version of the Rolls-Royce Nene which was fitted to the RAAF's Vampires of the 'fifties. As this was the first jet aircraft I flew, it was easy to interpret

the engine control system described in the manuals. It was also comforting to know that the aircraft was fitted with such a reliable engine as the Nene.

Having gathered all the necessary operating information and having obtained the necessary authorisations from the Australian Civil Aviation Authority I awaited the time when the aircraft would be ready to fly.

Given the difficulty of converting from the maintenance system of a foreign air force to the Australian civil system, it was not surprising that the preparation of the aircraft took a lot longer than the owners originally forecast. In the event we were ready to fly on 18 July 1991. Needless to say the weather in the morning was poor but it eventually cleared and we were able to make two flights on the big day.

I had planned the first flight without underwing tanks to ensure that the trim of the aircraft was correct before we fitted the tanks. I had planned to use the RAAF restricted area south-west of Avalon with return to Melbourne's Essendon Airport. In the event, I never got to the area because of the low endurance of the aircraft without underwing tanks.

One has to bear in mind that aircraft of that era consumed fuel at a

The Australian registered MiG-15UTI warbird which is the subject of the flight impressions by AVM Bill Collings RAAF (ret) in this chapter. (Wally Civitico)

Bill Collings (right) prepares to enter the cockpit of the MiG before taking it on its first post restoration flight on 18 July 1991. (Wally Civitico)

After engine start, Bill Collings conducts the vital checks. (Wally Civitico)

far greater rate than modern jet aircraft and any restrictions on operations in the Melbourne terminal area could cause serious problems. On reaching 27,000 feet in the climb I was already down to the fuel level I would need to carry out the required handling tests. I was therefore unable to look at the high Mach regime of the aircraft in the clean configuration. It was clear that for other than a short demonstration flight on the departure airfield, the normal configuration of the aircraft was with underwing tanks attached and filled.

The first impression one has of the cockpit, even compared with western aircraft of the same era, is of something agricultural. The Russians at that time certainly never wasted any effort on creature comforts for the crew. The emergency selectors for the pneumatic supply, for example, are large brass wheels and handles which look designed more for ships than aircraft. I have since learned through flying the Czech L-59 that the design of these controls is for the continental winter in Russia. The controls have to be of such a size because of the large gloves worn by the pilots for survival in the winter.

Apart from the appearance of the cockpit, everything was functional, except for one glaring exception: there is no park brake. This would not be a problem if the aircraft was fitted with foot brakes, but it is not. Like other East European and Russian aircraft it is fitted with the English system of differential air operated brakes using a lever on the control column.

For those of you not familiar with this system, I will explain. The air pressure for the operation of the brake shoes on the wheels is controlled by a lever like a bicycle hand brake lever on the control column. The aircraft is turned by deflecting the rudder pedal in the required turn direction and the lever operated to apply brake. The degree of braking is determined by the amount of travel on the lever.

The most difficult part with such a system is not turning but in keeping straight on landing during braking, particularly if the rudders are not strongly self centring. Fortunately, the MiG-15 is easy to keep straight during deceleration. One other area of concern with the cockpit is the canopy. It really is agricultural and it is relatively easy to drop the canopy off the aircraft if great care is not taken when opening it.

As with the original Nene, the starting sequence is fully automatic and after the usual rumbling on start, the motor is very well behaved. It is of course necessary to advance the throttle, or should I say power lever, slowly at low RPM, but once the RPM approach the operating range the engine response is very good. Maximum RPM on takeoff are about 11,300 depending on the mark of engine fitted.

The engine has twin fuel pumps and an isolation pump which will isolate both pumps in the event of failure of one of them. When we first operated the Nene in the RAAF we would take off with the isolation pump on and turn it off after takeoff before reducing RPM. The practice was discontinued and so with the Russian version in the MiG. Although there is an RPM governor for control of the top RPM, there is no temperature limiter and it is therefore essential that the pilot monitor the EGT on takeoff and reduce RPM if necessary to remain within the EGT limit of 690 degrees C.

In the climb, due to the design of the fuel control system, the RPM will increase with the same throttle setting and it is necessary to continually adjust the throttle in the climb to maintain the RPM or, if necessary, reduce RPM to stay within the EGT limit. Unlike modern fighter engines, there is a limit on the use of takeoff and climb power. The maximum continuous power in the MiG is 10,870 RPM and/or 640 degrees C.

Takeoff is straightforward but one has to be a little careful not to try to raise the nosewheel too soon as the aircraft is very light on it and over control is possible. After unstick at about 130 KIAS (knots indicated airspeed) the gear and flap are raised and the aircraft accelerated to initial climb speed: in this instance I selected 250 KIAS. The undercarriage selection is of interest and is one feature which is better than other aircraft I have flown. The gear selector has a neutral position which is selected after the gear is up and locked. During the retraction sequence, the brakes are automatically applied and the selection of neutral releases the brake pressure. I have not seen this system on another aircraft and it is definitely a worthwhile one.

There is little trim change with gear and flap retraction and the first thing that strikes one is the lightness of the

The MiG-15 taxies out for its first post restoration flight with pilot Bill Collings in the front seat and part owner of the aircraft, Barry Batagol, in the rear. (Wally Civitico)

flying controls. The aircraft's controls are aerodynamic with the ailerons being hydraulically boosted. Over the speed envelope the controls remain light and the stick force per G gradient remains positive throughout. This is very surprising for an aircraft of this type and is the most enduring impression of the aircraft that I have.

Low speed handling is uneventful and aerobatics with or without external tanks is straightforward. Although the ailerons are boosted, the rate of roll is not particularly high but the control force is light and well harmonised with the pitch channel.

After upper air work, descent is commenced. The speed brakes are limited to seven minutes of extension and one can either hold the selector on the stick or select them out with a switch on the left hand console. They are not particularly useful except for recovery from a high speed dive.

In the circuit, the gear and flap speeds are very useful. Takeoff flap can be selected at 243 KIAS and gear at 240 KIAS. Base turn is entered at about 160 KIAS, lowering flap when required to reduce speed to 130 KIAS at the runway threshold. The aircraft is very stable throughout and the landing is very straightforward with light elevator stickforces. On touchdown the nose wheel can be lowered as speed reduces and braking commenced.

As the aircraft has no anti-skid system it is essential to bring the stick fully back when braking if tyre skidding is to be avoided.

In a crosswind one has to control direction during braking by very careful small movements of the rudder pedals. If an oscillation develops, brakes should be released momentarily and then reapplied. With a little practice, one soon gets used to this old system. After landing, one turns off the gear master switch, a very good feature, and then selects neutral. I must say it takes a little courage to move the gear selector at all when on the ground! Flaps are then raised and the aircraft taxied back.

After several flights with the original owners, I had another opportunity

General view of a MiG-15UTI's cockpits. Note the side hinging front canopy. (Gerard Frawley)

to fly this aircraft with a new owner. This gave me the opportunity to fly from the back seat. Surprisingly, the view was better than most and the instructor's control was well suited to the task. It is interesting how well the hydraulic system was designed to allow override of the student without any electrical selectors. The only important thing to do when flying solo is to ensure that the rear seat hydraulic and electrical selectors are placed in neutral.

The MiG-15 is an aircraft of its time with few frills in the cockpit. But it is a very simple and workable machine. This comes from the requirement that it be capable of operating in the extremes of weather conditions encountered in Russia. It is a delight to fly with light well harmonised flight controls and even with a fairly hard suspension one can regularly turn in soft landings.

Jets Over Korea

A new era of air to air combat – jet versus jet – as the F-86 Sabre and MiG-15 meet over Korea.

JETS OVER KOREA

The division of Korea into North (communist) and South (democratic) elements came about as a result of the ending of World War II and the splitting of the previously Japanese occupied country into American and Soviet controlled halves, divided at the 38th parallel.

Attempts to unite the two halves in the late 1940s and early 1950s failed, each Korea claiming to be the true and legal government. As a result, tensions rose, and the communist North indulged in subversive activities coupled with a programme of propaganda designed to undermine the will of the South Koreans to remain associated with the United States and the rest of the Free World.

Subversion turned into full military action on the early morning of 25 June 1950 when the North Korean Peoples' Army (NKPA) launched two attacks across the border between the two Koreas. A breach of the peace was declared by the United Nations and member countries were called upon for assistance. The response was quick, the USA, Britain, Australia, South Africa and others contributing aircraft, troops and naval forces to the battle.

The war appeared to be all but over within four months with ground which had been lost in South Korea regained and an invasion of North

Korea going well with the capital, Pyongyang, in the hands of the allied forces and a push towards the Yalu River (the Chinese border) underway.

The nature of the Korean War changed dramatically in late October 1950 when allied troops were suddenly confronted by large numbers of Chinese soldiers. The entry of China into the war came as a complete surprise and immediately forced the UN forces into retreat. From here, the battle would be long and hard and the Korean War was not officially declared over until July 1953. At the end of it all, Korea remained divided.

In the air, the might of the UN forces – led by a large American presence – was virtually unchallenged for the first four months of the battle with bombers and strike aircraft able to attack any target with impunity. The North Korean Air Force (NKAF) possessed only modest strength with a fighter regiment comprising about 70 Yak-9 and La-7/11 piston engined fighters, 65 Il-2 ground attack aircraft and a few Yak-18 and Po-2 trainers.

Opposing them were US F-82 Twin Mustang night fighters, P-51 Mustang and F-80 Shooting Star fighters-bombers and B-29 Superfortress and B-26 Invader bombers. Allied air forces were also immediately involved, Australia and South Africa contributing Mustangs (Mete-

ors and Sabres, respectively, later on) while the Republic of Korea Air Force (ROKAF) itself had Mustangs. To this must be added substantial naval air power from the USA initially and then Britain and Australia. The NKAF was no match for all this and was quickly nullified.

This left the UN forces with complete air superiority and the freedom of movement which results from that. The American B-29s were particularly effective, ranging freely over North Korean strategic targets and destroying no fewer than 18 of them within two months of the start of hostilities. Steel plants, oil depots, railway yards, harbour facilities, explosives factories and chemicals plants all came under intense bombardment from the B-29s while the B-26 Invaders concentrated on night interdiction work against targets such as supply columns and trains.

Enter The MiG-15

If the unexpected entry of China into the battle in October 1950 was a large and unpleasant surprise for the troops on the ground, the date 1 November was equally memorable for those fighting the air war with the first appearance of the then unknown Soviet built MiG-15 jet fighter. Also unknown at the time was the fact that these Chinese MiGs were being flown

Sabres of the USAF's 18th FBW depart on another sortie over Korea.

USAF B-29 Superfortresses roamed the Korean skies virtually unmolested until the MiG-15 appeared. This aircraft departs for another mission under the watchful eye of an airfield defence gunner.

Lineup of 4th FIW F-86As at Kimpo in May 1951.

by Soviet pilots, as would many more the UN air forces would encounter over the next two-and-a-half years.

That first encounter set alarm bells ringing as here was a threat to all of the allied air effort in Korea as the security of the bombers could no longer be guaranteed as even the F-80 Shooting Star – very much a first generation jet fighter – could not match the fast, nimble and well armed MiG.

The first recorded jet versus jet combat took place on 8 November 1950 over the Yalu River when MiG-15s rose to intercept a force of B-29s which were on their way to bomb Antung. The bombers were escorted by F-80s from the USAF's 51st Fighter Interceptor Wing, one of which shot down a MiG-15 during the ensuing battle. A new era in aerial warfare had begun and despite this early and perhaps lucky victory by the USAF, it quickly became clear that this new Soviet fighter would – if in the right hands – make life very difficult for the Allied air forces in Korea.

The Soviet Union played a very large part in MiG-15 operations in Korea with its pilots and units rotating regularly during the course of the war and training the Chinese pilots who also flew the aircraft. The proximity of the Korean War to the end of World War II meant that many pilots on both sides had seen combat before.

The MiG-15 units were all based around Antung, north of the Yalu River in Manchuria, an area 'out of bounds' for UN pilots although they often did unofficially venture beyond the point of demarkation. As a result, most air battles took place south of the river in the triangular area on the north-western side of the country which quickly became known as 'MiG Alley' by the American pilots. The MiGs were more or less forced to operate from their Manchurian bases as constant raids on North Korean airfields by USAF bombers made them unusable.

The main role of the MiG-15s was to intercept the American bombers which were raiding the North. The MiGs would often take advantage of their superior altitude performance by lying in wait at heights of up to 45,000 feet, well above the bombers and their escorts with the obvious advantages involved. The MiG pilots were generally less inclined to get involved in dogfights than the Americans so the standard method of attack was to dive in from the rear, attack, and then take advantage of the MiG's high rate of climb to quickly escape from the scene.

When intercepting enemy aircraft, the MiGs were guided to their targets

CHINA

Manchuria

Yalu River

"MiG Alley"

Sea of Japan

Antung
Sinuiju
"N.E."
Sinuiju

*Taechŏn

*Huich'ŏn

*Uiju

*Namsi

*Sahmch'am

Sinanju
Osyo-ri
Yŏnsyn
Sunan

*Pyŏng-Ni

*Kangdong
*PYŎNGYANG
"Main", "Downtown"
& "East"

*Principal Communist Airfields

KOREA

● Principal UN Airfields

Anak

Hwangju

*Sariwŏn

*Sinmak

Yellow Sea

K-47 Ch'unch'ŏn

K-46 Hongch'ŏn

K-18 Kangnŭng

38°N

K-16 SEOUL
K-14 Kimp'o

K-13 Suwŏn
K-55 Osan
K-6 P'yŏngt'aek

K-5 ● Taejŏn

K-3 P'ohang

K-2 Taegu

K-8 Kunsan

K-37

K-9 Pusan East
K-1 Pusan West
K-10 Chinhae

K-4

0   km   150

Sabre, MiG-15 & Hunter   133

F-86E Sabres of the 51st FIW shortly after they replaced the Wing's Lockheed F-80 Shooting Stars in September 1951.

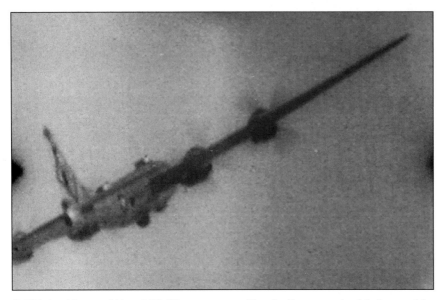

B-29 in trouble, caught by a MiG-15's gun camera. The situation swung back in favour of the bombers with the arrival of the Sabre.

by ground controllers operating Ground Control Intercept (GCI) radar, or if time permitted they would assemble near the anticipated target and loiter until the bombers and their escorts arrived. Updated information as to the whereabouts of the enemy aircraft was provided by the ground controllers. They would then attack, normally using the method described above. The MiG-15s usually flew in flights of six aircraft comprising three pairs – leader and wingman – the tactic universally adopted during World War II.

Sabres To Korea

The arrival of the MiG-15 in Korea prompted an immediate response from the USA, faced with a surprise new aircraft which was clearly superior to anything then operated by the UN forces including the F-80 Shooting Star, which was 75mph (120km/h) slower. By late 1950 the US Air Force had the new F-86A Sabre established in service and agreed to requests from the Far Eastern Air Force (FEAF) in Korea to send what was America's best fighter to the front. Strangely, there was some initial resistance to this idea from within the US government but this was quickly overcome and the proposal was approved on 11 November 1950.

The unit selected to first take the Sabre to Korea was the 4th Fighter Interceptor Wing (FIW) based at New Castle County Airport, Wilmington, Delaware. Three Fighter Interceptor Squadrons (FIS) – the 334th, 335th and 336th – made up 4 FIW and all had been equipped with the F-86A for well over a year by the time the order to move to Korea came. Most of its pilots were vastly experienced with many World War II combat hours and kills under their belts. This experience and quality of pilot would make the difference when the Sabre began meeting the MiG-15 in combat.

The 4th FIW arrived in Korea in early December 1950, their aircraft and personnel being shipped there aboard the jeep carrier USS *Cape Esperance* via Kisarazu in Japan. There it was discovered that the Sabres had been insufficiently protected from the elements for their journey with salt water corroding many parts and components including engines and electrics. Rectification work took

(left) Sabres of the 4th FIW aboard the jeep carrier USS Cape Esperance upon their arrival at Kisarazu, Japan, from the USA. Next stop Korea, but some maintenance work had to be performed first to deal with the salt water corrosion which had occurred on the way. (NAA)

Bombing up a Sabre of the 36th FBS/8th FBW at Suwin in June 1953. Although the Sabre's exploits against the MiG-15 gained most of the publicity, the ground attack role they performed was also of great value.

Two other groups converted to the Sabre whilst they were in Korea. Both were Fighter Bomber Groups, the 8th which swapped its F-80s for F-86F Sabres in April 1953 and the 18th, which kept P-51 Mustangs until the same year when it too converted to F-86Fs. The 8th FBG was made up of the 35th, 36th and 80th Fighter Bomber Squadrons and was based at Suwon (K13). The 18th FBG (12th, 39th and 67th FBS) operated from Chinhae (K10) and Osan (K55).

Operating with the 18th FBG were the F-86Fs of the South African Air Force's No 2 Squadron. This unit had arrived in Korea in November 1950 equipped with P-51 Mustangs and operated them until 1952 when it re-equipped with 22 Sabres provided by the USAF.

USAF KOREAN BASES	
No	**Name**
K1	Pusan West
K2	Taegu
K3	Pohang
K4	Sachon
K5	Taejon
K6	Pyongtaek
K8	Kunsan
K9	Pusan East
K10	Chinhae
K13	Suwon
K14	Kimpo
K16	Seoul
K18	Kangnung
K24	Pyongyang
K27	Yonpo
K37	Taegu West
K40	Cheju
K41	Chongiu
K46	Hoengsong
K47	Chunchon
K55	Osan

First Blood and Aces

The big moment for the 4th FIW arrived in the afternoon of 17 December 1950 when the Sabre met the MiG-15 in combat for the first time. On that day, a patrol of four Sabres led by Lt Col Bruce Hinton flew around MiG Alley. The flight used the existing F-80 Shooting Star radio calls and flight patterns in the hope of luring some MiGs into combat. The ruse worked, and four MiGs were soon spotted climbing towards what they assumed was a quartet of F-80s.

The fight was brief, and to Hinton went the honour of shooting down the first of 792 MiG-15 kills the America Sabre pilots would claim by the time the conflict ended. Hinton, flying F-86A serial number 49-1236, worked his way onto the tail of a MiG and gave it a long burst from 800 yards. The MiG was damaged and slowed, Hinton flying right up to the

two weeks to complete and the first seven aircraft arrived at their base at Kimpo on 13 December. The first sortie – a combat sweep officially described as an 'orientation flight' – was conducted two days later but without enemy contact.

The Americans gave their South Korean airfields alpha/numeric designations for ease of recognition. Kimpo became K14 and the others are listed in the table below.

With as many as 400 MiG-15s active at any one time initially (later estimates put the number at about 1,000) the need for another Sabre Wing was quickly recognised as be-

ing necessary. It was another nine months before this happened with the arrival of the 51st FIW (16th, 25th and 39th FIS) at Suwon, or K13. The 51st had replaced its F-80 Shooting Stars with F-86E Sabres, this improved model with all flying tail surfaces also being given to the 4th FIW at around the same time. The 51st later received the much improved F-86F with radar ranging gunsight and more power and between them this combined force of about 130 aircraft (of which less than half would be operational on a given day) regained air superiority in the face of much larger numbers of MiG-15s.

Captain Joseph McConnell, the top scoring US ace in Korea with 16 kills. McConnell survived the Korean War only to be killed in an F-86 accident in 1954.

Captain James Jabara, the first Korean War ace and the second top scorer overall with 15 kills.

Lt Col George Davis, 14 kills in Korea (plus seven in World War II) and the only Sabre pilot awarded the Medal of Honour. The award was made posthumously as Davis was killed in action.

crippled fighter, enabling him to have a good look at it. Despite its damage and the fact it was losing height quickly, the MiG needed finishing off, Hinton dropping back to do the job with another long burst which saw the MiG crash into the snow covered land below. The pilot stayed in his aircraft.

On his return to Kimpo, Hinton performed the traditional fighter pilots' victory roll at low altitude and high speed.

From there it was mainly Sabre ascendant but there were one or two hiccups on the way. The first came shortly after this first kill when the Sabre units had to temporarily abandon Kimpo for the safety of Japan when the airfield was overrun by

KOREAN WAR TOP 17 US ACES

Name	Kills	Remarks
Capt Joseph McConnell	16	all MiG-15s
Capt James Jabara	15	all MiGs, first jet ace
Maj George Davis	14	11 MiG-15s, 3 Tu-2s
Capt Manuel Fernandez	14	all MiG-15s
Col Royal Baker	13	12 MiGs, 1 La-9
Lt Harold Fischer	10	all MiG-15s
Col James Johnson	10	all MiG-15s
Capt Ralph Parr	10	all MiG-15s
Maj Frederick Blesse	10	9 MiGs, 1 La-9
Capt Lonnie Moore	10	9 MiGs, 1 La-9
Capt Iven Kincheloe	10	6 MiGs, 4 Yak-9
Lt James Low	9	all MiG-15s
Capt Robinson Risner	8	all MiG-15s
Lt Col Vermont Garrison	8	all MiG-15s
Capt Clifford Jolley	7	all MiG-15s
Capt Leonard Lilley	7	all MiG-15s
Lt Henry Buttelmann	7	all MiG-15s

Note: Of these, several also had WW2 kills to their credit, inclduing Jabara (1.5), Davis (7), Baker (3.5), Garrison (7.3) and Johnson (1).

Chinese forces. Other problems which had to be dealt with included the sheer number of MiGs in the sky compared with the number of Sabres. This was largely alleviated with the re-equipment of the 51st FIW with Sabres.

No fewer than 40 USAF pilots claimed ace status during the Korean War, all but one of them flying the Sabre. Of those, two were triple aces and six were doubles and between them these 39 Sabre pilots were responsible for the destruction of 305 MiG-15s.

The first to gain the distinction of being the world's first jet ace was Captain James Jabara of the 4th FIW's 334th FIS. Jabara achieved his fifth and sixth victories during a single sortie on 20 May 1951 despite ig-

Lt Col Richard Creighton was the fourth US ace of the Korean War. His 4th FIW F-86A is shown landing at Kimpo. (USAF)

noring orders and going into battle with one of his Sabre's (F-86A 49-1318) drop tanks 'hung up' after refusing to fall away from the aircraft when combat was joined. Jabara ended the war with 15 victories achieved over two separate tours of duty.

The top scoring ace was Captain Joseph McConnell Jr of the 16th FIS/4th FIW. McConnell ended the war with 16 MiG kills to his credit. As always, there was intense competition between the leading pilots as to the number of kills they achieved, a seesawing battle in the first half of 1953 between him, Jabara and Captain Manual Fernandez going on. McConnell survived being shot down himself in April 1953 to carry on, recording an amazing six kills the following month (including three in one day) to win the 'competition'. Fernandez ended the war with 14 kills to his name, as did Lt Col George Davis, who led the score comfortably until he was killed in action.

Sabre Versus MiG-15

The claimed 10 to 1 kill ratio of US Sabre pilots over the MiG-15 in Korea would appear to indicate that the Soviet fighter was something of a dud. The facts are that this is simply not the case, the MiG-15 being superior to the Sabre in many important respects.

A quick look at the accompanying comparison table shows some of the pertinent points: the MiG-15's better power-to-weight ratio (improved further with the arrival of the MiG-15bis in 1951) and its far superior rate of climb. This alone was a significant

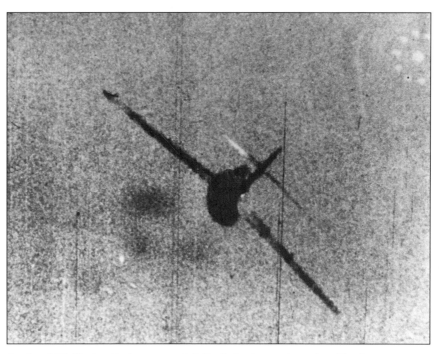

Another MiG-15 about to become a statistic, its final seconds captured by the camera gun of the pursuing Sabre. Note the sight 'pippers' on the right of the picture.

advantage. The MiG was about 10 per cent smaller than the Sabre and much lighter, resulting in a lower wing loading at typical weights and its better power-to-weight ratio.

The table also shows the Sabre's superiority in speed – a function of its higher limiting Mach number – but doesn't show that in some areas of the flight envelope the MiG was the better aeroplane (particularly at very high altitudes) and in others the Sabre was superior. The MiG-15's directional instability at high speeds and

its tendency to flick out of tight turns were definite minuses, the latter causing many a Soviet or Chinese pilot to lose his aircraft or his life in battle. Air battles tend to get lower and slower as they progress and in tight turning situations the Sabre's more docile characteristics could be an advantage.

Overall, however, the MiG-15 was more manoeuvrable than the Sabre, and that advantage was held until the F-86F-25 with wide chord '6-3' wings came along to help redress the bal-

F-86F 'Beauteous Butch II' of the 39th FIS/51st FIW, Joseph McConnell's second Korean War Sabre and the one in which he scored 11 of his 16 kills. The original 'Beautious Butch' (note spelling) was shot down in May 1953 but McConnell came back to finish the war with a flurry of kills.

Open air maintenance in Korea with an F-86A Sabre undergoing an engine change. Note the fuselage 'break' for easy access to the engine.

ance. At very high speeds the MiG was never a match for the F-86 under any circumstances and some aircraft were seen to suffer structural failures of their tail surfaces when they tried to turn with Sabres at top speed. The Sabre's wing structure was also better, being more rigid and therefore less prone to promote wing drop at high speeds. In addition, the Sabre's much better build quality helped maintain its aerodynamic characteristics, whereas the MiG's handling could vary from aircraft to aircraft due to varying manufacturing tolerances.

The MiG-15 was regarded as an unstable gun platform with a too slow rate of fire from its single 37mm and two 23mm NS-37 cannon, although their firepower was devastating. The introduction of the faster firing NR-23 gun on the MiG-15bis improved that situation. The lack of hitting power in the Sabre's six 0.50in machine guns was an area of great concern. Whereas it was calculated that one 37mm or two 23mm hits from the MiG's guns would be sufficient to bring down a Sabre, the American fighter needed an average 1,024 rounds of its machine gun ammunition to shoot down a MiG. It was not uncommon for a Sabre pilot to fire all his ammunition at a MiG-15 with no discernible result.

This hitting power imbalance resulted in the Gun Val programme described earlier in the book where some F-86Es and Fs were fitted with four 20mm cannon in place of the machine guns. The installation was tested in combat in Korea and although found to be generally satisfactory (six confirmed kills were recorded) was not adopted for the normal day fighter Sabres as some problems were found, including the almost universal one of the time of the ingestion of gases from the guns when they were fired causing engine surge and even flameout problems.

Other recognised weaknesses include insufficient armour protection on early Sabres and the lack of a radar ranging gunsight on all MiG-15 models and the early Sabres.

Many of the F-86A and E Sabres' weaknesses were addressed with the F model, which began to make its presence felt in Korea in 1953. The F-86F is generally recognised as being the best all round fighter of its time. Extra power gave greater speed and a much improved rate of climb (although it was still less than the MiG-15bis) and the new increased chord '6-3' wing in combination with the all flying tailplane first introduced on the F-86E gave the Sabre a handling advantage in just about every aspect of combat.

The new Sabre could fly faster and higher, could climb at a greater rate and turn tighter than before. It was a very stable gun platform and this in combination with a radar ranging gunsight gave the pilot every chance to shoot down his opponent.

Despite the various pros and cons of the two aircraft, the Sabre pilots had one major advantage – they were

A lineup of 4th FIW F-86F Sabres in 1953, with many kill markings apparent. (USAF)

The F-86Fs of the South African Air Force's No 2 Squadron flew with the USAF's 18th FBW.

one where a Sabre pilot radioed to his comrades (who were some distance away): "I've got 24 [or 30 or 40, depending on who's telling the story] MiGs cornered near Sinanju in case anyone isn't busy"!

The MiG-15 pilots' skills varied considerably ranging from very good for the mainly Russian mercenary 'hanchos' to poor and only fair for the 'recruits', the Chinese and North Koreans, who tended to sometimes eject at the first sight of trouble. This factor alone would account for much of the Sabre's amazing kill to loss ratio at the end of the day.

Many analyses have been written on the relative merits of the Sabre and MiG-15. Some have suggested that the American claim of 792 MiG kills is greatly exaggerated and that Sabre losses were understated. Perhaps this is true, perhaps not, but whatever the figures, the Sabres did shoot down many more MiG-15s than were lost, and all while being substantially outnumbered. The difference comes down to better pilots, training and tactics on the American side from the start, and with the arrival of the F-86F, a better aeroplane with which to exploit these advantages.

better. This advantage stemmed from superior training, previous combat experience in many cases and an attitude which simply did not allow them to consider defeat. The Sabres were usually outnumbered by a considerable margin when they fought the MiG-15s over Korea, yet despite the theoretical equality of the two aircraft in many areas, the Soviet fighter was shot down at the rate of 10 for every Sabre lost.

A classic and well recorded example of the Americans' attitude is the

COMPARISON – MiG-15 and F-86 SABRE					
	MiG-15	**MiG-15bis**	**F-86A-5**	**F-86E-5**	**F-86F-25**
Power (lb thrust)	5,000	5,950	5,200	5,200	5,910
Gross Weight Clean (lb)	10,595	11,177	14,108	16,512	16,860
Power/Weight Ratio	0.47:1	0.53:1	0.37:1	0.31:1	0.35:1
Wing Loading (lb/sq ft)	47.7	50.4	49.0	57.3	55.6
Internal Fuel (lb)	2,200	2,576	2,879	2,879	2,910
Max Speed S/L (mph)	652	668	676	666	695
Max Speed 45,000ft (mph)	575	580	585	582	595
Initial Climb (ft/min)	8,260	10,100	7,470	7,250	9,300
Service Ceiling (ft)	50,000	50,100	48,000	47,200	48,000

F-86A Sabre 49-1281 of the 4th FIW flown by Lt Col Glen Eagleston.

HAWKER
HUNTER

The first prototype Hawker P.1067 (WB188) over the English countryside and displaying the fine lines of the Hunter. (BAe)

HAWKER HUNTER

One of the best loved of all British aircraft, the Hawker Hunter represents several areas of importance in the history of military aviation: it was the Royal Air Force's first transonic fighter; it has been described as world's first genuinely multirole jet combat aircraft in its mature forms; and it was the last of a long line of fighters to come from the drawing board of Sir Sydney Camm and from the Hawker production lines before the company was absorbed into the nationalised Hawker Siddeley.

Regarded by many as the most aesthetically pleasing jet fighter ever built, the Hunter has also often been described as a 'pilots' aeroplane' and is an aircraft which has enjoyed a longevity of service which continues into the 1990s albeit on an ever reducing scale.

Total Hunter production amounted to 1,972 aircraft between the first flight of the prototype in 1951 and the rollout of the last new example just nine years later in 1960. In terms of time, this is a remarkably short production run for a 'modern' combat aircraft and with the benefit of hindsight it can be argued that many more Hunters should have been built

and that the aircraft was perhaps not as well developed as it could or should have been. The problem was one of perception as the supersonic 1950s progressed. Here was a subsonic (in level flight) aircraft which because of that characteristic, was regarded by many of the powers-that-be as obsolescent even while it was being built.

The very large numbers of Hunters which were subsequently rebuilt, upgraded and exported once the basic design had evolved into the fine ground attack aircraft it became, speaks for itself.

The Hunter was originally developed as an interceptor and carried a fairly hefty burden of early problems, many of them stemming from the 'Super Priority' status it was afforded by the British government in the early days. This resulted in the aircraft being rushed into production and service before it was ready, with the consequence that a fully battleworthy Hunter took some time to evolve, thus largely negating the perceived advantages of Super Priority.

But the Hunter survived all that to be developed into the effective multirole combat aircraft the world

has known for nearly five decades as a fighter, ground attack, reconnaissance and training aircraft serving with 21 nations in Europe, Asia, Africa, South America, the Far East and the Middle East.

The Hawker Heritage

The H G Hawker Engineering Company Ltd was established in November 1920 largely to replace Sopwith Aviation, the company which had provided some of World War One's most notable fighter aircraft but had folded earlier in 1920 after the British Treasury had served an enormous claim for Excess War Profits Duty.

Hawker took over Sopwith's premises at Canbury Park Road, Kingston-upon-Thames, in the south-west part of the Greater London area.

The company was named after the Australian pilot Harry Hawker, who had joined Sopwith in 1912 as a test pilot and who subsequently achieved fame as a pioneer. Hawker was appointed one of the original directors of the company which bore his name, but his life ended tragically in July 1921 when the Nieuport Goshawk he was testing for a race crashed, the

A formation of Sapphire powered Hunter F.5s of 41 Squadron RAF, photographed in 1955 shortly after delivery. (via Philip J Birtles)

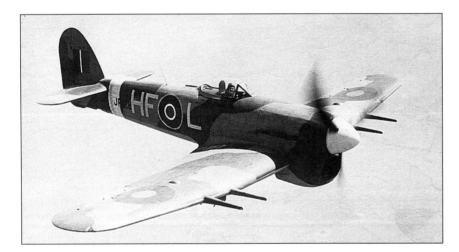

(left) Part of the rich aviation heritage which was Hawker (top to bottom): Demon, Hurricane, Typhoon and Fury, in this case the Rolls-Royce Griffon powered second prototype. (RAAF/BAe)

result of Hawker suffering a haemorrhage while pulling heavy 'g' loadings in tight turns. Hawker was just 32 years old.

But the company carried on, its golden years occurring during the 1925 to 1959 period when Sir Sydney Camm was the chief designer. The first new design to be launched under Camm's leadership was the Hornbill light fighter of 1926, the ancestor of the family of single engined biplane day bombers, fighter/bombers, army co-operation and general purpose military aircraft beginning with the Hart of 1928 and progressing through the 1930s with the Nimrod, Demon, Osprey, Audux, Hardy, Hind and other variants.

Following the same basic design was the smaller, single seat Fury fighter of 1931. Like its bomber counterparts, the Fury was ordered in quantity for the Royal Air Force and foreign customers.

Hawker became a public company in 1933 and assumed the new title Hawker Aircraft Ltd. On its flotation, the new company took over the assets of the old, which was eventually dissolved.

In 1934, Hawker took over another famous British aviation name, Gloster Aircraft, although the two companies retained separate identities until 1963 when they and other companies – including de Havilland, Armstrong Whitworth, Blackburn, Avro and Folland – were grouped together under the Hawker Siddeley banner.

In November 1935 Hawker flew the prototype of possibly its best known product, the Hurricane. The RAF's first monoplane fighter was typically evolutionary in its design, utilising the structural principals of the Hart/Hind/Fury series – all metal and fabric covered, the fuselage being of steel tube design – married to a Rolls-Royce Merlin engine and retractable undercarriage.

The RAF's first 300mph (483km/h) and eight gun fighter, the Hurricane soon acquired metal stressed skin wings and was developed into fighter/bomber, naval fighter and specialist ground attack variants. Its finest hour was the Battle of Britain in 1940, where it and smaller numbers of Spitfires helped save the day.

The Hurricane remained in production until 1944 when the 14,527th example was delivered. Of those, 1,077 were built by the Canadian Car and Foundry Company.

Two views of Hawker's first jet aircraft, the P.1040 VP401. This aircraft first flew in September 1947 and represented the first step in the line which would culminate in the Hunter. (BAe)

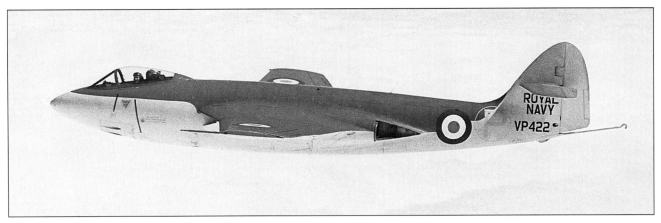

The P.1040 was developed and went into production as the Seahawk naval fighter, the first example flying in September 1948. (BAe)

Next came the series of more advanced piston engined fighters which culminated in the Fury and Sea Fury. The process began in 1937 when Sydney Camm and his team were investigating the development of a new 12 gun fighter powered by the advanced Napier Sabre 24 cylinder engine of horizontal 'H' configuration which promised power outputs of more than 2,000 horsepower (1,500kW).

The British Air Ministry issued Specification F.18/37 to cover such an aircraft, or specifically two, one powered by the Sabre (Type N) and the other by the Rolls-Royce Vulture 24 cylinder 'X' type engine (Type R). These fighters were named Typhoon and Tornado, respectively, and were similar designs apart from their powerplants and other details. Structurally, they offered an advance over the Hurricane by featuring a stressed skin semi monocoque rear fuselage design in combination with the traditional steel tube forward fuselage.

Problems with the Vulture and the pressures of Hurricane production in 1940 contributed to the Tornado being cancelled, efforts then being concentrated on the Typhoon.

This aircraft also suffered numerous teething problems including unreliability from the 2,100hp (1,565kW) Sabre I engine originally fitted, vibration, poor low speed handling and

After the P.1040 came two P.1052 prototypes with swept wings but the unswept tail surfaces of the original. VX272 was the first of them, flown in November 1948. This aircraft was later navalised and used in carrier trials. (BAe)

The third of the Hawker jets to fly before the Hunter was the sole P.1081 (VX279) converted from the second P.1052. First flown in its new form in June 1950, the P.1081 featured all swept flying surfaces – the next step was the Hunter. (BAe)

several failures of the monocoque structure behind the cockpit.

Despite these and a six month delay during 1940 while the production of Hurricanes had priority, the Typhoon entered service in 1941 with improved engines but lingering problems with the structural integrity of its rear fuselage, some 135 failures of which were reported before the problem was solved. The Sabre engine also continued to give some problems, and for a time many more Typhoons were lost due to these causes than for any other reason including enemy action.

Additionally, the Typhoon's climb and altitude performance were poor despite its power, making it unsuitable as a fighter, and the aircraft didn't find its *niche* until after D-Day when, fitted with rocket projectiles or bombs, it became an effective ground attack fighter, roaming across France and other parts of Europe on offensive sweeps against armour, trains and other targets on the ground.

The Typhoon's thick wing made it susceptible to the effects of compressibility at higher speeds, so by 1941 Sydney Camm had begun work on 'thin wing' development of the fighter.

Originally known as the Typhoon II, the new aircraft featured numerous changes over its predecessor and was renamed Tempest. The Tempest's thinner, semi elliptical wing meant moving some fuel capacity to the fuselage, resulting in a lengthening of that part of the aeroplane. Structurally, the Tempest was similar to the Typhoon.

Tempests were developed to be powered by three different engines, the Napier Sabre, Bristol Centaurus 18 cylinder radial and Rolls-Royce Griffon V12.

Production centred around the wartime Tempest V and the too late to see war service Tempest VI (both with Sabre engines) plus the Centaurus powered Tempest II, which also entered service too late to see action during the war. The Tempest II was generally regarded as being the best of the bunch and it was on this aircraft that early thoughts on a Centaurus powered 'Tempest Light Fighter' were based, this philosophy eventually resulting in the Fury and Sea Fury.

Of the 1,399 Tempests manufactured, 805 were Mark Vs. The type entered service in April 1944 and soon proved itself to be the fastest fighter at low altitude, topping

392mph (631km/h) at sea level and a remarkable 416mph (669km/h) at 4,600 feet.

The final stage in this evolutionary series of piston engined fighters came in September 1944 with the first flight of the Fury, a 'lightweight' version of the Tempest with reduced span wing thanks to the deletion of the centre section and other modifications. These changes resulted in a substantially redesigned aircraft which offered very high performance and represented the pinnacle of piston engined fighter design. The Fury was developed for the Royal Air Force and was first flown at a time when the world's leading air arms were already preparing for the introduction of jet fighters.

As a result, by far the most numerous Fury variants were navalised Sea Furies, the Royal Navy's last piston engined fighter and adopted by that service as a result of it not yet being fully committed to the jet engine.

The first navalised Fury was flown in February 1945 and 860 Furies and Sea Furies of all versions were built of which 615 were delivered to the Royal Navy. Export customers were Australia, Iraq, Egypt, Pakistan, Canada, the Netherlands (some built under licence by Fokker), West Germany,

Cuba and Burma. All production Furies and Sea Furies were powered by Bristol Centaurus radial engines although prototypes were fitted with Centaurus, Rolls-Royce Griffon and Napier Sabre powerplants.

The Sea Fury remained in production well into the jet age, with the last example coming off the line as late as 1954, largely due to export orders and the Royal Navy's operation of the aircraft in the Korean War. By then, Hawker was building large numbers of Hunter jet fighters for the RAF and the company would enter into a new phase of its history.

WB188 rotates from Boscombe Down on the occasion of its first flight on 20 July 1951. The 47 minute flight revealed no major problems.

The First Hawker Jets

Before the Hunter came a series of evolutionary and related Hawker jets, starting with the straight winged P.1040 (which in developed form was produced as the Sea Hawk for the Royal Navy), the P.1052 with swept wings and the P.1081 with swept wings and tail surfaces plus a straight through jet exhaust rather than the bifurcated design (with the exhausts exiting just aft of the wing roots) of the earlier aircraft. All were powered by Rolls-Royce Nene centrifugal flow engines.

Hawker's investigations into jets began in 1944 with a submission to the Ministry of Aircraft Production (MAP) in November of that year of its P.1035 design based on the piston engined Fury but with a mid mounted Rolls-Royce B.41 (later Nene) engine mounted amidships with wing root intakes and bifurcated exhausts. Numerous other concepts were also explored by the company, covering a variety of configurations.

Sydney Camm and his designers then refined the P.1035 concept, resulting in the P.1040 with a new tapered unswept wing and the pilot's cockpit situated well forward, allowing a large amount of fuselage space

to be set aside for fuel capacity. A simple and elegant design, the P.1040 (RAF serial VP401) was flown for the first time on 2 September 1947 from Boscombe Down. Built as a private venture, the P.1040 suffered from a lack of RAF interest – as had the Fury before it – and like its predecessor was instead adopted by the Royal Navy.

Specification N.7/46 for a naval fighter was written around it and the first of two fully navalised Sea Hawk prototypes was flown in September 1948. Production Sea Hawk F.1s began entering full Royal Navy service in March 1953 and six major production variants were developed, all but 33 of the 533 total being built by Armstrong Whitworth. The Sea Hawk was also exported to the navies of the Netherlands, West Germany and India, the last new aircraft not coming off the line until 1960 after having been reopened to fill these orders, a singularly remarkable fact when it remembered that the P.1040/Sea Hawk was very much a first generation jet fighter.

The prototype P.1040 was reconfigured as the P.1072 in late 1949 with a tail mounted Armstrong Siddeley Snarler rocket engine of 2,000lb thrust supplementing the standard Nene.

The availability of German research on high speed aerodynamcis shortly after the end of World War II had an effect on all designers around the world, those involved in jet fighter design immediately looking at the possibility of using swept wings to increase speed. Hawker was no exception, developing the P.1052 with sweptback wings and larger intakes but otherwise similar to the P.1040/Sea Hawk. The 5,000lb (22.4kW) thrust Nene powerplant was retained.

Two research prototypes (VX272 and VX279) were built to Specification E.38/46 and the first of them was flown in November 1948. These aircraft provided much useful research data into the science of swept wings and high speed flight. With a maximum speed of 594 knots (1,099km/h) at sea level, the P.1052 was some 80 knots (148km/h) faster than the straight winged Sea Hawk.

The third of the Hawker jet fighter projects to fly was the P.1081, the result of an Australian requirement to find a replacement for the RAAF's Meteors. Australia had expressed

A portrait of the first P.1067 Hunter (WB188) on the ground around the time of its first flight. Note the lack of armament and the bumps and bulges which would soon be applied to the aircraft plus the anti spin parachute fairing above the jetpipe. (BAe)

interest in a development of the P.1052 but powered with a more powerful Rolls-Royce Tay centrifugal flow engine with afterburner, this necessitating a redesigned configuration in which the engine exhaust exited through a single tailpipe rather the previous split, bifurcated arrangement.

The one and only P.1081 was converted from the second P.1052 (VX279) and incorporated not only the 'straight through' engine exhaust system but also redesigned and enlarged swept back tail surfaces. The Nene engine was retained in this prototype aircraft. VX279 first flew in its new form during June 1950 but crashed ten months later in an unexplained accident which claimed the life of Hawker's chief test pilot, Sqdn Ldr T S 'Wimpy' Wade.

By the time the P.1081 had flown, development of the P.1067/Hunter was well underway, and this in combination with official British disinterest in jet fighters powered by what were seen as 'old hat' centrifugal flow engines, killed off the P.1081 concept before it had a chance to prove itself. This disinterest also alienated the Australians, who had actually ordered 72 P.1081s in February 1950. These aircraft would have been built in Australia by the Commonwealth Aircraft Corporation (CAC) and powered by reheated Nenes which also would have been manufactured by the local company. The RAAF's P.1081s were cancelled later in 1950 and Avon powered Sabres (again built by CAC) were ordered instead.

Towards Hunter

The Hunter as it finally evolved was developed under Hawker Project No 1067 (P.1067), its initial impetus being provided by Air Ministry Specifications F.43/46 and F.44/46 (the latter a two seater) of 1946 for a twin engined fighter to replace the Meteor. It should be remembered that at the time the advances in military aircraft design – spurred on by rapidly ad-

The second prototype (WB195) was flown in May 1952 and like its immediate predecessor, was Avon powered.

vancing jet engine technology – were causing some confusion with new ideas and specifications coming forward regularly.

Sydney Camm and his team came up with the first P.1067 design which did not entirely meet the terms of F.43/46 and was designed around the forthcoming Rolls-Royce AJ.65 (later Avon) axial flow turbojet which was at that stage reckoned to produce about 6,000lb (26.9kW) thrust. Work progressed as a private venture, therefore, until early March 1948 when Specification F.3/48 was written around it.

Maintaining the great British military aircraft tradition of duplication, a specification was simultaneously issued to Supermarine for a similar aircraft, which would ultimately result in the unsuccessful Swift. Speculation still exists today as the to motive for this – was it as a back-up in case one of the designs didn't work, or was it because Britain's socialist government of the day wanted to spread the work around?

The Swift's problems were eventually largely solved but by then it was too late and the type saw only limited service with the RAF.

The original P.1067 design featured a wing swept at 42 degrees, a T-tail with unswept horizontal surfaces and a flattened oval section fuselage with annular nose air intake with a cone containing the radar ranging gunsight scanner in its centre. Engine exhaust exited through a single tailpipe, all fuel was carried in the wings and the armament of four 20mm Hispano cannon was in the lower forward fuselage. This design was quickly revised to feature a circular fuselage cross section, a semi delta tailplane (still in a T-tail arrangement) and the arrangement of the four cannon was revised with two in the original position and the remaining pair moved to the wing roots.

Three prototype P.1067s were ordered from Hawker in May 1948. Work progressed through 1948 with a mock up built and substantial wind tunnel work carried out. This had resulted in the revised fuselage and tailplane shape (and relocated guns) of the original design but further more radical changes were to be incorporated as 1948 wore on, eventually resulting in the layout and shape of the Hunter as we know it today.

These changes included the use of triangular wing root intakes for the engine – which had already proven themselves in the P.1040/1052/1081 series – the lowering of the horizontal tail surfaces to a point about 30 per cent up the redesigned fin, the incorporation of a revised broad chord wing with 40 degrees of sweep and 8.5 per cent thickness/chord ratio and a completely new forward fuselage shape with roomier cockpit and the gun ranging radar mounted in the now conventionally shaped nose.

This definitive P.1067 design would also be slightly faster than its predecessors with a maximum speed in level flight of Mach 0.94 compared with 0.88/0.90 for the earlier designs. The change from T-tail configuration

The third prototype (WB202) first flew in November 1952 and was the first Hunter fitted with an Armstrong Siddeley Sapphire engine. Note the channels for the guns and the ejector chutes below the leading edge wing root.

to the definitive design was a relatively late one and was incorporated well after the decision to switch to wing root intakes had been made.

A significant change in the definitive P.1067 in 1949 was the decision to move all fuel from the wings to the fuselage, a total internal capacity of only 333 Imperial gallons (1,514 l) being provided for the prototypes and early production versions. This wholly inadequate capacity continued another great British aviation tradition in that like so many fighters before it (and one or two since) great efforts subsequently had to be made to give the Hunter something resembling a decent endurance.

Engines and Guns

Although the Rolls-Royce AJ.65 Avon was always regarded as the primary powerplant for the P.1067 and several other new British types such as the Canberra and Swift, the first test runs of the Metropolitan-Vickers F.9 Sapphire axial flow jet in 1948 opened up options for the use of this alternative powerplant. The Sapphire was subsequently taken over and developed by Armstrong Siddeley.

In a similar power class to the Avon, the Sapphire differed in internal design to its Rolls-Royce counterpart. Whereas the Avon featured a nine stage axial compressor, eight combustion chambers and a single stage turbine, the Sapphire had a 13 stage compressor, a single annular combustion chamber and a two stage turbine. The Sapphire offered greater power in its early versions and was slightly wider (43.0in/109.2cm against 41.5in/1.05m), longer (133.8in/3.4m versus 125.0in/3.17m) and at 2,500lb (1,134kg) was 50lb (23kg) heavier. Theoretically, the Sapphire offered greater development potential at this point.

The P.1067's fuselage had been slightly widened during its design phase and was able to accommodate both engines. With that in mind (not to mention the question of 'insurance' should the Avon not live up to expectations), a contract was awarded in June 1948 for three prototypes with one of these to be powered by the Sapphire. At the same time it was decided that production aircraft would be powered by both engines, the Hunter F.1 with the 7,500lb (33.6kN) thrust Avon RA.7 and the F.2 with a Sapphire producing 8,000lb (35.8kN) thrust. Neither would be fitted with afterburning, and as it turned out, no production Hunter would have this feature.

The question of the Hunter's fixed armament was settled when it was decided to install four 30mm Aden cannon, its title derived from the

The Hunter's rival for large RAF orders was the Supermarine Swift, an aircraft which failed to live up to expectations and enjoyed only a short operational career.

names of its developers, the Armament Development Establishment (AD) and the Royal Small Arms Factory, Enfield (EN). This weapon had its origins in the wartime German MG213C gun which introduced some significant new features including a revolving cylindrical breech mechanism which allowed the very high rate of fire of 1,200 rounds per minute in both its 20mm and 30mm versions.

The MG213C saw limited service before World War II ended, and the design of the Aden was based on it. Both 20mm and 30mm variants were considered but the larger version was finally decided on and became the standard British weapon for some time.

The 'four pack' Aden installation in the Hunter's lower forward fuselage incorporated a clever detachable pack design which meant the aircraft could be rearmed in minutes. On returning from a sortie, the gunpack (containing the breeches and magazines) would be lowered from the aircraft, leaving only the barrels in place. A new pre loaded pack was then offered to the aircraft, the result being a substantial reduction in turnaround time. Assisting this process was sin-

gle point refuelling, and each of the Hunter's four Adens carried 150 rounds of ammunition, sufficient for seven seconds continuous firing.

Panic Production

Production of the P.1067 prototype jigs began in December 1949 and by the following April the first fuselage structure was largely complete. By now the aircraft had been given its name. Work continued at what might be described as a 'relaxed' pace, bearing in mind the badly run down state of the British aircraft industry at the time. All this changed in June 1950 when the Korean War broke out.

A state of near panic permeated Britain and its political masters, an immediate result being speeded up work on the Hunter prototypes and orders being placed in October 1950 for 200 Avon powered Hunter F.1s to be built by Hawker and a similar number of Sapphire powered F.2s which would be constructed by Armstrong Whitworth. Gloster Aircraft also received an order to manufacture 151 Hunters, but this had to be cancelled due to the company's inability to supply.

Another air-to-air view of WB188 emphasises the clean lines of the Hunter. (BAe)

The need to build lots of Hunters quickly – remembering that the first flight of the prototype was still many months away – and the British industry's state meant that a large number of tools, jigs and fixtures had to be sourced from Europe.

A change of government in Britain during 1951 which saw Winston Churchill return to power resulted in a new attitude to the nation's defence and the introduction of the Super Priority system under which certain projects would be rushed through the normal bureaucratic system of red tape and delays. As will be seen, this was of minimal benefit to the Hunter which suffered from its accelerated development and it would be some time before a fully combat worthy Hunter was flying with Royal Air Force squadrons.

Super Priority resulted in British Hunters being built at three different locations: by Hawker at Kingston and its associated Dunsfold aerodrome plus at Squire's Gate, Blackpool, in a factory which once built Wellington bombers and was reopened for the Hunter. Armstrong Whitworth contributed to the Hunter manufacturing programme through its Bagington (Coventry) facility. This production mechanism was in place even before the first aircraft had flown.

Into The Air

The first prototype Hunter was allocated the serial number WB188 and the second aircraft WB195. Both of these were powered by RA.7 Avons while the third aircraft (WB202) was powered by a Sapphire. WB188 was unarmed while the other two prototypes were equipped with the Aden gunpack, gun ranging radar and avionics and were therefore representative of the production Hunter F.1 and F.2, respectively.

Hawker's test flying plans had to undergo some reorganisation from April 1951 due to the tragic death of chief test pilot 'Wimpy' Wade in an unexplained accident in the one and only P.1081. His deputy, Neville Duke, took over the role as chief test pilot as a result and it was he who would take the pale green WB188 into the air for the first time on 20 July 1951 in a 47 minute flight.

The flight was conducted from Boscombe Down, the aircraft having been trucked there from the factory. The only real problems to emerge from the flight were excessively heavy elevator forces – somebody had decided to disconnect the hydraulic power boost system beforehand – and some lateral rocking which was caused by the extreme sensitivity of the boosted ailerons. Duke took the

Hunter to a maximum indicated airspeed of 350 knots (403mph/648km/h) and a height of 32,000 feet (9,750m) on this flight and within a month true airspeeds of 700mph (1,126km/h) at sea level were being recorded. The Hunter's first public appearance was at the 1951 Society of British Aircraft Constructor's show at Farnborough after only 11 flying hours had been logged.

High subsonic speeds revealed a severe tail buffet as the speed approached Mach 1 in a dive, a small bullet fairing at the rear of the tailplane/rudder junction solving that problem. Although WB188 had reached an indicated Mach 1.03 in April 1952, the date 6 June is the one recorded as being the day the Hunter officially went supersonic with a buffet free Mach 1.06 being reached in a shallow dive. The event was well recorded by those on the ground around Dunsfold thanks to the accompanying sonic boom.

These were the days when it was considered *de rigueur* to go supersonic at airshows, Neville Duke recording the first public demonstration of the sonic boom at Brussels in July 1952. The Hunter was regularly 'boomed' over the factory responsible for its rival Supermarine Swift, this aircraft not yet exceeding the magic Mach 1 and those involved were constantly reminded of the fact!

The first prototype was subsequently modified for a successful attempt on the world's air speed record and redesignated Hunter F.3, as described in the following chapter.

The second prototype (WB195) was flown on 5 May 1952 and the third, Sapphire powered aircraft (WB202) on 30 November of the same year. This Hunter was 7.5 inches (19cm) longer than the first two prototypes and that slightly extra length was adopted as standard for production aircraft. The second and third prototypes were extensively used for armament trials, while WB195 had a lot of effort expended on it trying to cure a nasty vibration which occurred during high-g pullups at high speed. The problem was apparently peculiar to that particular aircraft and inflicted no other Hunters.

What was apparent after testing of the three Hunters had been going on for a while was that the Sapphire powered aircraft had notably superior performance.

Serious Snags

What also became apparent were two problems which contributed greatly to the Hunter taking some time to become a fully operational and effective fighting machine. The first production Hunter F.1 (WT555) was flown in May 1953 and 'proper' deliveries to the RAF followed in May 1954 but it would be another year before the aircraft could be described as being fully fit for service.

Mass production of the Hunter had meanwhile begun and the seriousness of the problems can be gauged by the fact that the first 20 production aircraft were earmarked for trials.

Hunter F.1 production amounted to 139 aircraft – "139 prototypes", according to one wag.

The first problem concerned airbrakes. In the original design the flaps were also intended to operate as airbrakes. Incorporating small perforations, they were designed to remain fully open up to an indicated airspeed of 620 knots, above which they blew back to the closed position with the help of hydraulic relief valves. To counter the change of trim which resulted from the flaps' extension, small 'dive recovery flaps' were fitted to the underside of the wings. The flaps failed to work properly so alternatives were rapidly investigated – large numbers of Hunters were on the production lines after all. The final 'cobbled up' solution was the fitting of crude single surface, front hinged 'slab' airbrake under the rear fuselage. This became the standard Hunter airbrake throughout its production life and provided the hitherto beautifully clean airframe with its first external bulge.

The second problem was even more serious and concerned only the Avon powered Hunters – early Avons were prone to surge under some conditions and suffered from severe engine surge when the four Aden guns were fired under most conditions at heights above 10,000 feet. This phenomena sometimes resulted in flameout, the problem stemming from the massive blast from the guns disturbing the airflow into the engine. Interestingly, the Australian Avon-Sabre (which had only two Adens in the nose) suffered the same problem.

Presumably with a finely developed sense of the ironic, one leading aviation scribe has written that "Apart from being unable to fire its guns the

Hunter F.1 was a fine fighter", which is a bit like saying that "apart from the ability to diagnose and treat, Fred Bloggs was a fine doctor!"

The fact that the problem was largely missed during the Hunter's early armament trials is remarkable in itself but understandable to a degree when it is realised that the Sapphire powered third prototype was mainly used for these tests and the Sapphire ran as smoothly as silk under all circumstances. To illustrate the point, severe limitations were applied to the Hunter F.1 while the problem was being sorted out, among them gun firing with high explosive ammunition at no more than 25,000 feet and 250 knots indicated airspeed. The F.2, on the other hand, could fire its Adens at up to 48,000 feet and 550 knots indicated.

Once again the problem was exacerbated by the large numbers of Hunters (and Avons) which had begun pouring off various production lines in England during 1953. Soon, others would be coming from production lines established by Fokker in the Netherlands and Avions Fairey in Belgium as well. The problem was finally solved with the introduction of the 'surge proof' Avon 115 during the Hunter F.4's production run in 1955.

Other problems also had to be dealt with: like the damage being caused to the rear fuselage and tailplane by the ejected ammunition links when the guns were fired (solved by placing two collector blisters under the forward fuselage and thus providing the Hunter with its second round of protuberances), and the Hunter's chronic lack of range and endurance.

These and other Hunter modifications through the various mark numbers are discussed in the following chapter.

RAF Hunters: FGA.9 XK137 (top) of 45 Squadron in the early 1970s; and F.6 XG161 (bottom) of 229 OCU/234 Squadron. (BAe/MAP)

The prototype Hunter WB188 (top) in its F.3 world's air speed record form at Greenham Common in 1976. Carrying British Class B markings, this Hunter (bottom) is undergoing refurbishment at Dunsfold in 1973 for resale. (Philip J Birtles)

Switzerland was a major customer for the Hunter, taking delivery of 160 aircraft from both new production and refurbished sources. J-4101 (top) was the first refurbished Mk.58A delivered in 1971. (BAe/MAP)

Singapore was the only Pacific Rim customer for the Hunter, taking delivery of 38 refurbished single seaters and nine two seaters from 1970. (Greg Meggs/MAP)

Naval Hunters: GA(PR).11 WT723 (top) photographed in 1973; and T.8 'Admiral's Barge' XL584 (bottom) operated by the Flag Officer (Flying Training) Fleet Requirements and Direction Training Unit. (Philip J Birtles)

Export trainers: Omani T.66 (top) and Dutch T.7 (bottom), the latter delivered from new production in 1958. (MAP)

Non standard colour schemes: 'raspberry ripple' F.6 XG185 (top) of 4 FTS in 1973; and the sole Hunter Mk.12 XE531 (bottom) in its green and white scheme, photographed under a dark sky at Greenham Common in 1976. (Philip J Birtles)

Civil Hunters: The former Danish F.51 E-418 in private hands as G-HUNT (top); and Hawker Siddeley demonstrator G-BABM (bottom) as it appeared at the 1976 Farnborough Air Show, complete with customers' insignia on the nose. This former RAF FGA.9 (XF432) subsequently went to Singapore. (Philip J Birtles)

HUNTERS MANY AND VARIED

HUNTER F.1

The first production of model of the Hunter was built at two Hawker facilities, Kingston (113 aircraft) and the revitalised factory at Blackpool (26). Very many of the 139 Hunter F.1s were used for tests and trails associated with the problems described in the previous chapters and for testing generally.

The standard Hunter F.1 was powered by a 7,500lb (33.6kN) thrust Avon RA.7 Mk.113 and early production aircraft lacked the airbrake under the rear fuselage. Several different types of airbrake were tested (including underwing and under the forward fuselage designs) before the final 'slab' design was settled on, this relatively simple but effective (albeit not very aesthetically pleasing) modification resulting from the need to

find a quick solution as much as anything.

The Hunter F.1 featured no underwing hardpoints and therefore no opportunity to carry external fuel, the aircraft's lack of endurance being an quickly recognised problem which required urgent attention. As for the gun firing/engine surge problem, the Avon 113 was better than earlier engines in this respect but still by no means immune, as several pilots discovered when faced with a flameout. This resulted in operational restrictions which included limiting firing the guns to maxima of 25,000 feet and 250 knots indicated airspeed when using high velocity ammunition.

The Hunter F.1's problems left the RAF in an interesting position with both of its new fighters having difficulties. The Supermarine Swift (which

entered service slightly before the Hunter) was having serious difficulties of its own, this time in the area of flight control with 'runaways' of the electrically controlled tailplane the major area of concern. As a result, the Swift had its service clearance rescinded and the aircraft was very quickly withdrawn from service as a fighter. The Swift was Avon powered and also suffered engine surge problems but not on anywhere near the same scale as the Hunter. Later Swift variants had relatively successful but brief careers in the fighter reconnaissance role.

The first production Hunter F.1 (XT555) flew in May 1953 and production quickly built up to a rate of about three per week. All 139 F.1s had been completed by the end of 1954. The first 20 production aircraft

Finding an effective airbrake for the Hunter proved to be a problem, a simple slab type design Vnder the rear fuselage finally being settled on. It is displayed here in the fully open position on an 8 Squadron (RAF) Hunter FGA.9 over Aden. (via Philip J Birtles)

(left) NATO aerobatics. Hunter F.1 WW636 of 54 Squadron RAF leads a pair of Canadian Sabres and a USAF Lockheed T-33 trainer 'over the top' of a loop. According to the official caption to this 1955 photograph the formation "was completely unrehearsed [there just happened to be a photo aircraft there!] ... it was the first time that the pilots had done aerobatic formation flying together, and in view of the differing performance of the three types of aircraft, speaks highly of their skill". (via Philip J Birtles)

plus the prototypes were all allocated to various test roles, mainly at the Aircraft & Armament Experimental Establishment (A&AEE), Boscombe Down.

Trials Unlimited

Some of the Hunter F.1s used in these trials are listed below and give some indication of the effort involved. Some would have an effect on the physical characteristics of later model Hunters. The early production F.1s were in effect really pre production aircraft and were as clear an indication as any that the days of being able to built less than a handful of prototypes and then put a combat aircraft into production and immediate service were well and truly over.

Tests and trails Hunter F.1s included: WT555 (handling and performance); WT556 (engine); WT557 (radio); WT558 (gun firing); WT559 (canopy jettisoning); WT560 (engine handling, fitted with Avon 119); WT560 and WT561 (miscellaneous); WT562 (one-third span flaps); WT563 (all flying tail – this was one aspect of the Hunter's handling which was regarded as inferior to the F-86 Sabre); WT564 (combat tactics); WT565 (engine development); WT566 (airbrake development); WT567 (gun firing); WT568 (wing leading edge extensions); WT569 (full powered ailerons, drop tanks, tropical trails); WT570 (full powered ailerons); WT571 (area rule fuselage); WT572 (company trials); WT573 (engine); WT574 (engine); WT583 (first with modified Avon 113); WT611, WT612 and WT616 (Avon 115 trials); and WT656 (flap blowing).

The prototypes also contributed, all three being used for airbrake development work and the Sapphire powered WB202 for drop tank trials as well.

The use of WT569 and WT570 for trials with full powered ailerons came as a result of the extreme sensitivity of the powered flight control system as originally installed. This created aileron loads which were considered excessive at high airspeeds and the system was modified to a fully powered one with spring 'feel' incorporated.

WT659 was the first Hunter F.1 to be fitted with drop tanks.

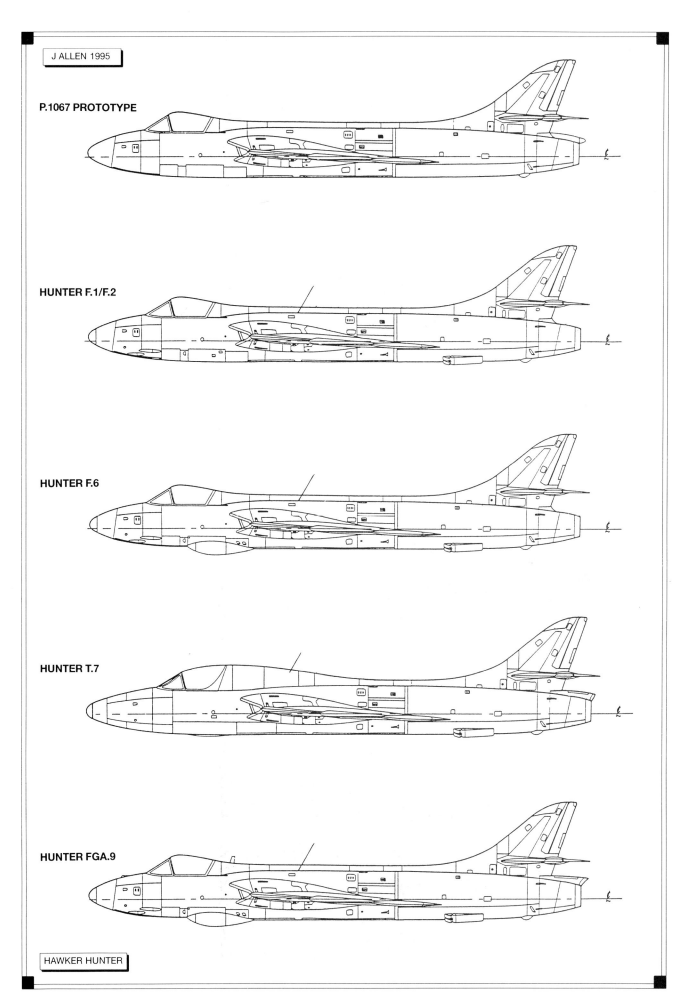

J ALLEN 1995

P.1067 PROTOTYPE

HUNTER F.1/F.2

HUNTER F.6

HUNTER T.7

HUNTER FGA.9

HAWKER HUNTER

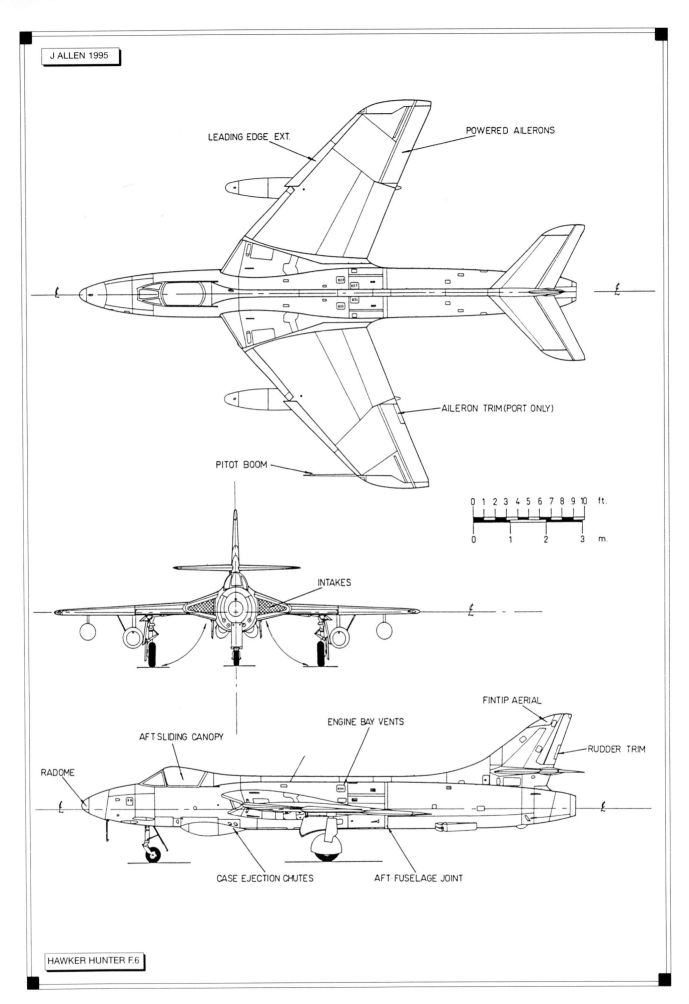

LEADING EDGE EXT.

POWERED AILERONS

AILERON TRIM (PORT ONLY)

PITOT BOOM

0 1 2 3 4 5 6 7 8 9 10 ft.

0 1 2 3 m.

INTAKES

FINTIP AERIAL

ENGINE BAY VENTS

RUDDER TRIM

AFT SLIDING CANOPY

RADOME

CASE EJECTION CHUTES

AFT FUSELAGE JOINT

HAWKER HUNTER F.6

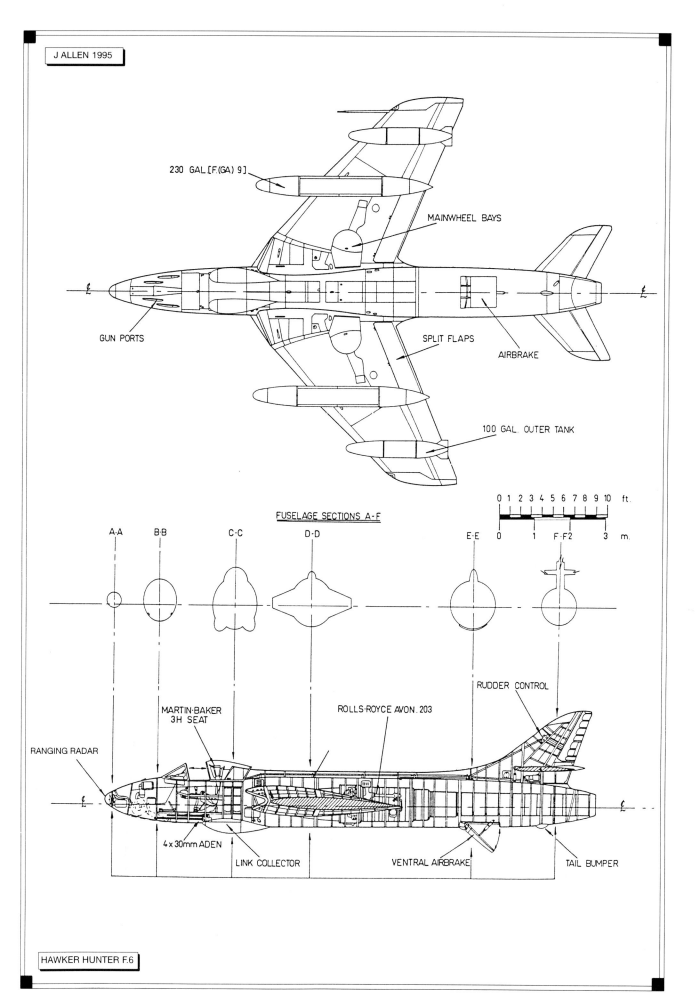

J ALLEN 1995

230 GAL [F.(GA) 9]

MAINWHEEL BAYS

GUN PORTS

SPLIT FLAPS

AIRBRAKE

100 GAL. OUTER TANK

FUSELAGE SECTIONS A-F

0 1 2 3 4 5 6 7 8 9 10 ft.

0   1   2   3   m.

A-A   B-B   C-C   D-D   E-E   F-F

RUDDER CONTROL

MARTIN-BAKER
3H SEAT

ROLLS-ROYCE AVON 203

RANGING RADAR

4 x 30mm ADEN

LINK COLLECTOR

VENTRAL AIRBRAKE

TAIL BUMPER

HAWKER HUNTER F.6

Hunter F.1 WT656 was experimentally fitted with blown flaps, seen here fully extended. Many of the 139 Hunter F.1s were used for trials of some sort, mainly in an attempt to sort out the type's early problems.

Of interest was Hunter F.1 WT571 with area rule rear fuselage, the so called 'Coke bottle' shape with pinched in sides. Theoretically, this reduced drag and made for greater speeds, but in the case of the Hunter this increase was found to be negligible as the drag rise at its maximum speed (Mach 0.93) was so great (as the speed was so close to Mach 1.0) that area ruling was of no great benefit. Sydney Camm had already voiced that opinion, but the boffins decided to go ahead with the experiment anyway ...

Another interesting experimental Hunter F.1 was WT656 which employed the principal of flap blowing – using air bled from the engine compressor and blowing it over the aircraft's flaps and thus increasing lift, reducing the stalling speed and as a result shortening the landing run. This too remained an experimental programme and no production Hunters were so equipped.

Several of the features which would be applied to later Hunters (underwing pylons, gun cartridge link collectors) were also tested on F.1s while the seriousness of the engine surge problem is indicated by the number of aircraft involved in engine trials generally, most of them with Rolls-Royce.

Brief Service

The Hunter F.1's RAF service began in May 1954 when the first examples began to reach the Central Fighter Establishment (CFE) at West Raynham, exercises quickly underlining the qualities of the aircraft and its problems. On the positive side, an early interception exercise against Canberra jet bombers resulted in the interception taking place *from above*, a hitherto unheard of tactic where the Canberra was concerned.

The Hunter's chronic lack of endurance was also brought home to CFE pilots when eight of them were forced to divert from West Raynham to nearby Marnham due to bad weather. Marnham was just 10 miles away but all eight aircraft ran out of fuel *en route*, forcing the ejection of six pilots. Two others landed wheels up at Marnham, and all this after a sortie which had lasted less than 40 minutes!

External tanks and/or increased internal fuel capacity were obviously needed urgently, Hawker quickly investigating two alternatives: a pair of detachable (but not jettisonable) 85imp gal (386 l) underwing tanks or 100imp gal (454 l) drop tanks. The latter was chosen as the best option and tested initially tested on WB202 from early 1954.

The Hunter F.1 served with three operational squadrons, No 43 at Leuchars becoming operational on the type in August 1954. No 222 Squadron (also at Leuchars) followed in December 1954 then No 54 in March 1955. The F.1's service history was quite brief with 54 Squadron exchanging its aircraft for F.4s in Octo-ber 1955 while Nos 43 and 222 had changed to F.4s by September 1956.

The F.1 also flew with the Empire Test Pilots School, the Fighter Weapons School and Nos 229 and 233 Operational Conversion Units. All pilots successfully converted to the Hunter despite the lack of a two seat operational trainer version, this development not appearing in service until 1957.

> ### HUNTER F.1
> **Powerplant:** One 7,500lb (33.6kN) thrust Rolls-Royce Avon 113 axial flow turbojet; internal fuel capacity 337imp gal (1,532 l).
> **Dimensions:** Wing span 33ft 8in (10.26m); length 45ft 10.5in (13.98m); height 13ft 2in (4.01m); wing area 340sq ft (31.6m²).
> **Weights:** Empty 12,128lb (5,501kg); loaded 16,350lb (7,416kg).
> **Armament:** Four 30mm Aden cannon in lower forward fuselage with 150 rounds per gun.
> **Performance:** Max speed 608kt (1,126km/h) at sea level, 539kt (998km/h) at 36,000ft, 524kt (970km/h) at 45,000ft; initial climb 5,800ft (1,768m)/min; time to 45,000ft 11.6min; service ceiling 48,800ft (14,874m); range (high altitude) 425nm (788km); sortie endurance 36 minutes.

HUNTER F.2

Equivalent to the Avon powered Hunter F.1 apart from its Armstrong Siddeley Sapphire engine, the F.2 turned out to be a more useful aircraft as a result. Engine surge was virtually unknown with this powerplant with the result that the gun firing limitations applicable to the initial model were unnecessary.

The other problems (lack of endurance, over sensitive controls, lack of effective air brakes initially and so on) still applied, but balancing this to some extent was the F.2's superior performance thanks to its more pow-

The prototype Hunter F.2 (WB202) was used for various trials including carrying four dummy de Havilland Firestreak missiles.

Only 45 Hunter F.2s were built of which this is the 20th (WN907) in the colours of 257 Squadron RAF. (Philip J Birtles)

erful engine. Rate of climb and there-fore time to height was notably better and the specific fuel consumption of the Sapphire was also slightly supe-rior to the Avon, although the F.2's marginally smaller fuel capacity nulli-fied this.

Only 45 Hunter F.2s were built, all of them by Armstrong Whitworth at Coventry. The first of them (WN888) was flown in October 1953 and the last was delivered to the RAF in No-vember 1954. The first seven aircraft were used for trials, the remainder going to the two squadrons which operated this version of the Hunter.

These were Nos 257 and 263 Squadrons at Wattisham, the F.2 en-tering service with them in Septem-ber 1954 and February 1955, respectively. Both squadrons began receiving improved Hunter F.5s (see below) in mid 1955 but kept at least

some examples of their original air-craft until 1957.

HUNTER F.2
Powerplant: One 8,000lb (35.8kN) thrust Armstrong Siddeley Sapphire 101 axial flow turbojet; internal fuel capacity 314imp gal (1,427 l).
Dimensions: Wing span 33 ft 8in (10.26m); length 45ft 10.5in (13.98m); height 13ft 2in (4.01m); wing area 340sq ft (31.6m²).
Weights: Empty 11,973lb (5,431kg); loaded 16,300lb (7,393kg).
Armament: Four 30mm Aden cannon in lower forward fuselage with 150 rounds per gun.
Performance: Max speed 610kt (1,130km/h) at sea level, 541kt (1,002km/h) at 36,000ft, 527kt (976km/h) at 45,000ft (13,725m); initial climb 6,600ft (2,011m)/min; time to 45,000ft 9.3min; service ceiling 49,100ft (14,965m); sortie endurance 36 minutes.

HUNTER F.3

The designation Hunter F Mk.3 was applied to the original P.1067 prototype (WB188) when it was modified for a successful attempt on the World's Absolute Speed record in September 1953. At that time the record was 715.754mph (1,151.8km/h), set by Lt Col William Barnes in a North American F-86D Sabre.

WB188 was substantially modified for the attempt, the most important change being the substitution of the normal non afterburning Avon with an engine featuring a two position, clamshell nozzle afterburner. In this configuration, the RA.7R Avon devel-oped 7,130lb (31.9kN) thrust dry and 9,600lb (43.0kN) with afterburner. In-creased internal fuel capacity of 400imp gal (1,818 l) was also fitted.

Externally, the Hunter F.3 featured a pointed nose cone and a reprofiled

A low sun puts Hunter F.2 WN899 almost in silhouette but emphasises the clean lines of the aircraft before the link collector tanks and airbrake were added. (via Lindon Griffith)

windscreen with a perspex fairing of increased rake to reduce drag. The aircraft was also fitted with petal style airbrakes on the rear fuselage sides, this being part of the overall airbrake type and position investigation going on at the time. WB188 also received an overall bright red colour scheme for ease of tracking.

Neville Duke was the pilot responsible for the new record, set on 7 September 1953. Flying over a three kilometre course off Rustington on England's south coast, Duke recorded an average 727.6mph (1,169.3km/h) over the required number of runs, bettering the previous mark by nearly 12mph (19km/h). Duke and WB188 also set a new 100 kilometre closed circuit record of 709.2mph (1,141.3km/h) a few days later, but the absolute record was beaten by Mike Lithgow in a Supermarine Swift just 18 days after it had been set. Taking advantage of the Libyan heat (and the higher speed for a given Mach number which results from that), Lithgow and the Swift set a new mark of 737.7mph (1,187.2km/h).

As far as the Hunter versus Swift rivalry of the time was concerned, that was the Supermarine aircraft's last hurrah, the Swift fading into obscurity and the Hunter overcoming its problems to become a classic.

HUNTER F.3
Powerplant: *One Rolls-Royce RA.7R rated at 7,130lb (31.9kN) thrust (dry) and 9,600lb (43.0kN) thrust with afterburner; internal fuel capacity 400imp gal (1,818 l).*
Weights: *Takeoff weight 17,850lb (8,097kg).*
Performance: *Max speed (record) 633kt (1,169km/h) at sea level, 542kt (1,004km/h) at 45,000ft; time to 45,000ft 5.7min.*

Two views of the Hunter F.3 WB188, converted from the first prototype and modified to break the world's air speed record by fitting an afterburning Avon and modifying the profile of the nose and windscreen. WB188 did its job and in the hands of Neville Duke set a new record of 727.6mph (1,169.3kmh) in September 1953. (Philip J Birtles)

HUNTER F.4

All the trials and tests conducted on the Hunter F.1 bore fruit with the Avon powered F.4. This version, along with the similar but Sapphire powered F.5 was the first truly combat worthy Hunter and incorporated numerous important modifications when compared to the original.

Firstly, the problem of engine surge when the guns were fired was largely solved with the installation of the Avon 115 engine after an intensive effort by Rolls-Royce. Although offering the same power as the previous model (7,500lb/33.6kN thrust), it incorporated modifications which eliminated surge. The first 156 F.5s were originally fitted with the F.1's Avon 113 but aircraft after that had 'surge free' Avons and the earlier aircraft were subsequently retrofitted. Other, basically similar marks of the Avon (notably the Mk.121) were also fitted to later Hunter F.4s.

The Hunter's lack of endurance was partially addressed by the installation of small bag tanks in the wing leading edges. These increased the internal fuel capacity of the F.4 to 414imp gal (1,882 l) a 22 per cent improvement, and therefore added about another 10 minutes to a typical sortie time.

Although this helped, the real breakthrough came with the introduction of inboard underwing pylons which were each capable of carrying a 100imp gal (454 l) drop tank or 1,000lb (454kg) bomb as an alterna-

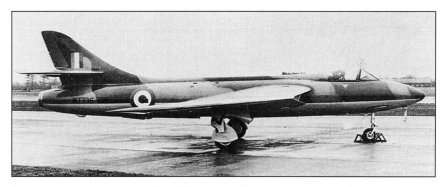

An early production Hunter F.4 (WT736), still without the ammunition link collector tanks under the nose.

tive. This instantly turned the Hunter into a much more useful aeroplane both in terms of potential endurance and for use as a fighter-bomber rather than as a straight interceptor.

These important developments were made available from the 114th Hunter F.4 on the Kingston production line (and the 27th at Blackpool) and could be retrofitted. This was supplemented halfway through the production run by the equally important Mod 228, which was the fitting of two outboard underwing pylons which were also able to carry the 100 gallon drop tanks or racks of unguided rockets for use in the air-to-ground role.

With all possible fuel tankage aboard, the Hunter F.4 could now carry 814imp gal (3,700 l) or 2.4 times that which was available for the Hunter F.1. The advantages this offered

for ferry flying (with overseas deployment of Hunters an important part of its operational history) and combat flexibility – particularly now that bombs and rockets could be carried – are obvious.

The Hunter F.4 also introduced some other innovations, including a full 'flying tail' (in which elevator movement activated the tailplane trim motor) and the single seat Hunter's next major external change, the introduction of gun ammunition belt link collector tanks in blisters under the forward fuselage.

Before this, both spent cartridge cases and the metal belt links had been ejected overboard through chutes in the lower fuselage. This was no problem for the cartridge cases as their weight carried them away from the aircraft, but the lighter links showed a tendency to strike the

Hunter F.4 of 130 Squadron RAF at Bruggen, Germany, during 1957. Note the link collector fairings under the fuselage. (via Philip J Birtles)

There's 16 Hunter F.4s in this 92 Squadron formation – count 'em! (via Philip J Birtles)

A fighter-reconnaissance nose (with five cameras) was fitted to Hunter F.4 WT780. The four guns were retained.

rear fuselage and in some cases the tailplane with resultant minor damage. In addition, the links could be reused if they were somehow collected.

The solution was found in the blisters which would become such a familiar part of the Hunter's outline from late 1955. This pair of 'bumps' were quickly nicknamed 'Sabrinas' after the well endowed actress of the time.

For Home And Abroad

The first Hunter F.4 (WF701) was flown in October 1954 and large scale production began immediately as this new model 'seamlessly' followed the F.1 down Hawker's production lines at both its factories. Total F.4 production for the RAF was 367 aircraft, 190 at Kingston and 177 at Blackpool. Deliveries continued until August 1956.

The F.4 equipped 21 RAF operational squadrons starting with the famous No 111 ('Treble One') at North Weald in January 1955 where the Hunters replaced Meteor F.8s. Two months later the first deliveries were made to a squadron based overseas, in this case No 98 at Jever in Germany, part of the RAF's 2nd Tactical Air Force in that country. Ultimately, 13 German based RAF squadrons were equipped with the Hunter F.4.

The F.4 enjoyed a slightly longer tenure of service with the RAF than its predecessor, but again it was relatively brief with most squadrons swapping their aircraft for much more capable F.6s by 1957. Only three retained the F.4 into 1958 – Nos 14, 74 and 93 – and their aircraft were quickly replaced by the F.6.

The wholesale withdrawal of the Hunter F.4 from RAF service had one disappointing sequel and that was the fact that many were quickly scrapped, most with very low airframe hours logged. Some were saved when the Hunter refurbishment programme got underway later on, but those lost airframes would have been invaluable at a time when Hawker was searching the world for Hunters to refurbish and resell.

The F.4 was the first Hunter variant to provide Hawker with export sales, both British built and manufactured under licence. British export orders for new build aircraft based on the F.4 were 120 for Sweden (designated F.50) and 30 for Denmark (F.51), these 150 aircraft bringing the British F.4 production tally to 517 aircraft.

Of the Swedish aircraft, 96 were built at Blackpool and the remainder at Kingston and were delivered in 1955-56; all the Danish Hunters were built at Kingston and delivered in 1956. It was that year which saw the peak of Hunter production with 230 aircraft leaving the assembly lines.

Hunter F.4 XF310 fitted Fairey Fireflash beam riding air-to-air missiles and lengthened nose.

The grand total of Hunter F.4 production reaches 723 aircraft when licence production in Belgium (95) and the Netherlands (111) is taken into account. Negotiations for licence production in these two countries for the respective air forces went ahead early in the Hunter's career, aided by US financial assistance and after evaluation by a US Air Force team which included 'Chuck' Yeager. The Dutch Hunters were assembled by Fokker-Aviolanda at Amsterdam in 1955-56 and the Belgian aircraft were bolted together by Avions Fairey and SABCA at Gosselies in the same years. The later Hunter F.6 was also built in both countries.

HUNTER F.5

The Sapphire engined equivalent of the Hunter F.4, the F.5 was the last of the Armstrong Siddeley powered variants to be built, future development instead being based around more powerful versions of the Rolls-Royce Avon.

Armstrong Whitworth built 105 Hunter F.5s, the first example (WN954) flying in October 1954, actually one day earlier than its F.4 stablemate. The first five aircraft were used for trials and the first service delivery was made in April 1955. The last F.5 was handed over to the RAF in August 1955.

The Hunter F.5 received all the modifications incorporated in the F.4 during the course of its production run, the leading edge fuel tanks, for example, coming on line on the 46th aircraft. This increased internal capacity to 388imp gal (1,764 l). Otherwise, the basic specification of the F.5 was similar to the F.2 including use of the same Sapphire 101 engine of 8,000lb (35.8kN) thrust.

The Hunter F.5 served with seven RAF Squadrons starting with 263 Squadron at Wattisham in April 1955. All but one of these squadrons had relinquished its F.5s by early 1958, only 1 Squadron hanging on to them for a few more months until June 1958 when they were replaced by F.6s. No 56 Squadron's Hunter F.5s replaced Supermarine Swifts after a brief and unsuccessful period of service. The F.5 achieved one notable feat in that it was the first Hunter mark to see active service, aircraft of Nos 1 and 34 Squadrons participating in the operations accompanying the Suez crisis of 1956.

HUNTER F.6

One of the factors which ultimately inhibited the development of the Hunter to what many considered to be a logical conclusion was the fact that it was subsonic in level flight. Another was that its potential as a ground attack aircraft was not recognised until well into its career and although the ability to carry external stores came with the Mks.4 and 5, it wasn't until the FGA.9 conversion became available in 1960 that this potential was fully realised. In the meantime, Hawker produced the F.6, the final expression of the Hunter interceptor.

There had been previous attempts to build a more advanced Hunter. As early as 1951 Hawker had plans to produce a supersonic Hunter powered by an afterburning Avon and featuring a thinner wing (six per cent thickness/chord ratio) of greater sweep (50 degrees). This project was developed under the company designation P.1083 and would have offered Mach 1.2 performance, greater offensive loads and various other aerodynamic refinements had it gone ahead.

A prototype was ordered and allocated the serial number WN470, a wooden mock-up was built and construction of the first aircraft got underway. By mid 1953 – when the original prototype (WB188) was flying

This Hunter F.5 (WN958) was used for trials designed to assess the type's potential as a fighter-bomber. In this shot the aircraft is carrying two 100imp gal (454 l) drop tanks and 24 three-inch rocket projectiles. WN958 was the fifth Hunter F.5 and lacks the ammunition link collector fairings.

The Hawker P.1099 XH833, prototype for the Hunter F.6. First flown in January 1954, the aircraft lacks the sawtooth leading edge characteristic of the F.6 and later marks, and the link collector fairings.

with an afterburning Avon for its attempt on the world's air speed record – construction of the P.1083 was well advanced and this Hunter was on its way to becoming the RAF's first supersonic fighter.

It was 80 per cent complete in July 1953 when the axe fell and the P.1083 was cancelled, partly due to the easing of international tensions with the end of the Korean War and the funding cutbacks which accompanied that. Instead, Hawker was informed that future developments of the Hunter should be less radical, using the existing basic airframe and wings and more powerful non afterburning versions of the Avon.

The result was the Hunter F.6 with a 200 series Avon offering 10,000lb (44.8kN) of thrust or one-third more than before. RAF Fighter Command would have to wait until 1960 before it had a supersonic fighter in squadron service, the English Electric Lightning.

The 'Large Bore' Avon

Fundamental to the Hunter 6 was the more powerful 200 series Avon, the so called 'large bore' model.

One of the mysteries of the Hunter development programme was the decision to stick with the in many ways troublesome Rolls-Royce Avon at the expense of the Armstrong Siddeley

Sapphire. Perhaps Rolls-Royce had greater political clout, but even the Sapphire had some minor mechanical problems and Armstrong Siddeley went to Rolls-Royce for help, the result being certain exchanges of information which allowed Rolls-Royce to incorporate some of the Sapphire's features in the 200 series Avon, particularly in its compressor design.

The Avon 200 was a largely redesigned engine with a 15 (instead of 11) stage compressor, annular (rather than straight through) combustion chambers and liquid fuel (iso-propyl nitrate) starting system – good for five attempts – in place of the previous cartridge system. Bench testing

Armstrong Whitworth built Hunter F.6 XF449 of 19 Squadron RAF, at this stage lacking the extended wing leading edges. (via Philip J Birtles)

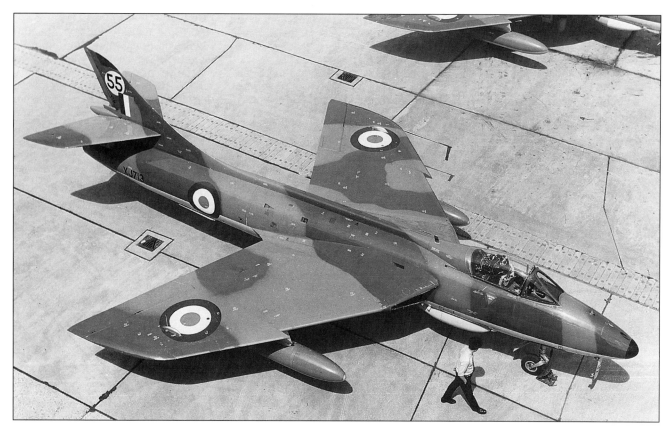

Looking down on Hunter F.6 XJ713 of 229 Operation Conversion Unit shows the definitive sawtooth wing leading edge. The aircraft was photographed at Hatfield in July 1968. (Philip J Birtles)

of the new Avon began in November 1951 and the first production engine was delivered in July 1953.

More Sorting Out

The Hunter F.6 was developed under the Hawker company designation P.1099 and the serial number XH833 was applied to the prototype. This particular aircraft used the centre and front fuselage plus the tail from the stillborn P.1083 in order to expedite construction. Flown by Neville Duke, XH833 flew for the first time on 23 January 1954.

The first production Hunter F.6 (WW592) would not fly until 16 months later in May 1955 and deliveries to the squadrons did not begin until October 1956 while various tests and trials were carried out and modifications incorporated. By the time squadron service began, about 100 Hunter F.6s had been completed but were languishing in Maintenance Units awaiting service clearance. Early Hunter F.6s were in several important ways very different to the definitive aircraft and were referred to as being to an 'interim' standard.

Several problems had to be dealt with, thus causing delays. Initially rated at 10,500lb (47.0kN) thrust, the Avon 203 (and 207) installed in the F.6 had to be derated to 10,000lb (44.8kN) thrust in the interests of engine life following a series of turbine blade failures early on.

Gun firing continued to present some problems with some engine surge still present as well as a new pitch down phenomena which presented itself when the guns were fired. Both required investigation and were ultimately solved, the pitch down cured by fitting blast deflectors which were attached to the gun muzzles. During the course of trials which dealt with these problems, one Hunter fired 40,000 rounds of ammunition whilst flying at maximum speed.

By way of contrast, the Hunter had always suffered from mild pitch up

The underside of Hunter F.6 XF389 displays a pair of 100imp gal (454 l) drop tanks and 24 three-inch rockets under the wings.

tendencies at high altitude and high indicated Mach numbers but the installation of the 'large bore' Avon with its extra power exacerbated the problem to the point where something had to be done.

The solution was found in a modified wing which incorporated extended and drooped outer leading edges which resulted in the distinctive 'sawtooth' leading edge characteristic of later Hunters. This modification increased the wing area slightly and was introduced during the F.6's production run from the 318th F.6 onwards in early 1957 and then retrofitted to earlier aircraft. Some F.4s and F.5s also received this modified wing.

Other changes to the F.6 over its predecessors included a rejigging of the rear fuselage internal fuel tanks due to the Avon 200's rearranged engine accessories. This resulted in a slight reduction in internal fuel capacity (including the wing leading edge tanks) to 392imp gal (1,782 l).

Spurred on by experience in Suez where the need for more range was once again emphasised, Hawker developed 230imp gal (1,045 l) drop tanks which could be fitted to the inner pylons. In combination with 100imp gal (454 l) tanks on the outer pylons, these provided the Hunter F.6 with a substantially increased maximum ferry range to nearly 1,600 nautical miles (2,960km). This range capability was proven in October 1958 when Hawker test pilot Hugh Merewether flew Armstrong Whitworth built F.6 XF374 non stop from Dunsfold to El Edem, Libya – a distance of 1,588nm (2,941km) – in 3 hours 19 minutes.

Production and Exports

Hunter F.6 production for the Royal Air Force amounted to 383 aircraft, of which 264 were built at Kingston and 119 by Armstrong Whitworth at Coventry. Several orders totalling nearly 200 aircraft were cancelled in the infamous Duncan Sandys 1957 Defence White Paper which in effect foretold the end of the manned combat aircraft and predicted a reliance on missiles instead. This theory was completely wrong but nevertheless resulted in the cancellation of several British military aircraft projects. The result was devastation for the British aircraft industry and a loss of impetus which was never really regained.

For the Hunter, this meant cancellation of orders (including all of those to be built at Blackpool) and the be-

Hunter F.6s of 229 OCU: XF387 (top) at Upper Heyford in August 1970 carrying 63 Squadron markings and XG131 (bottom) at Wattisham three years earlier with 234 Squadron markings applied. (Philip J Birtles)

The cockpit of a Hunter F.6 makes an interesting contrast with that of the F-86 Sabre illustrated elsewhere in this book.

mately flown by 19 RAF operational squadrons. Most had relinquished their aircraft by the beginning of 1961 as the Lightning began to take over although 19 Squadron kept its aircraft until November 1962 and 92 Squadron until April 1963. By then the days of the Hunter as a 'fighter' were over, but the full exploitation of its ground attack capabilities as expressed in the FGA.9 conversion (described later) ensured its RAF service had many years to run.

Perhaps the most enduring memory of the Hunter as far as the general public is concerned comes from No 111 Squadron's *Black Arrows* aerobatic team and its black painted aircraft. For the 1958 SBAC show at Farnborough, the team – augmented by aircraft from 43 Squadron – looped a formation of no fewer than 22 Hunters in absolute precision, creating a scene which will never be forgotten by those fortunate enough to witness it.

Export sales increased British Hunter F.6 production to 617 aircraft (including the prototype) to which must be added 237 others built under licence in the Netherlands by Fokker-Aviolanda (144 aircraft) and Belgium by Fairey and SABCA (93), in both cases following on from F.4 production and delivered between 1956 and 1958.

British built export F.6s were all manufactured at Kingston and went to India as the F.56 (145 plus 15 ex RAF delivered 1957-60), and to Switzerland as the F.58 (88 plus 12 ex RAF delivered 1958-60). Both subvariants were similar to the RAF's aircraft but featured braking parachutes. Both countries later became major customers for refurbished Hunters.

The last new build single seat Hunter was Indian F.56 BA360, first flown on 5 October 1960.

ginning of more emphasis on the aircraft's ground attack capabilities.

The last new build single seat Hunter for the RAF was F.6 XK156, first flown in July 1957 and delivered three months later. Subsequent single seaters from the production line were all for export, with aircraft for India following the last RAF aircraft down the line.

As noted above, Hunter F.6s began reaching RAF squadrons from October 1956 starting with Nos 19 at Church Fenton and 66 at Acklington, replacing Meteors and Sabres, respectively. Hunter F.6s were ulti-

Hunter F.6 XG274 of the RAF's 4 Flying Training School in July 1972. Note that the guns have been removed. (Philip J Birtles)

An important export customer for the Hunter was Switzerland, which ordered an initial 100 new build F.58s (equivalent to the RAF's F.6 but with braking parachutes) and refurbished aircraft later. This formation of Swiss Hunters is from the initial batch delivered in 1958-60.

Experimental Sixes

Several Hunter F.6s were used for trial developments, among them the P.1109 project for a Hunter equipped with AI.20 radar in an extended nose and two de Havilland Blue Jay (later Firestreak) missiles under the wings. Two of the Aden guns were removed.

The P.1109 was developed as a private venture by Hawker (with official encouragement, if not money) as

insurance against the failure of the Gloster Javelin all weather fighter. Three F.6s were converted in 1956-57, WW594 (the third F.6) as an aerodynamic prototype plus WW598 and XF378 in 1956-57.

WW598 was designated the P.1109A with the radar but not the missiles and XF378 became the P.1109B with all systems installed. Unfortunately for Hawker's invest-

ment in the P.1109, the Javelin went ahead as planned and the idea was quickly dropped despite being regarded as successful. WW598 went on to be used by the Royal Aircraft Establishment (RAE) for high speed, low altitude gust investigation as part of a data gathering programme for the BAC TSR-2 supersonic strike aircraft.

Another experimental Hunter 6 which flew was WG131 with tip

Three Hunter F.6s were converted to P.1109 configuration in 1956-57 for trials with radar in an extended nose and de Havilland Blue Jay (later Firestreak) missiles under the wings. XF378 was one of them and is photographed here at the Farnborough air show. (BAe via Philip J Birtles)

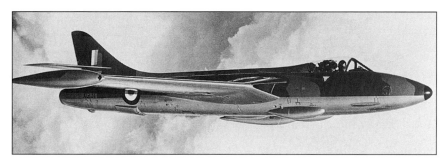

Hunter F.6 XG131 was also used for trials, in this case tip tanks. The idea was unsuccessful as the tanks produced high levels of buffet.

tanks, an idea which was an abject failure as the tanks produced high levels of buffet at relatively low airspeeds. This series of tests was flown in connection with a proposed two seat all weather fighter version of the Hunter (P.1114 with Avon and P.1115 with Sapphire) which went no further than the drawing board.

HUNTER F.6

Powerplant: *One 10,000lb (44.8kN) thrust Rolls-Royce Avon 203 axial flow turbojet; internal fuel capacity 392imp gal (1,782 l), provision for two underwing 230imp gal (1,045 l) or 100imp gal (454 l) drop tanks on inner pylons plus two 100imp gal (454 l) drop tanks on outer pylons.*

Dimensions: *Wing span 33ft 8in (10.26m); length 45ft 10.5in (13.98m); height 13ft 2in (4.01m); wing area 349sq ft (32.4m²).*

Weights: *Empty 14,122lb (6,406kg); normal loaded (clean) 17,600lb (7,983kg); maximum 24,000lb (10,886kg).*

Armament: *Four 30mm Aden cannon in lower forward fuselage with 150 rounds per gun; four underwing pylons for carriage of two 500 or 1,000lb (227/ 454kg) bombs (inner), two 500lb (227kg) bombs (outer) or 24 3-inch (7.6cm) rockets or combination of ordnance and drop tanks.*

Performance: *Max speed 622kt (1,150km/h) at sea level, 545kt (1,009km/h) at 36,000ft, 527kt (976km/h) at 45,000ft; max rate of climb (clean) 17,500ft (5,334m)/min; time to 45,000ft (clean) 6.7min; service ceiling 51,500ft (15,697m); radius of action (clean) 198nm (367km), with drop tanks and rockets 385nm (713km); max ferry range 1,595nm (2,954km).*

HUNTER T.7

One of the apparent anomalies accompanying the Hunter story is the length of time it took to get a two seat operational trainer version of the aircraft into production. Considering the Hunter was a new and more advanced type than the jet fighters which preceded it, the availability of a two seater pretty much right from the start would seem to be a fairly obvious requirement, but it was not to be. The RAF's philosophy was that stu-

dents would be able to convert to the Hunter from the Vampire or Meteor trainers and this is in fact what happened for some time.

When a replacement for the Vampire Trainer was eventually sought, the contract was won by the Folland Gnat. This aircraft was considered barely adequate for pilot training (but looked great at air shows in the hands of the Red Arrows) as it wasn't representative of any RAF operational aircraft, couldn't accommodate all pilots and could not be used in the increasingly important weapons training role. The Hunter two seater happily took over this job when it was eventually introduced, as well as conversion training.

Work on a Hunter trainer began in 1953 as a private venture under the Hawker designation P.1101, the company at that stage looking at a tandem seating arrangement. At that time the RAF was entering into its 'side-by-side seating for trainers' phase, Hawker was duly advised of this, and all design work on the

Hunter trainer now went along that train of thought.

The initial concept of the Hunter two seater was based around the apparently simple concept of the aircraft being identical with the then current single seater (the F.4) from the front fuselage transport joint (just behind the leading edge wing root) with an entirely new cockpit/nose section grafted on. The original idea was for a 'double bubble' shape to the twin canopies and very short fairings aft of them to the fuselage. Wing tunnel testing revealed this to be aerodynamically inefficient and a smoother canopy design was substituted, but later flight testing proved that greater modification was needed.

The new nose section also meant the Aden 'four pack' could not be fitted; individual single or twin gun installations were planned instead.

The Air Ministry issued Specification T.157D to cover the Hunter trainer in early 1954 and construction of the first aircraft was well underway before a government contract was placed for it and a second prototype in July 1954. The first P.1101 (XJ615) would be fitted with a 7,500lb (33.6kN) thrust 100-series Avon and two guns and the second aircraft (XJ627) would have a 10,000lb (44.8kN) thrust 'large bore' Avon 200.

XJ615 was flown on 8 June 1955 by Neville Duke, flight trials immediately revealing aerodynamic problems with the canopy, severe buffeting and unacceptably high cockpit noise levels being recorded due to airflow breakdown as the fairings aft of the canopy being too short. Various

One of the early Hunter T.7 canopy and aft fairing designs which was found to be aerodynamically inefficient.

An early Hunter T.7 trainer (XL564) formates with another Hawker product, the first Kestrel V/STOL fighter-bomber, XS688. The Kestrel was a stepping stone between the P.1127 prototypes and the production Harrier. (BAe)

Hunter T.7 XL596 of 4 Squadron RAF at Wittering in June 1970. (Philip J Birtles)

A March 1970 shot of Hunter T.7 XL579 of the Empire Test Pilots School early in its takeoff run at Hatfield. (Philip J Birtles)

(right) The Folland Gnat T.1 was found to be inadequate in several areas in RAF service and was replaced by the Hunter T.7 in the advanced training role.

'minimum change' configurations were tested – the idea still being to have the aircraft identical to the fighter version aft of the forward transport joint – but the task proved impossible. The problem was finally solved in late 1955 when a large area ruled hood fairing designed by Hawker's Cliff Bore was tested. This proved more than satisfactory and was adopted as the definitive configuration in early 1956. The new nose section added three feet (0.91m) to the overall length.

The second P.1101 with Avon 200 engine was flown in November 1956 and after initial flight trials spent a decade with Martin-Baker as an ejection seat testbed. Hunter trainers with the 'large bore' Avon would account for most export sales of the aircraft, but for the RAF and Royal Navy the smaller engine was settled on (Avon 121 or 122), along with a single Aden gun installed under the starboard forward fuselage.

The RAF initially ordered 65 P.1101s as the Hunter T.7, although this was quickly reduced to 45 so 10 could go to the Royal Navy as the T.8 (see below) and another 10 could be exported to the Netherlands. The production aircraft would be fitted with braking parachutes and the sawtooth extended wing leading edge which had appeared on single seaters. The first of them (XL563) flew in October 1957. Most T.7s were allocated to No 229 Operational Conversion Unit on delivery.

All Hunter T.7s were built at Hawker's Kingston facility, production amounting to 67 aircraft – 45 for the RAF, 20 for the Netherlands and two (as the T.53) for Denmark. The Danish aircraft lacked the extended wing leading edges.

Hunter T.7 XL571 with sawtooth wing leading edge.

This head-on shot of a Hunter T.7 shows the widened forward fuselage to good effect. Note the four 100imp gal (454 l) underwing tanks.

XF310 was one of five single seat Hunter F.4s converted to T.7s in 1959. Soon, Hawker would be doing the same to fill export orders. (BAe)

As an indication of things to come, the RAF also received six T.7s which had been converted from F.4s by Armstrong Whitworth. These were delivered in 1959 and were among the first of the many hundreds of Hunter conversions which would follow over the next decade and a half.

The designation T.7A was given to four RAF aircraft fitted with a TACAN navigation system in 1966.

Hunter T.8M XL602 with Blue Fox radar from the Sea Harrier in the nose. (BAe)

HUNTER T.7
Powerplant: *One 7,550lb (33.8kN) thrust Rolls-Royce Avon 122 axial flow turbojet; internal fuel capacity 414imp gal (1,882 l), provision for two 100imp gal (454 l) underwing drop tanks.*
Dimensions: *Wing span 33ft 8in (10.26m); length 48ft 10.5in (14.90m); height 13ft 2in (4.01m); wing area 349sq ft (32.4m²).*
Weights: *Empty 13,497lb (6,122kg); normal loaded 17,225lb (7,813kg); max loaded 22,000lb (9,979kg).*
Armament: *One 30mm Aden cannon in starboard lower forward fuselage; two underwing pylons each with capacity of 1,000kg (454kg).*
Performance: *Max speed 604kt (1,117km/h) at sea level, 574kt (1,062km/h) at 20,000ft; 528kt (977km/h) at 36,000ft; time to 45,000ft 12.5min; service ceiling 48,900ft (14,904m).*

HUNTER T.8

The Royal Navy's equivalent to the RAF's T.7, the Hunter T.8 differed mainly in having an arrestor hook fitted under the rear fuselage for use with airfield (not aircraft carrier!) arrestor gear.

Ten new production T.8s were delivered from Kingston in 1958 followed by 31 further aircraft converted from F.4s. Aircraft fitted with TACAN

navigational equipment were redesignated T.8Bs and T.8Cs. Three T.8s (XL580, XL602 and XL603) were later modified to test the Sea Harrier's Blue Fox radar in a redesigned nose radome and redesignated Hunter T.8Ms.

The first Hunter T.8 to fly was a conversion from an F.4 (WW664 in March 1958) while the first new build aircraft (XL580) flew two months later. Deliveries to RNAS Lossiemouth began in July 1958, training activities later concentrating on RNAS Yeovilton. Three well known Yeovilton T.8s (XE665, XL580 and XL584) were used by the Flag Officer (Flying Training) at Yeovilton's Fleet Requirements and Direction Unit (or Training Unit) – FRADU/FRADTU – and were conspicuous by their deep gloss blue and white 'Admiral's Barge' colour schemes.

HUNTER FGA.9

The Hunter FGA.9 represented the fully mature aircraft, developed for the ground attack role – at which it excelled – and forming the basis for

the numerous export sales Hawker achieved throughout the 1960s and into the '70s. Considering the effectiveness and commercial success of this Hunter variant, it's interesting to reflect that none of them (whether for the RAF or export) were newly built aircraft. All were converted from existing airframes.

As the 1950s progressed it became clear that the Hunter's days as a purely interceptor fighter were numbered as Britain slowly approached the supersonic age with the development of the English Electric Lightning. This aircraft finally entered service in 1960, by which time the USA, the Soviet Union and France all had supersonic fighters firmly entrenched in the inventories of their air forces.

This was a period of great change and uncertainty in the Royal Air Force. The infamous 1957 Duncan Sandys Defence White Paper had stated that the day of the manned interceptor was over and that future defences against nuclear attack should be based on the deterrent principle. At that time the Lightning

Royal Navy Hunter T.8 XL582 of the Yeovilton Station Flight at its home base in September 1967. Note the hook under the tail for arrested landings on dry land only, definitely not on aircraft carriers! (Philip J Birtles)

The FGA.9 represented the fully mature Hunter developed for the ground attack role, a role at which it excelled. This example has the big 230imp gal (1,045 l) tanks on the inner pylons and 100imp gal (454 l) tanks on the outer positions. (BAe)

Hunter FGA.9 XE624 of 1 Squadron with full external fuel at West Raynhman in September 1968. (Philip J Birtles)

A Hunter FGA.9 of the RAF's Middle East Air Force with typical load: drop tanks on the inner pylons and rocket projectiles outboard. (via Philip J Birtles)

Hunter FGA.9 XE532 of 208 Squadron RAF. (via Philip J Birtles)

was supposed to be the RAF's last manned fighter.

This theory was pure nonsense and did much damage to the RAF and the British aircraft industry before that fact was fully realised by the politicians. One factor they had not foreseen was that future wars would not be all out nuclear global conflicts but smaller disputes involving conventional weapons, men, vehicles and buildings on the ground. Aircraft to attack them would therefore be necessary!

Hawker had already done some investigation along these lines for the Hunter, but it was a 1958 RAF contest to find a replacement for the de Havilland Venom in the ground attack role in the Middle and Far East which resulted in the Hunter FGA.9.

A series of trials were conducted in Aden, examining the Folland Gnat, Percival Jet Provost and the Hunter. The Hunter was at first not included in the evaluation because a cheap solution to the Venom replacement problem was being sought, and the Hawker aircraft was regarded as being far too expensive.

Two Hunter F.6s took part nevertheless, in standard trim apart from having braking parachutes in the tail.

Not surprisingly, the Hunters romped it in, proving to be far and away the most effective of the trio in all aspects except cost. This detail was overcome by the simple expedient of converting existing Hunter F.6s to FGA (Fighter Ground Attack) Mk.9 configuration.

The Hunter Nine

The conversion of Hunter F.6 to FGA.9 resulted in several significant changes: fitting of the completely surge free Avon 207 of 10,150lb (45.5kN) thrust (early aircraft completed to an interim standard had Avon 203s); improved cockpit ventilation and air conditioning; increased oxygen capacity; local strengthening of the structure to allow greater operating weights; the fitting of a braking parachute; incorporation of a small cutaway on the outboard edges of the flaps to allow for the carriage of 230imp gal (1,045 l) drop tanks; fitting a bracing strut between these tanks and the wings so they could be retained in combat; and fitting a bobweight to tighten up the longitudinal control system.

The Hunter 9s fixed armament remained the Aden 'four pack' and the four underwing pylons were capable of carrying a load of up to 7,400lb (3,356kg) between them, comprising various combinations of 230 and/or 100 gallon drop tanks, 500 or 1000lb (227/454kg) bombs, and various air to ground rockets starting with the old 3 inch (76mm) weapon and progressing to 68mm SNEB rockets in Matra pods in RAF service. These rockets were very much the standard RAF armament (in combination with drop tanks) as the Hunter's radius of action fell off substantially when bombs were carried.

The RAF received 128 Hunter FGA.9s converted from F.6s over several contracts between 1959 and 1965. The first conversion was XG135 which was flown in its new configuration in July 1959. Deliveries began in January 1960, No 8 Squadron at Aden receiving the first aircraft. Six other operational squadrons also operated the Hunter FGA.9 (Nos 1, 8, 20, 43, 54 and 208) and Nos 45 and 58 also flew the aircraft for tactical training. The last operational squadron to use the FGA.9 was No 8 until December 1971. 1 Squadron's Hunters were replaced by another Hawker product – the Harrier – while Nos 43 and 54 converted to Phantoms. The remaining squadrons were disbanded.

As mentioned earlier, the Hunter FGA.9 formed the basis of many conversions for export customers. These are discussed below and in the following chapter.

HUNTER FGA.9

Powerplant: One 10,150lb (48.7kN) thrust Rolls-Royce Avon 207 axial flow turbojet; internal fuel capacity 392imp gal (1,782 l), provision for 230imp gal (1,045 l) or 100imp gal (454 l) underwing drop tanks.

Cockpit: Pressurised and air conditioned with Martin-Baker Type 2H or 3H fully automatic ejection seat; pressure differential 3.5psi (0.25kg/cm³).

Wing: Aspect ratio 3.33; mean chord 10ft 2.5in (3.11m); thickness/chord ratio 8.5; anhedral 1deg; incidence 1.5deg; sweepback at quarter chord 39.9deg.

Dimensions: Wing span 33ft 8in (10.26m); length 45ft 10.5in (13.98m); height 13ft 2in (4.01m); tailplane span 11ft 10in (3.60m); wheel track 14ft 9in (4.49m); wheelbase 15ft 9in (4.80m); wing area 349sq ft (32.4m²).

Systems: Air conditioning and pressurisation by engine bleed air; hydraulic system for undercarriage, wheel brakes, air brake, flaps, ailerons and elevators; dual 28 volt electrical systems for avionics, services, rudder trim tab and flying tail operation.

Weights: Empty 14,572lb (6,610kg); loaded (clean) 18,360lb (8,328kg); max loaded 24,422lb (11,078kg).

Armament: Four 30mm Aden cannon in lower forward fuselage; four underwing pylons with total maximum combined capacity of 7,400lb (3,356kg) for carriage of combinations of 230imp gal (1,045 l) or 100imp gal (454 l) drop tanks, 500 or 1,000lb (227/454kg) bombs, 12 x 3in (76mm) rockets, 24 or 37 2in (51mm) folding fin rockets. Typical RAF load two 230imp gal tanks on inboard pylons, two Matra pods each with 19 x 68mm SNEB rockets.

Performance: Max speed (clean) 622kt (1,150km/h) at sea level, 545kt (1,009km/h) at 36,000ft; economical cruise 400kt (740km/h); max climb rate (clean) 16,500ft (5,029m)/min, initial climb (typical load) 8,000ft (2,438m)/min; time to 40,000ft (clean) 5.5min, (loaded) 12.5min; service ceiling 50,000ft (15,240m); takeoff run (clean) 2,100ft (640m); landing roll (with parachute) 2,200ft (670m); radius of action (clean) 276nm (511km), radius of action (two 230gal tanks plus rockets) 472nm (874km); radius of action (two 1,000lb bombs and two 100gal tanks) 190nm (352km); max ferry range 1,595nm (2,955km).

Hunter FR.10 XF426 of 229 Operational Conversion Unit displays its lengthened, camera equipped nose. (via Philip J Birtles)

HUNTER FR.10

The final Hunter mark for the RAF, the FR.10 fighter-reconnaissance variant was also a conversion of the F.6. It incorporated the FGA.9 modifications plus the replacement of the nose mounted gun ranging radar with one forward and two oblique cameras in a lengthened nose which increased the aircraft's overall length by three inches (7.6cm) to 46ft 1.5in (14.06m).

Specification FR.146D was issued to Hawker in 1957 to cover this version and a trial camera installation was tested in F.6 XF429 from November 1958. Deliveries of 32 production conversions began in September 1960 and were completed the following year. The Hunter FR.10 fully equipped only two RAF Squadrons: Nos 2 and 4 in Germany.

Hunter FR.10 XE596 just airborne from Chivenor in August 1969. All 33 FR.10s were converted from F.6s. (Philip J Birtles)

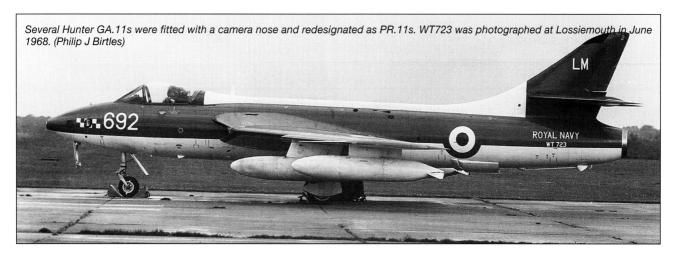

Several Hunter GA.11s were fitted with a camera nose and redesignated as PR.11s. WT723 was photographed at Lossiemouth in June 1968. (Philip J Birtles)

The Royal Navy received 40 Hunter GA.11s, all converted from F.4s. Note the Meteor trainer in the background of this shot. (BAe)

HUNTER GA.11

The need for a single seat weapons training aircraft for the Royal Navy resulted in the Hunter GA.11, another conversion variant roughly similar to the RAF's FGA.9 but with several differences, the most important one being that the GA.11 was based on the Hunter F.4 and therefore featured the 'small bore' Avon 100 series engine.

As the GA.11 was to be used for ground attack training using underwing stores, the Aden gun pack was removed and new items of equipment included a TACAN navigation system, a Harley Light in the nose for target acquisition at night in some aircraft, an airfield arrestor hook and the ability to carry naval air-to-surface weapons such as the 2in (50mm) podded rocket.

Forty F.4s were converted to GA.11 standards in 1962-63, the first 26 of which featured only two underwing stores pylons while the remainder had four pylons. All had sawtooth extended leading edge wings. Some were fitted with camera noses and designated PR.11s.

The first GA.11 conversion was XE712 which flew in April 1962. Royal Navy operators of the aircraft include Nos 738, 739 and 764 (training) Squadrons and the Fleet Requirements and Air Direction Unit (FRADU).

HUNTER Mk.12

While most of the refurbished and exported Hunter two seaters featured the big Avon 200 series engine, all the RAF and RN two seaters – expect one – were powered by the smaller Avon 100.

The exception was the sole Hunter Mk.12 (XE531) which in previous lives had been an F.6 and FGA.9. After conversion, this Hunter was delivered to the Royal Aircraft Establishment (RAE) at Farnborough in 1963 for use as systems development aircraft for the BAC TSR.2 strike aircraft. When the TSR.2 was cancelled the Hunter 12 was used for various tests and trials for which it was equipped with a head up display (HUD) and a vertical nose camera.

Painted a distinctive green and white, XE531 survived until March 1982 when it crashed on takeoff at Farnborough.

HUNTER T.66

The designation Hunter T.66 broadly covers the many Avon 200 powered two seat aircraft which were rebuilt (exclusively from single seaters) and subsequently exported to various air forces around the world.

There were many variations on the Hunter T.66 theme, but fundamentally the aircraft featured the powerplant

Hawker's famous Hunter T.66 demonstrator, civil registered as G-APUX and armed with two working 30mm Aden cannon. T.66 was the general designation given to Hunter trainers powered by the Avon 200 series engine. (BAe)

The finished product. This Jordanian Hunter T.66B started life as a Dutch built F.6. (Hawker via Philip J Birtles)

and underwing stores capacity of the FGA.9 along with two Aden guns mounted in the lower forward fuselage.

Some new production T.66s were also built, 22 for India in 1959-60 and a single T.66B for Jordan in 1960. This was the last new build Hunter to emerge from Hawker's factories. All these T.66s were built at Kingston.

Perhaps the best known Hunter T.66 was Hawker's demonstrator, G-APUX. Designated the Hunter Mk.66A, this aircraft is probably the only one ever to appear on the British civil register armed with two working 30mm Aden cannon!

The aircraft was built up from the parts of various other Hunters including the centre and rear fuselage of a Belgian F.6, the wings, fin and rudder of another Belgian aircraft, the engine and gearbox of an ex RAF F.6 (XE378) and the forward fuselage/cockpit of ground display unit originally prepared for exhibition at the 1959 Paris Air Show.

First flown in August 1959, G-APUX was used for demonstration flights and various trials including the fitting of nosewheel braking and unique 350imp gal (1,591 l) ferry tanks. From 1963 the aircraft was leased to a number of air forces including Iraq, Jordan and Lebanon and after refurbishment was sold to Chile as a T.72 in 1967.

REFURBISHED EXPORTS

Having established that just about any Hunter variant could be converted to any other thanks to the FGA.9, T.7 and T.8 conversion programmes for the RAF and RN, Hawker in 1962 embarked on a lucrative and successful 'second life' for the aircraft involving the refurbishment and resale of Hunters for export. The overall programme involved nearly 400 aircraft and continued until early 1975. Because of the general lack of former RAF Hunters for conversion (due to many aircraft being scrapped and others converted to FGA.9s and trainers) many of the export conversions were based on former Belgian and Dutch aircraft.

Negotiations resulted in Hawker obtaining aircraft from these sources in 1962-63, many with very low hours on their airframes. It is interesting to note that all of Hawker's export sales contracts had a clause which gave the company first option in repurchasing any Hunters which came up for disposal once they were no longer wanted by the purchasing air force. This was originally intended to prevent the aircraft 'falling into the wrong hands' but in this case came in very handy once the idea of the refurbishing programme was established.

Another Jordanian Hunter (an FGA.73A) which started life as something entirely different, in this case an RAF F.4. The rebuild resulted in an aircraft equivalent to the very different FGA.9. (Philip J Birtles)

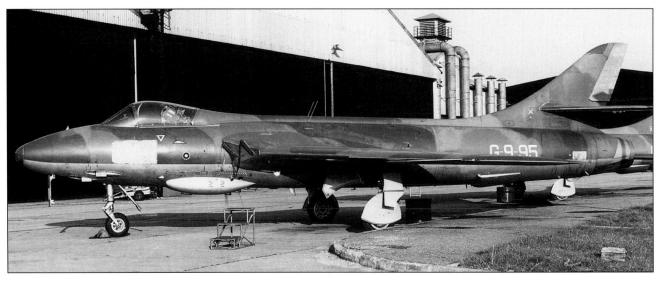

The unfinished product! A former Belgian Hunter F.6 awaits its turn for refurbishment. This particular aircraft was converted to an FGA.59 for Iraq. (Hawker via Philip J Birtles)

All the conversion work was performed by the manufacturer, most single seaters ending up in a form equivalent to the RAF's FGA.9, while most two seaters had a specification similar to the T.66 described above. Trainers with designations in the T.70 series were generally of the lower powered type and were therefore similar to the RAF's T.7.

Hunters were also sourced from the RAF as the programme progressed and retired F.6s became available, while ex RAF F.4s and Swedish aircraft to the same standard were also used. At the height of the programme, the cancellation of orders and destruction of Hunter airframes was becoming bitterly regretted as there is no doubt that Hawker could have sold many more refurbished – and new – aircraft had they been available.

Down but not out. Hunter F.4 WV326 at the end of its RAF flying life after retirement in 1960. It spent 12 years as an instructional airframe (as 7669M) before returning to its manufacturer to be rebuilt as an FR.71A for Chile. (Philip J Birtles)

HUNTER PRODUCTION

New Build Aircraft

Note: This table summarises new Hunter production between 1951 and 1960 and amounts to 1,972 aircraft of which 959 were built at Kingston, 299 at Blackpool, 269 by Armstrong Whitworth at Coventry, 256 in the Netherlands and 189 in Belgium. Production by mark was 6 prototypes, 139 F.1s, 45 F.2s, 725 F.4s and export equivalents, 105 F.5s, 852 F.6s and export equivalents, 67 T.7s and export equivalents, 10 T.8s and 23 T.66s.

Abbreviations: del – delivery; ff – first flight; Qty – quantity.

Model	Qty	Serial Nos	Factory	Customer/Remarks
P.1067	1	WB188	Kingston	1st prototype ff 20/07/51
P.1067	1	WB195	Kingston	2nd prototype ff 05/05/52
P.1067	1	WB202	Kingston	3rd prototype ff 30/11/52
F.1	41	WT555-WT595	Kingston	RAF del 07-09/54
F.1	50	WT611-WT660	Kingston	RAF del 08-11/54
F.1	22	WT679-WT700	Kingston	RAF del 10-11/54
F.1	12	WW599-WW610	Blackpool	RAF
F.1	14	WW632-WW645	Blackpool	RAF
F.2	34	WN888-WN921	Coventry	RAF, WN888 ff 14/10/53
F.2	11	WN943-WN953	Coventry	RAF del 11/54-04/55
F.4	23	WT701-WT723	Kingston	RAF del 02-05/55 WT701 ff 20/10/54
F.4	47	WT734-WT780	Kingston	RAF del 03-05/55
F.4	17	WT795-WT811	Kingston	RAF del 04/06-55
F.4	29	WV253-WV281	Kingston	RAF del 05-06/55
F.4	21	WV314-WV334	Kingston	RAF del 06-07/55
F.4	50	WV363-WV412	Kingston	RAF del 06-10/55
F.4	3	WW589-WW591	Kingston	RAF del 11/55
F.4	20	WW646-WW665	Blackpool	RAF del 03-05/55
F.4	33	XE657-XE689	Blackpool	RAF del 05-08/55
F.4	17	XE702-XE718	Blackpool	RAF del 07-11/55
F.4	36	XF289-XF324	Blackpool	RAF del 11/55-03/56
F.4	14	XF357-XF370	Blackpool	RAF del 03/56
F.4	22	XF932-XF953	Blackpool	RAF del 04-04/56
F.4	33	XF967-XF999	Blackpool	RAF del 05-08/56
F.4	2	XG341-XG342	Blackpool	RAF del 07/56
F.4	96	N-101/N-196	Holland	Netherlands del 1955-56
F.4	112	ID-1/ID-112	Belgium	Belgium del 1955-56
F.50	24	34001-34024	Kingston	Sweden (F.4 equiv) del 08/55-10/56
F.50	96	34025-34120	Blackpool	Sweden (F.4 equiv) del 1956-58
F.51	30	401-430	Kingston	Denmark (F.4 equiv) del 01-08/56
F.5	39	WN954-WN992	Coventry	RAF del 03-05/55
F.5	50	WP101-WP150	Coventry	RAF del 05-06/55
F.5	16	WP179-WP194	Coventry	RAF del 06-08/55
P.1099	1	XF833	Kingston	F.6 prototype ff 22/01/54
F.6	7	WW592-WW598	Kingston	RAF trials built 1955
F.6	36	XE526-XE561	Kingston	RAF del 01-03/56
F.6	50	XE579-XE628	Kingston	RAF del 04-06/56
F.6	14	XE643-XE656	Kingston	RAF del 07-08/56
F.6	11	XG127-XG137	Kingston	RAF del 08-10/56
F.6	19	XG150-XG168	Coventry	RAF del 1956
F.6	4	XG169-XG172	Kingston	RAF del 08-10/56
F.6	27	XG185-XG211	Kingston	RAF del 09-10/56
F.6	15	XG225-XG239	Kingston	RAF del 09-11/56
F.6	24	XG251-XG274	Kingston	RAF del 11/56-01/57
F.6	10	XG289-XG298	Kingston	RAF del 12/56-02/57
F.6	15	XJ632-XJ646	Kingston	RAF del 01-03/57
F.6	23	XJ673-XJ695	Kingston	RAF del 02-05/57
F.6	7	XJ712-XJ718	Kingston	RAF del 03-05/57
F.6	21	XK136-XK156	Kingston	RAF del 05-10/57
F.6	17	XF373-XF389	Coventry	RAF del 1956
F.6	50	XF414-XF463	Coventry	RAF del 1956
F.6	33	XF495-XF527	Coventry	RAF del 1956
F.6	93	N-201/N-293	Holland	Netherlands del 1956-58
F.6	144	IF-1/IF-144	Belgium	Belgium del 1956-58
F.56	32	BA201-BA232	Kingston	India (F.6 equiv) del 10-12/57
F.56	112	BA249-BA360	Kingston	India (F.6 equiv) del 08/58-12/60
F.58	88	J-4013/J-4100	Kingston	Swiss (F.6 equiv) del 06/59-04/60
P.1101	1	XJ615	Kingston	trainer 1st prototype ff 08/07/55
P.1101	1	XJ627	Kingston	trainer 2nd prototype ff 17/11/56
T.7	17	XL563-XL579	Kingston	RAF del 12/57-11/58
T.7	1	XL583	Kingston	RAF del 07/58
T.7	2	XL586-XL587	Kingston	RAF del 08/58

Model	Qty	Serial Nos	Factory	Customer/Remarks
T.7	7	XL591-XL597	Kingston	RAF del 09-10/58
T.7	2	XL600-XL601	Kingston	RAF del 11/58
T.7	1	XL605	Kingston	RAF del 12/58
T.7	15	XL609-XL623	Kingston	RAF del 12/58-02/59
T.7	20	N-301/N-320	Kingston	Netherlands del 07/58-02/59
T.53	2	35-271/35-272	Kingston	Denmark (T.7 equiv) del 11-12/58
T.8	3	XL580-XL582	Kingston	Royal Navy del 05-08/58
T.8	2	XL584-XL585	Kingston	Royal Navy del 10/58
T.8	2	XL598-XL599	Kingston	Royal Navy del 12/58
T.8	3	XL602-XL604	Kingston	Royal Navy del 12/59-01/59
T.66	16	BS361-BS376	Kingston	India del 04/59-03/60
T.66	6	BS485-BS490	Kingston	India del 07-11/60
T.66B	1	714	Kingston	Jordan del 07/60

SUMMARY OF HUNTER EXPORT CONVERSIONS

Note: This table excludes resales and covers only countries which took delivery of conversions from the manufacturer up until 1975.

Customer	Model	Qty	Date	Notes
Rhodesia	FGA.9	12	1963	ex RAF F.6
Peru	F.52	16	1956	ex RAF F.4
	T.62	1	1960	ex RAF F.4
India	F.56	16	1957	ex RAF F.6
	F.56A	36	1966-67	ex Begian/Dutch F.6
	F.56A	8	1968-69	ex RAF F.6
	F.56A	3	1969	ex RAF F.6
	F.56A	6	1969-70	ex RAF/Dutch F.6
	T.66D	12	1966-67	ex Belgian F.6
	T.66E	5	1973	ex Belgian F.6
Kuwait	FGA.57	4	1965-66	ex Belgian F.6
	T.67	5	1965-69	ex Belgian/RAF F.6
Switzerland	F.58	12	1958	ex RAF F.6
	F.58A	30	1971-73	ex RAF F.4/F.6/GA.11, Dutch T.7
	F.58A	22	1974-75	ex RAF F.4/F.6
	T.68	8	1974-75	ex RAF F.4/Swedish F.50
Iraq	FGA.59	24	1964-65	ex Belgian/Dutch F.6
	FGA.59A	18	1965-67	ex Belgian/Dutch F.6
	FGA.59B	4	1966	ex Dutch F.6
	T.69	5	1964-65	ex Belgian/Dutch F.6
Saudi Arabia	F.60	4	1966	ex RAF F.6
	T.70	2	1966	ex RAF T.7
Jordan	FGA.73	2	1968	ex RAF F.6
	FGA.73A	13	1969-71	ex RAF F.4/6, Dutch F.6
	FGA.73B	3	1971	ex RAF F.4, Dutch F.6
	T.66B	2	1966-69	ex Dutch F.6
Lebanon	T.66C	3	1965-66	ex Belgian F.6
	FGA.70	4	1966	ex Belgian F.6
Chile	FGA.71	28	1966-74	ex Begian/Dutch F.6, RAF F.4/6
	FR.71A	6	1968-74	ex RAF F.4/6
	T.72	7	1968-74	ex Belgian/Dutch F.6, RAF F.4/6
Singapore	FGA.74	12	1970-71	ex RAF F.6
	FR.74A	4	1971	ex RAF F.6
	FR.74B	22	1972-73	ex RAF F.4/6
	T.75	4	1969-70	ex RAF F.4, RN T.8, Dutch T.7
	T.75A	5	1972-73	ex RAF/RN F.4/GA.11
Abu Dhabi	FGA.76	7	1970-71	ex RAF F.4
	FR.76A	3	1971	ex RAF F.4/6
	T.77	2	1970	ex Dutch T.7
Qatar	FGA.78	3	1971	ex Dutch F.6
	T.79	1	1971	ex Dutch T.7
Kenya	FGA.80	4	1974-75	ex RAF F.4/6
	T.81	2	1974	ex RN T.8

RAF AND RN CONVERSIONS

Conversion	Qty	Delivery
T.7 from F.4	5	02-05/59
T.8 from F.4	18	1958-59
T.8B from F.4	3	1964
T.8C from F.4	10	1954-65
FGA.9 from F.6	128	1959-65
FR.10 from F.6	33	1960-61

Fleet Air Arm

London

R.N.A.S. Yeovilton

T.8

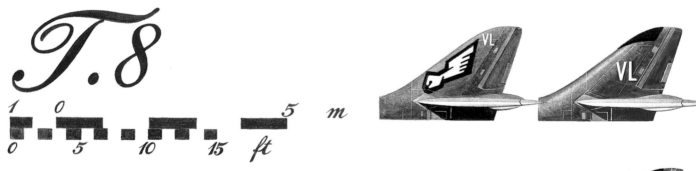

VL

VL

VL

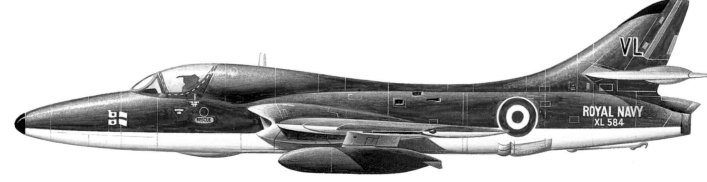

RESCUE

ROYAL NAVY

XL 584

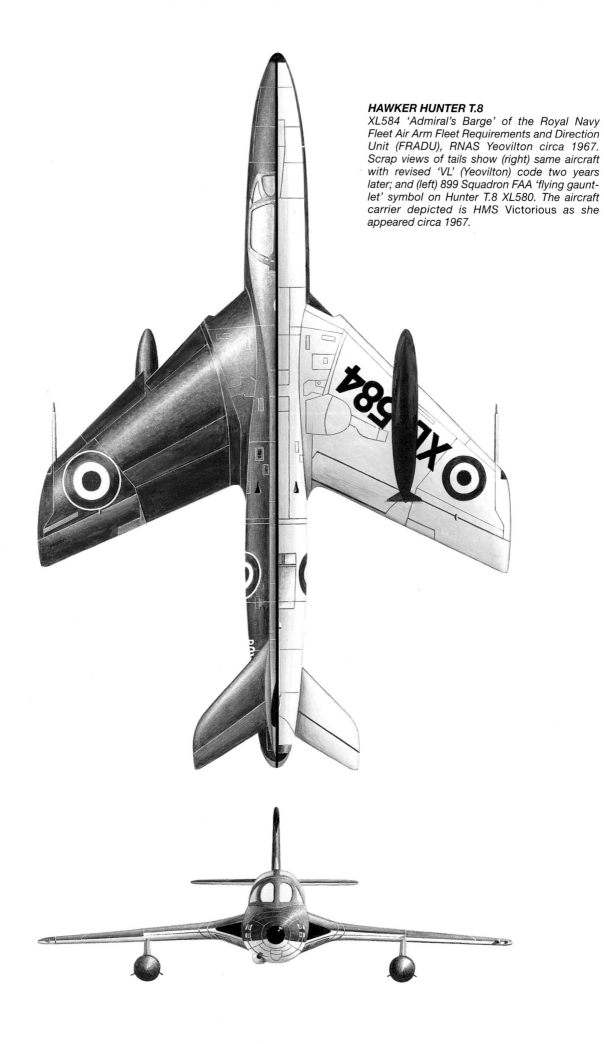

HAWKER HUNTER T.8
XL584 'Admiral's Barge' of the Royal Navy Fleet Air Arm Fleet Requirements and Direction Unit (FRADU), RNAS Yeovilton circa 1967. Scrap views of tails show (right) same aircraft with revised 'VL' (Yeovilton) code two years later; and (left) 899 Squadron FAA 'flying gauntlet' symbol on Hunter T.8 XL580. The aircraft carrier depicted is HMS Victorious as she appeared circa 1967.

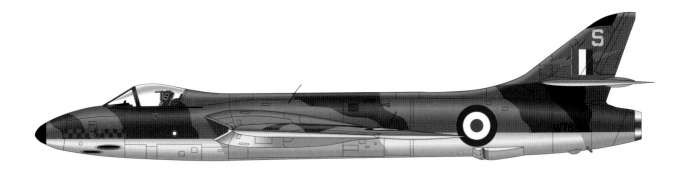

Hunter F.1 WT692/S of 54 Squadron RAF 1955.

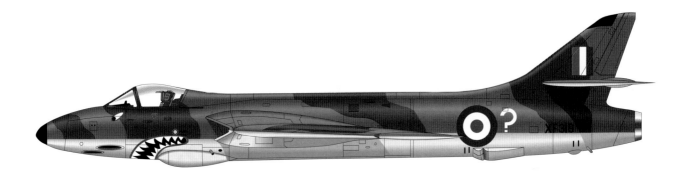

Hunter F.4 XF319/? of 112 Squadron RAF.

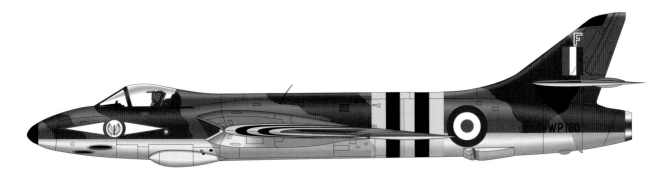

Hunter F.5 WP180/F of 1 Squadron RAF during Suez Crisis November 1956.
Note black and yellow identification bands.

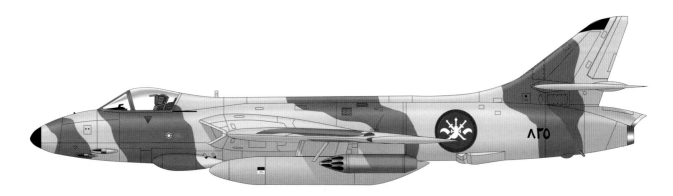

Hunter FGA.9 of 6 Squadron Sultan of Oman's Air Force.

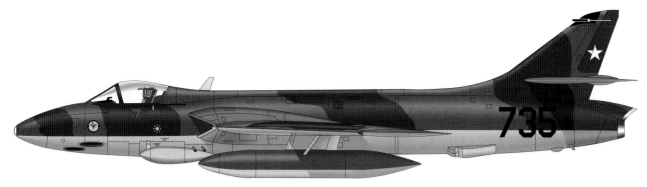

Hunter FR.71A J-735 of Gruppo 8 Chilean Armed Forces.

Hawker P.1067 prototype WB188 at time of first flight 20 July 1951.
Note anti spin parachute fairing above jetpipe.

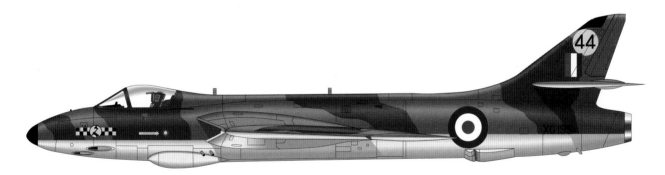

Hunter F.6 XG199/44 of 229 Operational Conversion Unit/63 Squadron RAF 1969.

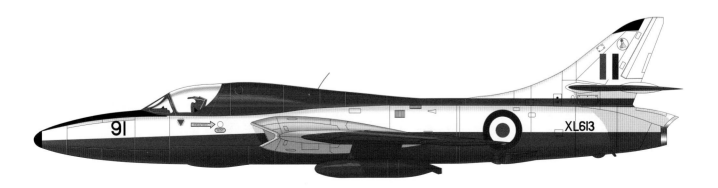

Hunter T.7 XL613/91 of 4 Flying Training School RAF.

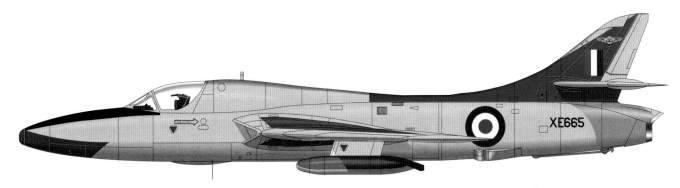

Hunter T.8 XE665 of 208 Squadron RAF 1980.

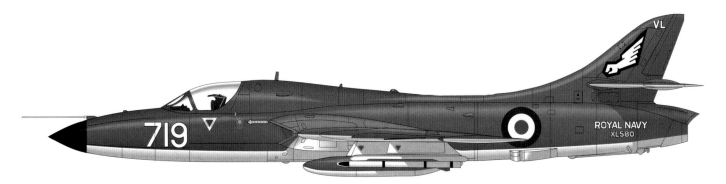

Hunter T.8M XL580/717 of 899 Squadron Royal Navy Fleet Air Arm 1980.
Note revised nose with Blue Fox radar.

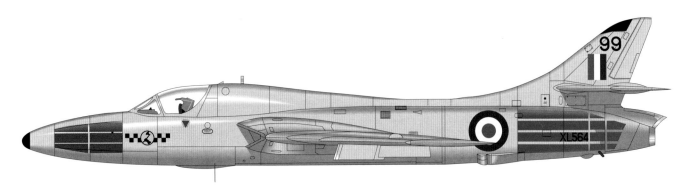

Hunter T.7 XL564/99 of 229 Operational Conversion Unit/63 Squadron 1968.

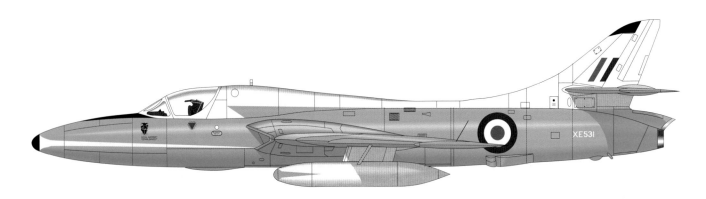

Hunter Mk.12 XE531 of Royal Aircraft Establishment, Farnborough.

HUNTERS AROUND THE WORLD

The Hawker Hunter saw widespread service around the world as a front line combat aircraft from the mid 1950s until well into the 1970s and 1980s in some cases, flying with the air forces of 21 nations. Even as the 21st century approaches, a handful of countries still operate the Hunter, but in rapidly diminishing numbers.

Two major users of the type – Britain's Royal Air Force and Switzerland – retired the Hunter in 1994 after 40 and 35 years' service respectively. This length of service gives some clue to one of the Hunter's major assets, its longevity thanks to sturdy construction and adaptability.

Many of the Hunter's operators purchased aircraft which had been refurbished and upgraded in most cases to a mark and standard totally different to that which it had originally been built. Some 600 Hunters out of the total production run of 1,972 were refurbished in this way, of which about two-thirds were exported (or 're-exported' in many cases).

This refurbishment programme was remarkable in itself and pre-empted by some years a fact of combat aircraft life which is taken for granted in these days of budget restrictions and the need to extend the life and capability of aircraft as a matter of necessity. The Hunter's ability to be relatively easily modified from any mark to any other (including single to two seaters) made it ideal for this kind of programme and great export success was achieved as a result.

New aircraft were also exported to Denmark, Sweden, India, Switzerland and Jordan from British production lines (a total of 407 aircraft) while licence production in the Netherlands and Belgium accounted for a further 445 Hunters.

The sales to NATO members Belgium, Denmark and the Netherlands were of great significance to the Hunter programme. They came about as a result of the appearance of the Soviet MiG-15 fighter over Eastern

Europe at a time when many European air forces were run down. The threat was recognised and several countries took delivery of F-86 Sabres with the help of US money, while others looked closer to home for their new fighters.

Because any purchase by European nations would be largely financed by American 'off shore' funding, the Hunter was extensively evaluated by a US team in 1952-53 and found to be more than satisfactory in most respects. The result was licence production in Belgium and the Netherlands and direct sales to Denmark, which did not have its own aircraft manufacturing industry. These purchases were all made with the considerable help of the Americans, although the Hunter's early problems in British service caused a few heartaches and resulted in the much improved Mk.4 being the basis of the first export models.

Another significant European order was that by Switzerland, a country

Swiss Hunters regularly operated from a most unusual airfield during exercises – stretches of road such as this.

Hunter F.6 XE587 – minus its guns – of the Empire Test Pilots School at Boscombe Down in March 1971 to celebrate the 50th anniversary of the Aeroplane & Armament Experimental Establishment. (Philip J Birtles)

noted for its thorough evaluation methods. Its decision to order Hunters after a competitive evaluation against several other types undoubtedly influenced others to look closely at the British fighter.

What follows is a summary of the nations which operated the Hawker Hunter:

Abu Dhabi

One of several small Arab states which established air forces with the help of the British after its withdrawal from the Persian Gulf area, Abu Dhabi ordered 12 refurbished Hunters from Hawker in 1969. These comprised seven FGA.76s and three FGA.76As (converted from ex RAF F.4s and F.6s) and two 'small bore' T.77s which were former Dutch T.7s.

The aircraft were delivered in 1970-71 and featured braking parachutes and provision for target towing. They served with a single

squadron at Sharjah until 1975 when they were presented to Jordan to help replace Hunters lost in the 1973 Yom Kippur War. They were replaced by Mirages.

Belgium

The evaluation of the Hunter by US personnel for use by NATO nations resulted in the Hunter F.4 being selected for use by the *Force Aerienne Belge/Belgishe Luchtmacht* with licence production undertaken in Belgium by Avions Fairey and SABCA at Gosselies. The 112 licence built F.4s entered service in 1955 and flew with Nos 1, 7 and 9 Wings as part of NATO's 2nd Tactical Air Force.

Production switched to the Hunter F.6 in 1956, 144 of these being built between then and 1958. The Hunters served Belgium until the mid 1960s when they were replaced by Lockheed F-104 Starfighters and many aircraft were bought back by Hawker

from 1962 for use in the refurbishment programme. Most aircraft had very low airframe hours logged with many aircraft spending most of their lives to that point in storage.

Chile

The *Fuerza Area de Chile* (FAC) has been a major user of the Hunter since the mid 1960s and retains the type in service three decades later. Chile has had a turbulent political relationship with Britain, falling out of favour in 1974 and returning to the 'good books' in the early 1980s. Chile provided assistance to Britain during the Falklands War.

Chile purchased 41 refurbished Hunters in several batches between 1966 and 1974, comprising 28 FGA.71s, six FR.71As and seven T.72s. All but one of these Hunters were converted from Belgian, Dutch and RAF F.4s and F.6s, the exception being one of the T.72s which had

Belgian built Hunter F.4 ID-60.

Chilean Hunter T.72.

previously served as Hawker's famed civil registered demonstrator, G-APUX.

Equipping two squadrons, the serviceability level of the Chilean Hunters suffered with the imposition of a British arms embargo, but while the Falklands War was raging, more Hunters were shipped from Britain to the South American air arm. Further batches delivered later in 1982 raised the number of 'new' Hunter FGA.9s shipped to Chile during the year to 16 along with a stock of spare parts.

By late 1994 Chile still had about 30 Hunters in service. A recent programme to upgrade them with the fitting of radar warning receivers and chaff/flare dispensers indicates they will remain on strength until about the turn of the century, despite the arrival into service of more modern types such as the Mirage 50 and Northrop F-5E.

One of the contributing factors in Britain's 1974 decision to place an embargo on Chile was the overthrow of President Allende in 1973. In September of that year, FAC Hunter FGA.71s were used in a rocket attack on the presidential palace.

Denmark

The Royal Danish Air Force placed an order for 30 Hunters to F.4 standards in July 1954 as part of the NATO/US deal which saw Belgium and the Netherlands building the aircraft under licence. Denmark's much smaller order was placed directly with Hawker, and deliveries of the aircraft (designated F.51) were carried out between January and August 1956. The serial numbers 401 to 430 were applied.

These aircraft lacked the wing leading edge 'sawtooth' extensions which were applied to most British F.4s and this feature was also missing from the two Hunter T.53s (equivalent to the RAF's T.7) delivered late 1958.

Two of the F.51s were later converted to trainers.

The Hunters were flown by a single *Kongelige Dansk Flyvevaben* unit (ESK 724) until 1974 when the 21 survivors were retired. Most found their way back to Britain for issue to museums, although at least one (Spencer Flack's G-HUNT) stayed in the air as a civil operated warbird.

One particular survivor (aircraft number 415) achieved some fame just a few weeks after having been delivered to Denmark. The aircraft suffered a flameout while on the approach to Skrydstrup, the pilot ejected about three miles out and the Hunter continued on its merry way to make a perfect wheels up landing on the runway! Damage was minimal and the Hunter was soon repaired and back in service.

India

A substantial operator of the Hunter with more than 250 aircraft entering service from both new production and refurbished sources, the Indian Air Force remains in the mid 1990s the world's biggest operator of the type with at least 80 aircraft still in service in late 1994.

India's Hunter purchases are notable for a couple of firsts, particularly with the regard to the 'large bore' Avon variants in that it was the first overseas order for the new family of aircraft, in both single and two seat forms.

Indian interest in the Hunter began in late 1954 and after a series of evaluations (and the arrival of the much improved Mk.6) an order for 160 aircraft was placed in July 1957. Similar to the RAF's F.6 apart from the addition of a braking parachute, these aircraft were designated the F.56 for Indian service and deliveries were able to begin within three months. The order came at an excellent time for Hawker, which had just suffered cancellations for Hunters in the wake of the 1957 British Defence White Paper.

The first 32 Indian Hunters were completed from the part of the cancelled RAF order and the next 16 were only slightly second hand former RAF aircraft which were refurbished and modified to Indian standards. These Hunters were all delivered by the end of 1957, the remaining 112 were delivered to India between 1958 and 1960 and serialled BA201 to BA360. A further order for 22 two seaters (T.66s) was placed and the aircraft delivered in 1959-60 as BS361-376 and BS485-490. Indian Air Force Hunters initially served with Nos 7, 20 and 27 Squadrons at Ampala and Nos 5 and 17 Squadrons at Poona.

A further 65 refurbished Hunters entered IAF service between 1966 and 1970, ordered as a result of attrition sustained in normal peacetime flying and losses recorded during the 1965 India-Pakistan war. Comprising 53 F.56A single seaters (all to FGA.9 standards) and 12 T.66D trainers, these aircraft were converted from a mixture of former Belgian, Dutch and British Hunters. The last Indian Hunter order was for five T.66Es (refurbished from ex RAF F.6s) delivered in 1973. The T.66, T.66D and T.66E differed mainly in their avionics fit and all featured braking parachutes.

In late 1994 the Indian Air Force

India received more than 250 Hunters from both new and refurbished production. BS361 is a T.66 delivered new in 1959. (via Philip J Birtles)

Indian Hunter F.56A A1012, converted from a Dutch F.6.

still had more than 80 Hunters in service comprising at least 60 F.56/As and 20 T.66s.

India's Hunters have seen more combat than any others and have been used operationally on four recorded occasions: the 1965 and 1971 wars with Pakistan, border clashes with China in 1962 and during the invasion of the Portuguese colony of Goa in 1961. Hunters were reportedly used to provide top cover during this operation, while the border dispute with China saw Indian Hunters engaging Chinese MiG-17s.

The major conflicts in which Indian Hunters were involved are the two wars with Pakistan in 1965 and 1971. The first was fought over the integration of Kashmir into Pakistan in 1957, the uneasy peace which followed being shattered in September 1965. India had six operational Hunter squadrons at the time (Nos 7, 14, 17, 20, 27 and 37) and their aircraft were used for both air defence and ground attack duties.

This so called '17 Day War' saw Pakistani F-86F Sabres destroy nine Hunters for the loss of six of their own. In one celebrated incident a single Pakistani Sabre pilot shot down a flight of five Indian Hunters. Taken by surprise, the first Hunter was dismissed by a Sidewinder missile and the remainder by the Sabre's guns. Subsequent information revealed the Hunter pilots had been trained only for ground attack duties and were extremely inexperienced in the art of air combat tactics.

The December 1971 war with Pakistan started with the secession of East Pakistan from the Pakistani Union and resulted in the formation of the new state of Bangladesh in its place. Lasting just under two weeks, the battle saw heavy losses sustained by both sides including undoubtedly exaggerated claims for 32 Indian Hunters and 54 Pakistani Sabres. Seventeen appears to be a more accurate estimate of the number of Hunters lost.

The Hunters were employed almost exclusively in the ground attack role and indeed took on the bulk of this role in daylight and were usually escorted by Gnats. The Hunter squadrons involved were the same six as listed for the 1965 conflict. Of the Hunter losses, six fell to the guns of Sabres, four to Mirages, three to Shenyang F-6s (MiG-19) and the remainder to ground fire. Indian Hunters shot down two Sabres and one F-6, this relatively low figure reflecting the fact they were used mainly for ground attack duties.

Iraq

The Iraqi Air Force was the first customer to place a contract with Hawker for refurbished Hunters under the programme which started in 1963, initially receiving 24 FGA.59s in 1964-65 converted to full FGA.9 standards from former Belgian and Dutch aircraft. These were followed by 18 FGA.59As (1965-67), four FGA.59Bs (1966) and five T.69s (1964-65). Before that, the IAF had received 16 F.6s transferred from the RAF in 1957. Several Hunters were converted to FR.10 fighter-reconnaissance standards.

The IAF had 64 Hunters in service at the beginning of the Six Day War between Israel and various Arab nations in 1967. The aircraft were used mainly for border patrols during that conflict and six were lost on the ground during Israeli air strikes on airfields.

By the time of the 1973 Yom Kippur War, Iraq still had 48 Hunters in service and these flew top cover for Syrian Sukhoi Su-7 attack aircraft. The Hunters often engaged in air combat with Israeli A-4 Skyhawks and Dassault Super Mysteres and claimed about a dozen kills for the loss of seven Hunters, two of them to ground fire.

Iraqi Hunters also took part in the 'Gulf War' between Iran and Iraq which raged for eight years from 1980. In this long and often vicious conflict the remaining Iraqi Hunters were used almost exclusively in the ground attack role including – it has been reported – for the purpose of dropping chemicals (including mustard gas) on Iranian troops. Iraqi Hunters were also used in the long running battle against the Kurds in the north of the country.

Iraq's Hunter force gradually declined during the 1980s and by the time of the 1991 Gulf War the type was effectively out of service with any remaining aircraft disappearing during that conflict.

Jordan

Jordan has been traditionally linked with Britain over the years and an association with the Hunter began in 1958-60 with the supply of 12 ex RAF F.6s and a single T.66B. Eight FGA.9s were transferred from the RAF in 1964. A refurbished Hunter T.66B (from a Belgian F.6) was delivered in 1966.

Serving with the Royal Jordanian Air Force's No 1 Squadron, this entire force of Hunters was destroyed or damaged beyond repair on the ground in an Israeli strike on the Mafraq base during the 1967 Six Day War. Three single seaters were subsequently given to Jordan by Saudi Arabia and more refurbished Hunters were ordered from Hawker to help make up the losses. These comprised 18 FGA.73s, 73As and 73Bs

Iraq received 67 Hunters from 1957 including 46 FGA.59s. They saw action in the 1967 and 1973 wars with Israel. (via Philip J Birtles)

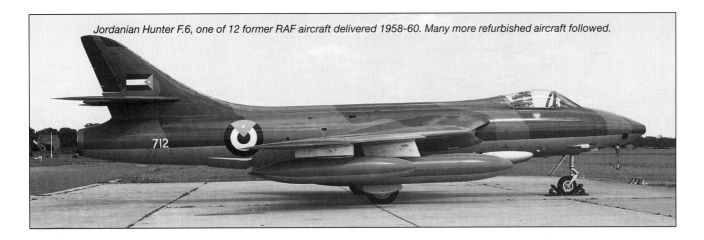
Jordanian Hunter F.6, one of 12 former RAF aircraft delivered 1958-60. Many more refurbished aircraft followed.

(plus a single T.66) delivered between 1968 and 1971.

The Hunter was due for retirement from RJAF service in 1973 when the Yom Kippur war with Israel broke out, with the result that their service lives were extended slightly due to the lack of a replacement. By early 1975 Jordan had 19 Hunters left and these were supplemented by Abu Dhabi's entire strength of 12 Hunters, presented to Jordan by Abu Dhabi's rulers.

Later in 1975 all of Jordan's 31 aircraft were in turn given to the Sultan of Oman's Air Force.

Kenya

Kenya was the last customer for refurbished Hunters, receiving four FGA.80s and two T.80s in 1974-75. The single seaters were rebuilt from former RAF F.4s and F.6s and the trainers had previously seen service with the Royal Navy as Hunter T.8s. The T.81s retained the 'small bore' Avon. The Hunters remained in Kenyan service only until 1980 when the five survivors (one T.81 had been lost) were sold to Zimbabwe.

Kuwait

Kuwait obtained four Hunter FGA.57s and five T.67s between 1965 and 1969 as part of a defence pact with the United Kingdom. The single seaters were operated until 1976 when they were replaced by McDonnell Douglas A-4KU Skyhawks, while the two seaters remained in service as trainers for a short time after that.

Lebanon

Lebanon received six ex RAF Hunter F.6s in 1958-59 with the help of US funding, equipping the Lebanese Air Force's only fighter squadron of the time. Four refurbished FGA.70s and three T.66Cs (all converted from Belgian F.6s) were subsequently delivered in 1965-66. An order for a further six FGA.70s (from RAF FGA.9 stocks) was placed in 1975 and although the first three air-

One of four Kuwaiti Hunter FGA.57s delivered (along with five T.67s) between 1965 and 1969. (via Philip J Birtles)

craft were delivered the following year, the remainder were delayed until late 1977 while Britain awaited the outcome of Lebanon's civil war.

The bloody civil war and the Israeli invasion of Lebanon in 1982 saw the Hunters in action, some of them reportedly operating from a highway near Beirut. Lebanon's ongoing instability has run its air force down to the point where it is no longer an effective and functioning service. Six Hunters were still flying in 1994 (five FGA.70s and a single T.66C) and these were apparently the only operational combat aircraft.

The Netherlands

As had been the case with fellow NATO nations Belgium and Denmark, the Netherlands selected the Hunter as its standard fighter. Financed mainly by US money, 96 F.4s and 93 F.6s were manufactured under licence by Fokker-Aviolanda at Amsterdam with the earlier aircraft delivered to the *Koninklijke Nederlandse Luchtmacht* (RNethAF) in 1955-56. These Hunters served with Nos 324, 325 and 327 Squadrons.

The Hunter F.6 began coming off Fokker's assembly line in 1956 and the last of them was delivered two

The Hunter F.4 and F.6 were built under licence in the Netherlands by Fokker-Aviolanda for the RNethAF. N-176 is an F.4 (with sawtooth leading edge) delivered in 1956.

An Omani Hunter modified to carry a pair of Sidewinder air-to-air missiles.

The Hunters entered service with *Escuadron Caza* 14, part of *Gruppo* 12 which also boasted a squadron of F-86F Sabres. Later, when they were replaced in the fighter role by Mirage 5Ps, the Hunters flew with *Escuadron Caza* 12 as ground attack aircraft but as two pylon Hunters they were not entirely suited to this role. They were replaced by Sukhoi Su-22s in 1976 but remained on FAP strength for a time after that.

The single seaters were supplemented in 1960 by a single Hunter T.62, converted by Hawker from a former RAF F.4.

Qatar

This small, oil rich Arab state received three refurbished Hunter FGA.78s (converted from former Dutch F.6s) and a single T.79 (from a Dutch T.7) in 1971. The Hunters remained in service until 1987.

Rhodesia/Zimbabwe

The then Royal Rhodesian Air Force ordered 12 ex RAF Hunter F.6s upgraded to FGA.9 standards in late 1962. The aircraft were delivered in 1963 for operation by No 1 Squadron and were quickly subject to the lack of spares and support resulting from a trade embargo imposed when Rhodesia declared its Unilateral Declaration of Independence in 1965.

Despite this, the by now simply Rhodesian Air Force (RhAF) managed to keep the aircraft not only flying but also involved in almost continuous action against Soviet backed insurgents trying to overthrow the white government of Ian Smith and replace it with a government representing the black majority. The Hunters saw much action in the ground attack role during this period and at least one was lost towards the end of the conflict in 1979.

A black government was duly installed and the country's name changed to Zimbabwe. Five more Hunters (four FGA.80s and a T.81) were obtained from Kenya in 1980.

years later. These aircraft flew with the F.4 squadrons listed above plus Nos 322, 323 and 326 and they were modified to carry the Sidewinder air-to-air missile. Complementing the Hunters were three squadrons of F-86K Sabre all weather fighters. The Netherlands began retiring its Hunters from 1963 and many were repurchased by Hawker Siddeley for use in the company's refurbishment programme.

The RNethAF also purchased 20 British built Hunter T.7s which were delivered between July 1958 and February 1959, some of which could also carry Sidewinders.

Oman

The Sultan of Oman's Air Force (later Royal Air Force of Oman – RAFO) received the Royal Jordanian Air Force's entire inventory of 31 Hunters in 1975, comprising 29 single seat FGA.73/A/Bs, F.6s and FR.10s plus three T.66Bs. This fleet was itself gained from a variety of previous sources including Saudi Arabia, Abu Dhabi and aircraft remanufactured by Hawker. Two ex Kuwaiti T.67s were acquired in 1980 and Omani single seat Hunters were later modified to carry a pair of Sidewinder air-to-air missiles.

Oman's Hunters were flown operationally by No 6 Squadron at Thumrait and for intermediate training duties, with about 18 normally operational and the remainder in storage as attrition replacements and for spares. The aircraft were more often than not flown by RAF pilots on loan to the RAFO and by mercenaries.

When the Hunters were delivered Oman was in the middle of a ten year war in the south of the country against communist insurgents from South Yemen with backing from the Soviet Union and China. The Hunters were immediately called into action and were used for strikes against enemy insurgents on the ground and then against targets in Yemeni territory. These actions were performed with the help of Iran, at that time still ruled by the pro West Shah. These demonstrations of air power had an impressive effect on the insurgents and their backers and by the end of 1975 the south of the country was declared safe.

The RAFO's well used Hunters were retired in August 1993, replaced by British Aerospace Hawk 200s.

Peru

One of the earliest export customers for the Hunter, the *Fuerza Aerea del Peru* received 16 ex RAF F.4s in 1956, these aircraft having been made available with introduction of the Hunter F.6 to RAF service. The Peruvian Hunters were redesignated as the F.52 and were of the pre Mod 228 standard with a single stores point under each wing.

Peruvian Hunter T.62 '681', converted from an RAF F.4. (via Philip J Birtles)

Rhodesia acquired 17 refurbished Hunters from 1963 which were subsequently involved in almost continuous action as the country went through its internal troubles. (via Philip J Birtles)

Vicious internal fighting broke out again three years later, and in a guerilla attack on Gwelo (Thornill) air base in July 1982, seven Hunters, a newly delivered BAe Hawk and a Lynx helicopter were destroyed and another Hunter and three Hawks badly damaged.

The surviving Hunters remained in Air Force of Zimbabwe service until the late 1980s.

Saudi Arabia

The United Kingdom's 'Magic Carpet' arms sales deal with Saudi Arabia saw four ex RAF Hunter F.6s and two T.7s delivered to the Royal Saudi Air Force (RSAF) in 1966 as a temporary expedient pending delivery of new BAC Lightnings. It's worth noting that these aircraft are sometimes referred to as F.60s and T.70s, although this is not an official designation.

The Hunters served with the RSAF's No 6 Squadron, which was deployed to Kamis Mushayt in the southwest of the country to act as a deterrent to numerous incursions into Saudi airspace by Egyptian MiG-21s and Il-28s. No interceptions were made due to a lack of proper ground control facilities, but some attacks on ground targets were made.

The three surviving F.6s were donated to Jordan in 1967 to help make good its heavy losses in the Six Day War against Israel and the T.7s were returned Britain in 1974.

Singapore

The Republic of Singapore Air Force (RSAF) became the Asia-Pacific region's only operator of the Hunter when the first of an eventual total of 47 refurbished aircraft was delivered.

The aircraft were delivered in several batches between 1970 and 1973 and comprised 12 FGA.74s, 26 FR.74As and Bs and nine T.75/As. The Hunters equipped the RSAF's Nos 140 (Osprey) and 141 (Merlin) Squadrons at Tengah and were used for tactical reconnaissance, air defence and army support duties. An extensive armament upgrade programme was performed by Lockheed Air Services enabling the Hunters to carry Sidewinder air-to-air missiles and additional weapons stations.

Singapore still had 32 Hunters in service by the end of the 1980s, at which time retirement was close and the type was withdrawn shortly after that.

One of the six Hunters delivered to the Royal Saudi Air Force in 1966 as a temporary measure pending the arrival of new BAC Lightnings. (via Philip J Birtles)

Sweden received 120 new Hunter F.50s from British production in 1955-58. The F.50 was similar to the RAF's F.4. (via Philip J Birtles)

Somalia

Somalia's extremely unstable political situation in recent times has meant the state of its Aeronautical Corps has been unclear. It is known that seven Hunter FGA.76s, one FR.76A and one T.77 which had once seen service with Abu Dhabi were delivered probably in 1983 and that they operated alongside Shenyang F-6s (MiG-19s), MiG-17s and MiG-21s from Berbera, flown mainly by former Rhodesian Air Force pilots. Since the overthrow of the Somalian government, little information has been available on the Hunters' status.

Sweden

One of the first export customers for the Hunter was the *Kungl Svenska Flygvapnet* (Royal Swedish Air Force), which after evaluation of the type ordered 120 examples in June 1954. Designated the F.50, these Hunters were equivalent to the RAF's F.4, although the first 24 aircraft were equipped with the surge prone Avon 113 or 115. These early aircraft (built at Kingston) were later upgraded, while the remaining 96 F.50s were built at Blackpool.

Deliveries began in August 1955 and continued into 1958. In Swedish service the Hunter was designated J34 and flown by four *Flottiljer* (Wings): F.8, F.9, F.10 and F.18. The aircraft were serialled 34001 to 34120.

The Swedish Hunters were not fitted with the sawtooth wing leading edge extension and early aircraft initially lacked link collector tanks and gunblast deflectors. They were nevertheless subject to some upgrading, the main one being the ability to carry Sidewinder air-to-air missiles.

The Swedes conducted an interesting experiment with one Hunter when they installed an afterburning system designed and built by *Svenska Flygmotor* (Volvo). First flown in 1958, the Hunter demonstrated remarkably improved time to height figures (four minutes to 39,400 feet/12,000m) but also returned unacceptably high fuel consumption which had a dramatically detrimental effect on the radius of action.

Withdrawn from front line service in 1966, a few Swedish Hunters remained on strength until the end of the decade for weapons training and the vast majority were scrapped at a time when Hawker Siddeley was looking for as many Hunters as it could find to refurbish. It was mentioned earlier that Hawker's sales contracts for the Hunter included a clause which gave the company first option on repurchasing them when they were retired. In the case of Sweden's order, this clause had been inadvertently omitted!

Switzerland

Switzerland's *Schweizerische Flugwaffe* (Swiss Air Force) was an early, major and important customer for the Hunter, taking delivery of a total of 160 aircraft in two distinct phases and involving a mixture of factory new and refurbished examples.

The original Swiss order for 100 Hunter F.58s (similar to the RAF's F.6) was important to the whole Hunter programme because of its influence

The first Swiss Hunter F.58 (J-4001) was a former RAF F.6. It was delivered to its new owner in April 1958. (via Philip J Birtles)

A Swiss Hunter F.58 from the first batch climbs away from an Lugano in June 1973. Switzerland eventually received 160 new and refurbished Hunters and retired the last of them only in 1994. (Philip J Birtles)

on several other purchasers. Switzerland is known for the care it takes before ordering any new equipment for its air force, its high standard of evaluation and the knowledge that any Swiss purchase is likely to remain in service for a long period of time and be constantly upgraded in the process.

So it was with the Hunter, the first aircraft entering service in 1958 and retirement from front line service not coming until 1994.

Swiss interest in the Hunter began in 1953 when Hawker test pilot Bill Bedford demonstrated the third (Sapphire powered) prototype at Dubendorf. A lengthy period of evaluation followed during which the Hunter was compared with several other fighters from west and east, among them the Canadair Sabre, Dassault Mystere IVA, Folland Gnat, Saab J-29 and the S-103, a Czech built version of the MiG-15bis. February and March 1957 saw two Hunter F.6s in Switzerland undergoing extensive trials and tests (with good results) and two aircraft were then loaned to the Swiss for a month for further 'in service' evaluations complete with a stock of bombs and rockets.

This extensive and unusual series of evaluations paid off for Hawker – in January 1958 the *Flugwaffe* ordered 100 Hunter F.6s which would be designated the F.58 in Swiss service. The serial numbers J-4001 to J-4100 were allocated to the new aircraft.

The first 12 aircraft were drawn from existing RAF stocks in order to

The remarkable 'Kavernen', in which Swiss aircraft can be housed in a completely self contained underground hangar, each capable of accommodating 18 Hunters in two tiers with the top layer hanging from the ceiling.

An especially decorated Hunter F.58 marks the 30th anniversary of the famed 'Patrouille Suisse' aerobatic team in 1994, the same year Switzerland finally retired its Hawker fighters. (Philip J Birtles)

speed up initial deliveries and these Hunters were handed over to the Swiss from April 1958. The remaining 88 were new build aircraft delivered between June 1959 and April 1960. Basically similar to the British Hunter F.6, the F.58 differed mainly in its avionics fit and the fact it was equipped with a braking parachute.

The second phase of Swiss Hunter purchases was between 1971 and 1975 when 60 refurbished aircraft were acquired, comprising 52 F.58As and eight T.68s. The single seaters were serialled J-4101 to J-4152 and the two seaters J-4201 to J-4208.

Swiss Hunters served with *Fliegerstaffeln* (squadrons) Nos 1, 2, 3, 4, 5, 6, 7, 8, 11, 15, 18, 19, 20, 21 and 24 during their years of service, operating under the Swiss system of flying from different peacetime and wartime bases, the latter used in exercises during which the aircraft were housed in extraordinary underground nuclear resistant hangars or *Kavernen*. Each of these hangars was a self contained

unit capable of accommodating 18 Hunters in two tiers with the top layer hung from the ceiling. Full workshop and storage facilities were provided and part of the Hunters' *modus operandi* during these exercises was to operate from stretches of highway.

The Swiss Hunters underwent several stages of modification during their careers, starting in with provision to carry Sidewinder air-to-air missiles and being fitted with a Saab bombing computer. Later on, they were able to carry a pair of AGM-65A Maverick TV guided air-to-surface missiles.

The final major Swiss Hunter update was carried out in the early 1980s. Under the 'Hunter 80' programme, the aircraft were fitted with a nose mounted radar warning receiver, chaff/flare dispensers and extra wing pylons allowing them to carry up to 28 80mm unguided rockets and Hunting BL755 cluster bomb units.

By 1994 Switzerland still had 87 Hunters in service, seven of them two

seaters. The fighter was finally withdrawn in that year after 36 years service and the aircraft were scheduled to be dismantled by early 1995. Coincidentally, 1994 also marked the 30th anniversary of probably the best known Hunter aerobatic team, the *Patrouille de Suisse*.

United Kingdom

Some of the Hunter's British service is covered in the previous chapters, but in summary it's worth noting that (excluding prototypes) nearly 1,100 new production aircraft were delivered to the Royal Air Force and these served with 38 front line operational squadrons. To those must be added the numerous Operational Conversion Units, Tactical Weapons Units and other RAF establishments which also operated Hunters, plus the various Royal Navy units which had Hunters on strength.

The last RAF Hunters were officially retired in March 1994 after 40 years of service. This left the Royal Navy as the final custodian of operational British Hunters and those still in service in March 1994 were: Hunter T.8C – WT722, WV396, XE665, XF289, XF357, XF358, XF994 and XL598; Hunter GA.11 – WT744, WV246, XE685, XE689, XE707, XF300 and XF368, a total of 15 aircraft all serving with the Fleet Requirements and Direction Unit (FRADU) at RNAS Yeovilton in Somerset.

One other Hunter was also flying in 1994, T.8M XL602 operated for British Aerospace.

Three of the GA.11s (WT744, XE685 and XE707) were auctioned in November 1994 – along with eight

An RAF Hunter FGA.9 of 43 Squadron patrolling over Aden, an area in which the aircraft saw action. (via Philip J Birtles)

The RAF's No 229 Operational Conversion Unit put up this formation of all its aircraft types in August 1969: Hunter F.6 leading, Meteor T.7 on starboard side and Meteor F.8 on port side, Hunter T.7 in middle and Hunters FR.10 (starboard) and FGA.9 (port) at the rear. (Philip J Birtles)

other Hunters – XE707 commanding the top price of £6,500.

The RAF's Hunters were involved in several skirmishes around the world during their long period of service, starting in 1956 with the crisis which erupted following Egypt's nationalisation of the Suez Canal. The French and British mounted *Operation Musketeer* to regain control of the vitally important canal, including the involvement of Hunter F.5s from the RAF's Nos 1 and 34 Squadrons.

Operating from Akrotiri, the Hunters were initially used to provide a fighter escort for the RAF and Fleet Air Arm aircraft attacking targets on the ground in the area, but their inadequate endurance (even with 100 gal-

lon drop tanks fitted) made them unsuitable for this. As a result, the Hunters were reassigned to the job of providing an air defence for Cyprus in case of an Egyptian attack, but no combat was seen.

An event which would have a familiar ring to it 30 years later occurred in 1961 when Iraq was threatening the sovereignty of the Arab state of Kuwait. Assistance from Britain was requested and two Hunter FGA.9 squadrons (Nos 8 and 208) joined other RAF aircraft in the area along with a strong Royal Navy and Royal Marines presence. Flying from Bahrain, the Hunters were ready to attack the Iraqi armour which has assembled near the Kuwaiti border, but no

fighting occurred as the British presence was sufficient to deter Iraq from its invasion plans.

The period of Confrontation with Indonesia involved Britain, Australia and New Zealand, this troubled time resulting from the formation of Malaysia in September 1963, the joining of Malaya, Singapore, Sarawak, Brunei and Sabah (North Bornea) into a single union. Singapore later dropped out of the federation. This act was contrary to the plans of then communist Indonesia, which saw the establishment of an Indonesian empire incorporating Malaya and the Philippines.

Indonesia backed a rebellion in Brunei and Sarawak and Indonesian

Gunless Hunter F.6 XG185 of 4 Flying Training School at Bentwaters in May 1973, resplendent in the then new red and white Training Command livery.

Some good detail in this shot of Royal Navy Hunter T.8 XF995 at Hatfield in October 1967. The aircraft belongs to 764 Squadron, Fleet Air Arm. (Philip J Birtles)

aircraft regularly entered Malaysian airspace. Guerilla incursions kept the troops on the ground busy, while in the air, the Hunter FGA.9s of 20 Squadron joined other RAF, RAAF, RNZAF and Royal Malaysian Air Force units. The Hunters were used to provide air defence capability (and had permission to shoot down Indonesian aircraft which encroached), their very presence providing a deterrent for any such activity. Later, the Hunters were also called on to perform numerous rocket and cannon strikes on Indonesian paratroops which had landed in Western Malaysia.

The crisis ended in late 1965 when the Indonesian government was ousted by a *coup* and a peace treaty between Indonesia and Malaysia was signed the following year.

Hunters were also used for strikes against ground targets in the ongoing troubles in Southern Arabia, centred

RAF OPERATIONAL HUNTER SQUADRONS

Sqn	Model	Dates	Base/s	Sqn	Model	Dates	Base/s
1	F.5	09/55-06/58	Tangmere, Akrotiri, Stradishall	65	F.6	12/56-03/61	Duxford
	F.6	07/58-06/60	Waterbeach	66	F.4	03/56-10/56	Linton-on-Ouse
	FGA.9	03/60-07/69	West Raynham		F.6	10/56-09/60	Acklington
2	FR.10	03/61-03/71	Germany	67	F.4	01/56-04/57	Germany
3	F.4	05/56-06/57	Germany	71	F.4	04/56-04/57	Germany
4	F.4	07/55-02/57	Germany	74	F.4	03/57-01/58	Horsham St Faith
	F.6	02/57-12/60	Germany		F.6	11/57-12/60	Coltishall
	FR.10	01/61-05/70	West Raynham	79	FR.10	12/60 only	Germany
	FGA.9	09/69-03/70	West Raynham	92	F.4	04/56-05/57	Linton-on-Ouse
8	FGA.9	01/60-12/71	Khormaksar		F.6	02/57-04/63	Middleton St George,
	FR.10	04/61-05/63	Muharraq, Sharjah				Thornaby, Leconfield
14	F.4	05/55-12/62	Germany	93	F.4	01/56-02/58	Germany
	F.6	04/57-12/62	Germany		F.6	02/58-12/60	Germany
19	F.6	10/56-11/62	Church Fenton, Leaconfield	98	F.4	03/55-07/57	Germany
20	F.4	11/55-10/57	Germany	111	F.4	01/55-11/56	North Weald
	F.6	08/57-12/60	Germany		F.6	11/56-04/61	Wattisham
	FGA.9	08/61-02/70	Tengah	112	F.4	04/56-05/57	Germany
26	F.4	06/55-09/57	Germany	118	F.4	03/57-05/57	Germany
	F.6	06/58-12/60	Germany	130	F.4	04/56-05/57	Germany
28	FGA.9	05/62-01/67	Kai Tek	208	F.5	01/58-02/58	Tangmere
34	F.5	02/56-01/58	Tangmere		F.6	01/58-03/59	Nicosia, Kenya
41	F.5	08/55-01/58	Biggin Hill		FGA.9	03/60-09/71	Stradishall, Khormaksar,
43	F.1	08/54-08/56	Leuchars				Muhrraq
	F.4	03/56-12/56	Nicosia	222	F.1	12/54-08/56	Leuchars
	F.6	12/56-1960	Khormaksar		F.4	08/56-11/57	Leuchars
	FGA.9	1960-10/67	Khormaksar	234	F.4	05/56-07/57	Germany
45	FGA.9	08/72-06/76	West Raynham, Wittering	245	F.4	03/57-06/57	Stradishall
54	F.1	03/55-10/55	Odiham	247	F.1	06/55-07/55	Odiham
	F.4	09/55-01/57	Stradishall		F.4	07/55-03/57	Odiham
	F.6	01/57-03/60	Waterbeach		F.6	03/57-12/57	Odiham
	FGA.9	03/60-09/69	West Raynham	257	F.2	09/54-03/57	Wattisham
56	F.5	05/55-11/58	Waterbeach		F.5	07/55-03/57	Wattisham
	F.6	11/58-01/61	Wattisham, Nicosia	263	F.2	02/55-10/55	Wattisham
58	FGA.9	08/73-06/76	Wittering		F.5	04/55-10/57	Wymeswold
63	F.6	1956-10/58	Waterbeach		F.6	10/57-07/58	Stradishall

around the Aden Protectorate. The root cause of the troubles was the strong anti British sentiments held by Egypt at the time and that country was behind most of them. An attack on the British High Commissioner which killed two and injured 52 others in 1963 inflamed the situation.

There had been regular skirmishes in the area for some time before three RAF Hunter FGA.9 squadrons (Nos 8, 43 and 208) arrived on the scene. These were later joined by 1417 Flight's Hunter FR.10s. A revolution in Yemen in 1962 saw the situation hot up and the incorporation of Aden into the Federation of South Arabia

the following year added fuel to the fire with various tribal and political groups fighting each other and the British.

The Hunters were employed in the ground attack role during the various attempts to quell the situation, in May and June 1964 alone flying 642 sorties, firing 2,508 rockets and using 183,900 rounds of 30mm ammunition. All three British services were involved in this messy affair in which the security forces had to deal with dissident tribes, incursions from Yemen and terrorist activities in Aden. No fewer than 25 RAF Squadrons equipped with various aircraft types were involved.

The climax of the affair came in 1964 with a Special Air Services attack on a fort near Harib, an insurgent stronghold. The Hunters attacked the fort with rockets and bombs before the SAS paratroopers dropped in under cover of darkness and after some 30 hours' fighting the battle was won. Other insurgent positions were also attacked, the Hunters playing a major part in this activity. The British withdrew from the area in 1967 after more fighting had taken place, leaving Aden to its own fate.

Royal Navy Hunter GA.11 XF291 of 738 Squadron's 'Rough Diamonds' aerobatic team. Photographed at Yeovilton in September 1969. (Philip J Birtles)

FLYING THE HUNTER

Air Vice-Marshal Bill Collings RAAF (ret) looks back 35 years to his training at the Empire Test Pilots School at Farnborough and presents his impressions of the Hawker Hunter from the pilot's seat.

I flew the Hunter during my test pilot training at the Empire Test Pilots School at Farnborough in the United Kingdom, flying the F.4 and T.7. It was a long time ago, and it might therefore be useful to describe flying the Hunter in the context of the state of aircraft design at that time, since it is difficult for pilots trained in the present era to appreciate what enormous advances have been made in aircraft design.

When I underwent my training at Farnborough in 1960, the Flight Manuals for aircraft were small books in a blue cover in black and white print and illustrations. One was given the Pilot's Notes, as they were then called, and told to read them. When one felt comfortable with the aircraft's systems and the operating data, one familiarised oneself with the cockpit and advised one's tutor that one was ready to go. He would approve the flight profile and off one went.

One had to read the flying orders and sign them before flying. These orders gave detail of important information that had not yet been included in the Pilot's Notes. In the Hunter, the most important matter was the engagement of the flight control hydraulic boost system. In these early days of powered flight controls there were two design schools of thought. The British system was to provide manual reversion in the event of failure of the hydraulic boost system in any of the three channels. To engage the boost system, one selected hydraulic boost and then ensured that the engagement indicator indicated correctly and full control travel was available. Failure to ensure correct engagement would result in a semi engaged condition with subsequent handling difficulty.

It is interesting to note that the type of indicator used in that era was the magnetic doll's eye. The indicator was a flip-flop shutter in a window in the instrument panel. One side was white and the other black. The instrument panel was painted black and if the black side of the indicator was in the window the pilot could not see any change in the panel and the system was therefore normal. If the system was faulty, the white side would show and the pilot would notice it in the black panel. Failure indicators have improved since then!

The Hunter was a typical Hawker aircraft, very strong with a wide track undercarriage. Because the cockpit did not have a bubble canopy, one could not see very well to the rear. In my cockpit evaluation of the Hunter as a training exercise, I compared it unfavourably with the Australian Sabre. My tutor was not very happy and would not believe that one could see one's tail in the Sabre without great difficulty!

The Hunter was powered by a 200 series Rolls-Royce Avon turbojet. This was a state-of-the-art axial flow engine at that time. The earliest Avons were of the first generation of axial flow engines and suffered operating problems which the centrifugal types did not.

For example, in the early engines, as the RPM increased there was a drop in RPM as the two position inlet guide vanes changed to the high RPM position. The engine would then continue to accelerate. If there was a cross wind on the runway, one often had to run up the engine into wind until the guide vanes and the bleed valves changed to the high RPM position, then align the aircraft with the runway while releasing the brakes.

It was therefore a pleasure to fly an aircraft where the engine acceleration was smooth and continuous, a condition we would not consider remarkable today.

Takeoff in the Hunter was straightforward, although one was monitoring the aileron performance to verify that the boost was properly engaged. Once cleaned up the aircraft is accelerated to 450 KIAS (knots indicated airspeed) for the climb, changing to 0.8 Mach. The first part of the familiarisation flying involved the usual manoeuvring, low speed handling and aerobatics.

For the Hunter 4 at that time, low speed handling was limited by airspeed because of its pitchup characteristics. Early swept wing aircraft suffered from pitchup at the stall due to the spanwise flow induced by the swept wing. This would cause thickening of the boundary layer on the outer wing which would stall before

RAF Hunter T.7 XL567 of 4 Flying Training School photographed at Leeming in November 1967. (Philip J Birtles)

The Hunter T.7 cockpit.

the inner wing with a subsequent movement forward of the centre of pressure and pitchup. The cure was either wing fences or, as the later marks of Hunter had, a leading edge extension on the outer wing.

On the second familiarisation flight one explored the aircraft's behaviour at high Mach number. With the Mark 4 and earlier Hunters, control in the pitch channel above Mach 0.93 reduced drastically. This was because the elevator, being in stagnant airflow behind the shock wave, lost effectiveness. One could move the stick through full travel fore and aft without significantly affecting the aircraft's pitch attitude. The only way to recover control was to reduce power

and extend the speed brakes until the Mach reduced below 0.93.

Circuit and landing in the Hunter was also straightforward. For those not used to the older 2000psi systems, lowering the undercarriage caused quite a change in the hydraulic pressure with accompanying noises. Once the pressures had recovered and three greens were obtained, one lowered flap as required to hold about 150 KIAS on base on a curving approach, aiming to cross the threshold at about 130 KIAS The aircraft sits down nicely but a soft landing is difficult as the gear damping is hard. The aircraft is directionally stable on the ground due to the wide track undercarriage.

Later in the course, we carried out spinning in the T.7, which had a fully flying tailplane and leading edge extensions on the wing. The lower limits of the envelope could therefore be fully explored. On the other hand, this type of aircraft had spinning characteristics which were largely controlled by the ailerons. This was the norm for many aircraft of the time and led to a fundamental revision of the procedure for spin recovery. The old standard spin recovery action was: power off, full opposite rudder, stick forward.

The ETPS T.7, which had been used for spinning trials, was equipped with turn lights to indicate the direction of rotation of the spin. The lights were coloured red and green for quick reference. The spin demonstration was as follows, for an initial left hand spin. One entered the spin using full back stick, full left rudder and full right aileron. Once the spin was established, the direction of turn was confirmed using the turn lights and the effect of ailerons was demonstrated by slowly moving them to the right. As the stick moved to the right of neutral, the aircraft would rapidly reverse the direction of the spin, entering a spin to the right.

At the order to recover from the spin, the student invariably applied full right rudder, because that is what he had previously been trained to do. On being shown the direction of the spin on the spin lights, the light would dawn! The standard spin recovery was amended at this time to: power off, determine the direction of rotation of the spin, apply full rudder opposite to the direction of rotation of the spin, stick forward.

As an interesting aside, the RAF Central Flying School was authorised

Hunter T.7 XL564 of the Empire Test Pilots School at Fairford in July 1994. (Philip J Birtles)

to carry out spinning training on the T.7 and immediately lost one. The reason wasn't incorrect recovery technique, but the fact that the pilot didn't apply the recovery action long enough to allow the aircraft to respond. He had tried ten recovery actions in the space of the same number of spin rotations and then abandoned the aircraft!

The Hunter was a very pleasant aircraft to fly. It had good performance for its time and was very rugged, as attested to by the fact that there are still Hunters in regular service with several air forces. It suffered from many of the design problems of its time, but the later marks incorporated all of the refinements we take for granted today, but which were then part of the ongoing development which has resulted in the modern jet fighter.

A Naval Aviator's View

Commodore Norman Lee RAN (ret) flew numerous aircraft types during his career with the Royal Australian Navy, including Fireflies on active service in Korea. Exchange duties with the Royal Navy gave him the opportunity to fly many British types, including the Hunter.

My introduction to the Hunter was tragically marred by the loss of the commanding officer of the Royal Navy squadron I had just joined on exchange, in a Hunter Trainer.

He had been practising for an air display and had rolled the aircraft inverted at low level over the airfield. Witnesses saw the nose of the aircraft drop and before the pilot could recover, the aircraft had struck the ground.

The subsequent investigation determined that it was not possible to tighten down the combined parachute and seat harness fully, and that he had probably dropped several inches out of his seat when inverted, enough to affect the control of the aircraft. I did not get to fly the Hunter Trainer until quite some time later but can categorically state that it had one of the worst seat harness arrangements I have ever come across; it was just not possible to tighten yourself hard down in the seat even though it was fitted with a negative 'g' strap.

Apart from that, the Hunter was a magnificent machine, well deserved of all the praise that has been heaped on it over the years. Unfortunately my first association with the aircraft was somewhat brief as we only used it as a transition vehicle to the Scimitar, Vickers Armstrong's final attempt at designing a fighter.

All told we flew some ten hours in the T.8 which was the Royal Navy version of the Trainer, gaining a swept wing instrument rating as part of the conversion. The T.8 was developed from the RAF T.7, the main difference being the fitting of an airfield arrester hook which enabled the use of the emergency arrester wire system set up at all naval airfields. Apart from the ejection seat harness, the only other small criticism that could be levelled at the aircraft was that it was possible to scrape the tailcone on landing if you held off for too long.

The Hunter Trainer was a beautifully co-ordinated machine with fully powered controls and joy of joys, electric trim for elevator and aileron controlled by a four way switch on the top of the control column. This might seem old hat nowadays but it was a quantum leap in development from the old trim wheels mounted in a box on the floor of the aircraft under your left hand.

The Hunter's thoroughbred lineage clearly stemmed from the other two Hawker aircraft I had flown, the Sea Fury and the Seahawk; there was something distinctive in the design philosophy.

I don't think any of us had any problems in the transition to swept-wing aircraft, even instrument flying was fairly straight forward. The only thing that one needed to watch was the stall and a tendency to pitchup. The RAF, however, had a few problems with inexperienced pilots getting themselves into inverted spins in their T.7's.

One remarkable incident occurred when two pilots could not recover from an inverted spin and the captain gave the order to eject. He went out under considerable negative 'g', well clear of his seat cushion and suffered fatal back injuries. The other pilot tried to eject but the seat failed to operate. He made a number of unsuccessful attempts to fire the seat but just about at the time he was preparing himself to meet his Maker, he noticed that the aircraft had recovered from the spin by itself. Despite considerable difficulties resulting from the absence of the canopy, he took control and flew the aircraft back to base!

Subsequent analysis determined the change in airflow with the loss of the large canopy was most likely what had caused the aircraft to recover from the spin. It subsequently became SOP (Standard Operating Procedure) to dwell a pause after jettisoning the canopy if in an unrecoverable spin, on the off chance that the changed airflow might help spin recovery.

Hunter T.8 WT772 of the Fleet Requirements Unit at Yeovilton. This aircraft started life as a single seat Hunter F.4. (Philip J Birtles)

All told, I only flew about 15 hours in the T.8 which from memory was all fairly straight forward with nothing untoward happening in that short association.

My next encounter with the Hunter was some eight years later when I was on the staff at Australia House in London. As Staff Officer (Air) I was allowed to do 25 hours a year and from memory the Royal Navy charged £125 per flying hour for the Hunter. Amusingly, when I flew RN Wessex helicopters the charge was spelt out down to the last sixpence, something like £112/12/6!

I duly made arrangements to return to Lossiemouth for a week's flying on the single seat GA.11 which was a conversion from the RAF F.4. With the phasing out of the Seahawk, the Royal Navy had identified a requirement for a single seat weapons trainer and the GA.11 proved to be an ideal aircraft.

On arrival, my hosts apologised for only having a T.8B available for my dual check. This aircraft had been developed as the instrument trainer for the Buccaneer which was fitted with strip instruments. As with cars of the same period, strip reading instruments were a failure, being no substitute for the good old fashioned round dial. It has certainly been my experience that one doesn't read an instrument but rather notes where the needle is on the dial and this doesn't seem to work with linear readouts.

Lossiemouth, despite being located in the north of Scotland, has one of the best weather factors in the United Kingdom due to the mountains to the west and south taking the strength out of any weather coming from that direction. However I must have picked the only week when there were continuous strong winds and as luck would have it, the two runways were neatly bisected. How-

ever, with my time almost up, the wind at last abated and I was finally let loose in the single seater.

It was the fastest conversion I've ever done. Several day's flying were crammed into the one day remaining to me with two sorties in the morning and two in the afternoon, and I thoroughly enjoyed every minute of them. I had experienced high speed sub sonic flight in the Scimitar so could more easily mentally relate to the expanded time and space demands of an aircraft of the Hunter's calibre. I must admit, however, that this was greatly aided by TACAN which took all the fun out of wondering where you were!

It would be presumptuous of me to attempt to sum the aircraft up after such a brief association, however if I had to do so I would liken it to a super Seahawk. One could not bestow a greater accolade.

Hunter GA.11 WV382 of the Fleet Requirements Units. Note the Harley light in the nose for the night acquisition of targets. (Philip J Birtles)